E.M.
BOUNDS

A Francis Asbury Press Book

E.M. BOUNDS

MAN OF PRAYER

LYLE WESLEY DORSETT

ZondervanPublishingHouse
Academic and Professional Books
Grand Rapids, Michigan

A Division of HarperCollins*Publishers*

E. M. Bounds
Copyright © 1991 by Lyle Wesley Dorsett

Requests for information should be addressed to:
Zondervan Publishing House
Academic and Professional Books
1415 Lake Drive, S.E.
Grand Rapids, Michigan 49506

Library of Congress Cataloging-in-Publication Data

Dorsett, Lyle W.
    E.M. Bounds : man of prayer / Lyle Wesley Dorsett.
      p. cm.
    Includes bibliographical references.
    ISBN 0-310-53931-5
    1. Bounds, Edward M. (Edward McKendree), 1835-1913. 2. Methodist
Church–United States–Clergy–Biography. I. Bounds, Edward M.
(Edward McKendree), 1835-1913. Selections. 1991. II. Title.
BX8495.B66D67 1991
287'.6'092–dcB –dc20   91-7928
                                                          CIP

Designed and edited by Robert D. Wood
Cover designed by Foster Design Associates

Printed in the United States of America

91 92 93 94 95 96 / AK / 10 9 8 7 6 5 4 3 2 1

CONTENTS

This book is dedicated
to my mentor and friend,
Dr. Robert E. Coleman, who
introduced me to E. M. Bounds.

PREFACE

Edward McKendree Bounds did not look like a man of power. Even in shoes he stood only five feet, five inches tall. Before age forty his hairline had receded, and his beard and temples were marked with dense swatches of gray. A slender, almost diminutive man, Bounds's most striking features were piercing, hazel-colored eyes accentuated by heavy, bushy brows.

But God frequently chooses the weak things of the world to confound the strong. Indeed, this little man who was born in obscurity and died without fanfare, who had little formal schooling and held no lofty church offices, wielded a profound impact on North American Christians. During his lifetime he set countless souls ablaze with his preaching, praying, and writing. Since his death in 1913, his books, especially those on prayer, have helped thousands, perhaps millions, find a deeper life in the Lord Jesus Christ.

Nearly a decade ago Dr. Robert E. Coleman introduced me to the writings of Edward McKendree Bounds. The little book *Preacher and Prayer*, originally entitled *Power Through Prayer*, had a revolutionary impact on my spiritual life. This volume, as well as some other books Bounds wrote on prayer, drove me to my knees with renewed vigor, vision, and expectation. The stimulating effect of these works caused me to search for other things he had written. I also set out to discover more about the life of this author whose books had so revitalized my faith in a living and powerful Christ.

As I embarked upon a quest to read more Bounds and learn about his life, three things became apparent. First, few books on prayer have had a greater impact on the Christian faithful than *Power Through Prayer* (*Preacher and Prayer*). Originally published in 1907, this little classic has been in print in one form or another for nearly ninety years. Countless editions and printings have given it unusually wide distribution. Indeed, few books written in this century, except for some by C. S. Lewis, have reached and influenced so many people. Second, although Bounds's eight little books on prayer are in print and readily available, few people, even devoted Bounds readers, have seen his three long-out-of-print and extremely rare books *Satan, Heaven,* and *The Resurrection.* Likewise his edifying but long-forgotten articles have not been read by more than a handful of people since they were published in the late nineteenth century. Third, very little is known about E. M. Bounds. Except for a five-hundred-word sketch in *Who Was Who in Church History* (Moody, 1962) by E. S. Moyer, Dr. Melvin Dieter's brief portrait for *Dictionary of Christianity in America* (InterVarsity, 1990), Dr. Robert E. Coleman's two-page introduction to the Christian Outreach edition of *Preacher and Prayer* (1981), Willis Irvin, Jr.'s, sixteen-page typed but unpublished *Prayer Warrior: A Mini-Biography of E. M. Bounds,* and a half-page sketch in Warren Wiersbe's *Walking With the Giants* (1976), nothing is available on the life of E. M. Bounds.

The purpose of this book is to fill the gaps. Part One is the first biography of Bounds that is more than a few hundred words in length. It is also the first publication on Bounds that is based upon research in all the available primary sources in the National Archives, Washington, D. C., and from the states of Missouri, Tennessee, and Georgia. Part Two contains Bounds's own writing, much of it never reprinted since its initial publication and limited circulation between seventy-five and one hundred years ago.

To put a fine point on the central purpose of this book, I pray that as many people as possible will have the deeply edifying and life-changing encounter with E. M. Bounds that I have had. The fruit of my research is here for you to feast upon.

ACKNOWLEDGMENTS

My greatest human debt in preparing this book is to Dr. Robert E. Coleman. I dedicate this volume to him because he introduced me to the writings of Edward McKendree Bounds a decade ago. Both Coleman and Bounds have been key spiritual mentors, sent to me by God at critical times in my life and ministry. I will be eternally grateful.

Mary Dorsett, my wife and my best friend, is another spiritual mentor who offered immeasurable assistance. She took two research trips with me, one to Georgia and Missouri in 1989 and another to Tennessee in 1990. As always she helped me find and interpret sources. She also took photographs and did a critical reading of the text.

I owe much thanks to two gracious Georgians who offered us southern hospitality at its finest: Mrs. Rosemary Reynolds of Washington, Georgia, and the Reverend Willis Irvin, Jr., of Augusta. Mrs. Reynolds is Edward M. Bounds's granddaughter. She invited us to her home, gave us a personal tour of the cemetery where her grandfather and his family are buried, and provided photographs of Dr. and Mrs. Bounds. Mrs. Reynolds also gave me photocopies of a collection of letters and documents related to Dr. Bounds's life and career. The Reverend Willis Irvin also invited us to his home. He pointed me to sources on the deceased preacher and author, and he allowed me to take notes from his privately produced and handsomely illustrated booklet entitled *The Prayer Warrior: A Mini-biography of Dr. E. M. Bounds*. This little book contains sixteen pages of narrative text, a bibliography, several photographs, and photocopies of some documents as well as five editorials Bounds wrote for the *Christian Advocate* published in Nashville. Reverend Irvin also gave me a copy of this unpublished mini-biography.

Because of its limited circulation I deposited my copy in the Billy Graham Center Library, Wheaton, Illinois.

Mrs. Doris Martin of the Washington-Wilkes Historical Museum (Bounds's home from 1894–1913) was a cheerful guide through the rooms where Dr. Bounds lived, wrote, and prayed. Mr. Charles Irvin of the Mary Willis Library showed us numerous primary sources related to Bounds, and he allowed us to photocopy many documents.

Thanks are due to the staff of the Missouri Historical Society, St. Louis, for giving me access to their holdings. I am grateful, too, for help from the Wheaton College (Illinois) Library staff in locating and ordering microfilm of the *Christian Advocate*.

I am grateful to Dr. Patricia Ward, my colleague and academic dean at Wheaton College. Her father, the Reverend H. Blair Ward, was a Nazarene pastor in New York. He owned a copy of one of Bounds's books with a letter and inscription from Homer W. Hodge. Reverend Blair also owned the only copy that I have seen of Hodge's *Prayer: "The Forgotten Secret of the Church."* The latter book contains Hodge's memories of his visits with Bounds. In brief, Patricia Ward gave me these books from her late father's library. This gesture on her part is typical of her generosity and love for learning.

Diane Garvin on the staff of the Institute of Evangelism, Billy Graham Center, Wheaton College, cheerfully typed the manuscript with speed and accuracy. Ginny Feldmann typed transcripts of *Christian Advocate* editorials. To both of these friends I offer thanks.

Finally, I am extremely grateful to Robert D. Wood, my able editor at Francis Asbury Press of Zondervan Publishing House, for enthusiastically sharing my vision to get Bounds's life story and his long-ignored writings into print.

Lyle W. Dorsett
Wheaton, Illinois
September 1990

PART ONE

The Life of
E. M. Bounds

CHAPTER 1

EARLY LIFE AND CONVERSION

In 1823 Hester A. Purnell married Thomas Jefferson Bounds in Worcester County, Maryland. They were both twenty-two years old, in the prime of life, and brimming with high hopes about raising a family and getting a stake in the new nation. Like many young people born into the poorer classes, they moved westward in search of inexpensive land and economic opportunity.[1]

In quest of a better life the Bounds family had settled in Kentucky by 1827; but a few years later they made their way to Missouri where land was reportedly equally fertile and much less expensive. Settling first in the rich lands of Marion County on the western edge of the Mississippi River, they found competition for farmland and town lots was already keen among the emigrants from Kentucky and Virginia. By 1834 they had moved about forty miles west of the thriving river town of Hannibal and had settled into a village that later became part of Shelby County. Thomas Bounds, obviously an ambitious man with a promoter's heart, helped organize the county in 1835. He also was one of the original landholders in the county seat named Shelbyville.[2]

Bounds, who as a boy had been apprenticed to a mercantile businessman in Baltimore, decided against farming once he arrived in Missouri. Leaving plowing and planting to others, he turned his hand to construction, town promotion, and local politics. As soon as the county was organized in 1835 he ran for county clerk. His election a success, Bounds used his own house for court sessions, and hired himself out to do construction on private dwellings and county projects.[3]

While he worked in politics and construction, his wife labored at home making clothes, tending a garden, and raising their ever-growing family of children. By 1840 there were six little Boundses: three boys and three girls.[4] The next to the youngest was a boy whom they christened Edward McKendree. No one knows with certainty who this child was named for, but it is likely that his middle name was inspired by the Methodist bishop of the Western Conference, William McKendree.

McKendree was the principle person responsible for planting Methodism in Missouri. A zealous man with searching eyes, set chin, and firm lips, he made a "covenant with poverty" and chose never to marry once he heard the call to preach. A tireless preacher led to do the work of an evangelist, McKendree was sent in the early 1800s from his native Virginia by Francis Asbury to plant churches, first in Kentucky and eventually in Missouri. So called "McKendree churches" were planted all the way from the Atlantic seaboard to western Missouri by this ardent Wesleyan who lived most of his ministerial life on horseback.

Bishop McKendree was a household name by the time that Hetty and Tom Bounds married. Over the years they probably heard him preach, or perhaps they had worshiped in one of his churches somewhere in Kentucky and Missouri during the 1820s and early 1830s. In any case the eminent old Wesleyan evangelist died in March 1835 at age seventy-eight.[5]

Later that same year, on August 15, Hetty gave birth to a boy and named him Edward McKendree. It is tempting to believe he was the namesake of that venerable old preacher and first American-born Methodist bishop who chose to remain single and childless for the sake of taking the gospel to the wilderness West. But if no proof exists, the coincidence is symbolic. Indeed, it was a portent of what was to be.

Perhaps some of Shelbyville's Methodist saints saw the name connection. But if they held hopes for young Edward McKendree to pick up the torch, they had a long wait. Although the youngster, like his brother and sister, was baptized in and later joined the Methodist Episcopal Church, there were no particular signs of sanctification or calling.

By the early 1840s the Bounds family was comfortable and

relatively prosperous. The county, like the state, was growing. Shelby County boasted two grain mills and over three thousand settlers. Likewise, several hundred slaves were involved in a diversified agricultural economy. One historian writing in 1884 said that Shelby County was beginning to boom by the early 1840s. Log cabins were being replaced by brick and frame structures, and Shelbyville, "the only town in the county worthy of the name, was a thriving little village with fair prospects for the future."[6]

Thomas J. Bounds appeared to be doing well by earthly standards. By 1840 he had six healthy children and a good wife. Although he did not follow the fashion of prosperous farmers and buy slaves, he did imitate the status symbol for slave state townspeople. He rewarded his faithful wife by hiring a slave woman and her child to live in the house and take charge of the heavy chores. Thomas Bounds could afford this forty-dollar-a-year extravagance because during the 1840s he was continually reelected county clerk. He also oversaw the planting of locust trees and rose bushes around the public square, and he secured numerous local contracts, among them one to build a fence around Shelbyville's public buildings and square.[7]

If the Boundses depended on family relationships and economic stability alone to bring them happiness, they were in trouble by the late 1840s. A daughter died before her tenth birthday, and Thomas Bounds passed away in 1849 at age forty-eight, in their twenty-sixth year of marriage.[8]

Edward McKendree Bounds was fourteen when his father died. No evidence survives to show the impact of this dreadful loss, but it is clear that he was an ambitious young man with no eyes for Christian ministry. As a boy Bounds had been an able student, and he mastered reading and writing in Shelbyville's one-room school. Being continually exposed to court proceedings with his father serving as county clerk, the young man set a flint-like gaze upon the legal profession.

During the early 1800s a person could qualify to practice law and be admitted to the bar with no college or university education. While some lawyers were college graduates, most men who entered the legal profession before the Civil War had no formal legal training, especially if they lived south of the

Ohio and west of the Mississippi rivers. Instead, candidates for the bar studied law under the tutelage of an attorney. They read law books, memorized key cases, and then sat for the bar examination as soon as they felt qualified. Abraham Lincoln, for example, studied law in Illinois and was admitted to the bar in 1836 at age twenty-seven. Although E. M. Bounds sought a law license in a younger and less-developed state than Illinois, his achievement is extraordinary by any standards. On June 9, 1854, two months before his nineteenth birthday, he passed the bar and was licensed to practice as an attorney-at-law in any court of record in Missouri.[9]

For the next five years E. McKendree Bounds, as he signed his papers, conducted a successful legal practice in Monroe and Shelby counties. Still rather young for such an aggressive and competitive profession, he nevertheless won the respect of judges, lawyers, and clients alike. An unusually effective communicator, Bounds convinced the citizens of northeastern Missouri that he was one of the most intelligent and able attorneys in the area.

Because of his stellar reputation, colleagues and acquaintances of this young lawyer with so much promise were stunned when he announced the closing of his law office in 1859. A call that brooked no refusal had come. He finally was going to live up to that McKendree name.

CHAPTER 2

THE TRAINING OF AN EVANGELIST: HIS FIRST GREAT TRIAL

E. McKendree Bounds had been a Christian as long as he could remember. During infancy a Methodist Episcopal minister baptized him in Shelby County. Then twelve years later young Bounds confirmed the faith in which his parents had raised him and joined the church. Never a particularly errant lad, he attended church regularly with his family. Like the other Boundses, he trusted the promises of Christ for salvation and did his best to live a moral life in a frontier society where hard drinking, gambling, and general rowdiness were the order of the day.

In 1859 something dramatic evidently happened to this decent, God-fearing, young lawyer. The details are lost to history, but apparently sometime near the tenth anniversary of his father's death, Bounds felt overwhelmed by God's grace in a new and profound way. He surrendered his will to Christ and experienced a keen sense of the Holy Spirit's presence. In the wake of this second blessing he experienced power to tell others about Christ's love for all people, and he knew that God was calling him to a full-time preaching and evangelism ministry.

Within a few months of this heart-warming encounter with God, Bounds took down his shingle, closed his law office, and began a serious study of the Scriptures and theology. He voraciously read the Bible and devoured John Wesley's sermons. Now twenty-four years old, he read widely in the field of Christian autobiography and biography, finding Jonathan Edwards' work on David Brainerd and a life of John Fletcher to be particularly helpful. Before Christmas of 1859 he was preaching and evangelizing in a little Methodist Episcopal Church, South,

in the village of Monticello, nearly forty miles as the crow flies
from his hometown of Shelbyville. By February 1860 the
Hannibal Station Quarterly Conference certified, "E. McKendree Bounds, in accord with the discipline of said church [is]
Licensed to preach the Gospel of Christ."[10] Three days later the
eager new preacher was brought into the Connection as a
deacon and sent halfway across the state to take a church in the
Missouri River town of Brunswick.

It is important to understand that seething sectional
tensions over slavery were buffeting everyone in Missouri by
1860. Dedicated Christians were no exceptions. Indeed, the
institutional church was so embattled that people were forced to
take sides. Back in 1843 when the Methodist Episcopal Church
refused to take a stand for the immediate abolition of slavery, a
significant body of Methodists seceded and formed the Wesleyan
Church. During the Methodist Episcopal General Conference in
1844 a great struggle again arose over slavery, this time when a
member of the Baltimore Conference, who by marriage became
a slave owner, refused to free his slaves. The result was that the
conferees sympathetic to slavery, except those in Maryland and
Delaware, seceded from the larger body. On May 1, 1845, a
separate Methodist Episcopal Church, South, divorced itself
from the larger body, taking with it approximately half a million
members, numerous church buildings and parsonages, as well as
many schools and institutions of higher learning.

Because Missouri was a border state, not everyone agreed
on the morality of slavery. Certainly there was no unanimity
over the propriety of splitting the denomination and comman-
deering property. Few states suffered more internal strife over
slavery and preservation of the Union than Missouri. Originally
a slave state settled by slave owners from Virginia and Kentucky,
it quickly attracted a more diverse population. By the late 1840s
many antislavery immigrants, especially the Irish and Germans,
had moved into Missouri. In brief, the state was marred by
dissension. Missouri had become, in effect, a microcosm of a
war-destined sectional rift.

The Bounds family was caught in the eye of this storm.
Although the family had hired a slave woman as a household
servant, they were neither partisan defenders of slavery nor

secessionist in sentiment. In fact, the two oldest Bounds sons, Thomas and Charles, joined the Union Army once the Civil War started. E. McKendree, on the other hand, ultimately became a chaplain in the Confederacy.

How these brothers ended up on different sides of such a bloody conflict is a strange and tangled story. In February 1861 Bounds assumed the pastorate of the Methodist Episcopal Church, South, congregation at Brunswick, Missouri. Located in proslavery Charitan County, this Missouri River Valley land was settled by Virginians and Kentuckians who used slave labor to plant cash crops including tobacco and hemp. Most central Missourians, however, did not want to secede from the Union. All they wanted was to be left alone to mind their own interests. Indeed, General Sterling Price, the political leader of this part of Missouri, was a Mexican War veteran who had distinguished himself in military affairs. After the border war he served as governor of Missouri as well as a member of the United States House of Representatives.

As soon as Abraham Lincoln was elected president of the United States, southern states began to secede from the Union. But Price, a conditional Unionist, wanted to keep Missouri in the Union as long as the rights of slave owners were recognized. To that end he led a state convention in 1860 and counseled Missourians to remain loyal to the Union. But in the summer of 1861, just a few months after Bounds assumed his Brunswick pastorate, President Lincoln sent federal troops to occupy Missouri and make certain that the state did not secede. Although Lincoln expressly instructed his generals not to free any slaves (because he did not want to offend pro-Union slaveholders), troops under John C. Fremont and Nathaniel Lyon began freeing slaves and confiscating property belonging to slave owners.

Charitan County's favorite son, General Sterling Price, consequently took charge of a Missouri state militia of five thousand men. Their goal was to defend the state from the likes of Fremont and Lyon. Price was rapidly driven from Missouri, and civil war began in earnest in the deeply divided border state.

As a result of this unpremeditated conflict, Unionists not only freed more slaves, they confiscated the church buildings, schools, and parsonages of all Methodist Episcopal, South, churches. This, they claimed, was merely regaining property stolen by proslavery partisans when the Methodist Episcopal Church split in 1845. Bounds, while uncomfortable supporting slavery, found himself the pastor of a church that was, as people in his county saw it, invaded by hostile forces. Ultimately somewhere between five hundred and a thousand men from Charitan County joined Confederate regiments under Sterling Price while only 130 Charitan men volunteered for Union service.[11]

By 1861 Missouri had approximately 48,800 Methodist Episcopal Church, South, members with 243 traveling preachers. The northern wing of the church had 6,619 members and 69 traveling pastors. These statistics notwithstanding, Union troops and unauthorized bands of ruffians whose sympathies lay with the North confiscated property and then arrested most preachers and pastors who admitted being under orders from the Methodist Episcopal, South, denomination.

Sometime during autumn 1861 the Reverend E. M. Bounds was arrested while he worked in the twelve-year-old red brick church in Brunswick. Union troops who took him into custody argued that he was disloyal to the Union because of his denominational affiliation. The evidence suggests that he was treated rather harshly—no doubt roughed up, hastily tried, and then placed in a federal prison at St. Louis. If he had ever entertained the thought of joining his brothers and supporting the Union cause, circumstances and Providence moved him to the other side. By the time the leaves were turning brown and falling from the trees in Missouri in 1861, E. M. Bounds was imprisoned with a collection of criminals, rebel soldiers, and Confederate sympathizers. Immediately he began ministering to scores of angry and defeated souls. He was a de facto Confederate chaplain even though he had neither volunteered nor signed a loyalty oath in support of the Confederate States of America.[12]

Bounds spent nearly a year and a half in a St. Louis federal prison before being freed at the end of 1862. On New Year's Eve Major General Samuel R. Curtis ordered his release from prison with the stipulation that he be "sent South and beyond the lines of the United States forces; he will not be permitted to return to the State of Missouri during the War."[13]

Early in 1863 the twenty-six-year-old prison-weary native Missourian was taken to Memphis where he remained under Union guard for a few days. Then he and many other Confederate prisoners were exchanged in Arkansas for U.S. troops captured by Jefferson Davis's army. By February Bounds, who had two brothers armed and dressed in Union blue, found himself thoroughly enmeshed in the Confederacy simply because he had protested the Union occupation of a church building that was constructed three years after the Methodist Episcopal Church, South, was formed. Inasmuch as Methodist Episcopal, South, people donated the land and built the forty-by-fifty-foot structure with their own rather than confiscated funds, the young pastor refused to hand it over to the representatives of the rival denomination. For this stand he was declared disloyal to the United States, spent eighteen months in prison, and found himself banished from the state of his birth. No opportunity was given to take an oath of loyalty to the United States as he left prison. He was an enemy prisoner who was bartered away in a larger prisoner exchange.

In February 1863 the one-time reluctant rebel now had ample reasons to side with the secessionists. His brothers notwithstanding, he would commit his allegiance to the Southern people who quickly got him out of his old clothes and into a grey uniform with brass buttons. He made his way to Port Gibson, Mississippi, and was sworn in as a regular chaplain for the Third Missouri Volunteer Infantry Regiment. He once again had a congregation of fellow Missourians to oversee.[14]

The Confederate Army was as desperate for good chaplains as it was for able-bodied fighting men. The pay was poor (Bounds eventually earned eighty dollars a month),[15] the conditions dangerous and demanding, and the reception from the men was at first mixed. Although the vast bulk of the Confederate soldiers were at least nominal Christians, they did not always welcome chaplains. They were so used to preachers joining them as chaplains and then deserting or resigning when the going got rough that they eyed every newcomer with suspicion and aloofness. Battle-seasoned soldiers had seen too many zealous ministers come and then leave them for the comforts of home-front callings. These veterans also observed that some chaplains ministered only in camp, behind the lines in hospitals, or on the fringes of combat near the tent surgeries.[16] Chaplain Bounds may have been little in stature, but he was not short on courage. To be sure, he ministered in the hospitals and led prayer meetings and worship in camp, but he traveled on foot with the army, and he never dodged the front lines of battle. He won the deep respect of his men because he loved them, marched with them, and never flinched from the heat of battle. In brief, Bounds was the kind of chaplain the Confederacy craved. He bravely served the men, and his preaching and pastoring shored up the men's morale.

Bounds's courage and commitment to his flock in the face of combat was nowhere more apparent than at the bloody battle of Franklin, Tennessee. In November 1864 Confederate General John Bell Hood, commander of the Army of Tennessee, who had been overwhelmed and forced to retreat from Atlanta in September, was in the midst of his last-ditch strategy to stop Union General William T. Sherman's ruthless march to the sea. Because Hood's greatly outnumbered forces could not stop Sherman when they fought head-to-head, his plan was to swing around, pull up northward, and try to sever Sherman's communications that stretched back to Tennessee. During the last of November 1864, Hood tried to slip between a force commanded by General George Scofield at Pulaski, Tennessee, and another large Union force seventy-five miles to the north at Nashville. But when Scofield detected Hood's plan, he pulled his entire force of thirty thousand men back to a defensible point on the Harpeth River at Franklin.

General Hood, who had taken command of these Confederate troops four months earlier, had complained that they did not like to fight unless they were well fortified in trenches. If this was ever true, and it is doubtful that it was, the rumor was laid to rest forever after November 30. On that beautiful Indian summer day in 1864, Hood's men made contact with Scofield's outposts at noon. General Hood, who was furious that he had missed earlier opportunities to punish the Yankees, determined to make a frontal assault.

Several of Hood's corps-commanding generals counseled against this plan. The Confederates were outnumbered thirty thousand to eighteen thousand. The Union was on high ground and solidly entrenched, complete with four-to-one artillery superiority. General Scofield himself was so confident of his superior numbers and strength that he announced to the Carter family, who owned the farmhouse where the Union set up a command post, that they were sure to be safe. The Confederates, he argued, would never be foolish enough to attack given their artillery and numerical disadvantages and the terrain.[17]

Counsel and odds notwithstanding, General Hood made preparations to attack the Union lines. Tension mounted all afternoon among the two corps of men from the Army of the Tennessee. For three to four hours regiments moved into position and waited for the imminent call to charge. During this time when men's hands were sweaty, their toes curled tightly in well-worn boots, and thoughts turned to home and eternity, Chaplain Bounds made the rounds of the combat-ready Missouri regiments. During what must have seemed like an interminable delay, he walked in front of a massive line of soldiers with positioned muskets and fixed bayonets so that he could go from one front-line Missouri regiment to another in order to pray with as many men as possible.

Bounds presented an incredible sight to the men lined up and ready to engage in heavy combat. Suddenly their tense eyes fixed on the Confederate chaplain walking directly in front of them and carrying all of his gear, including a large nap sack. Because Bounds was so short and his backpack so massive, one nervous rebel soldier quipped, "Look at that backpack walking out there with a soldier on its back!" The humorous remark lightened the eerie mood of the unseasonably warm and sunny afternoon. Immediately chuckles rolled up and down the line as Bounds waved, smiled, and went to pray with more of his men.[18]

As the clocks in the Carter farmhouse struck 4:00 p.m., Hood finally gave the order to attack. According to the foremost authorities of the Battle of Franklin, the next five hours would be the worst in the entire war for the attackers. From 4:00 to 9:00 the battle stormed on. Both sides fought stoutheartedly in a mass of carnage where the blood flowed ankle deep in some places of heavy hand-to-hand combat. As the authors of *The Battle of Franklin* phrased it, "In terms of the number of Confederate casualties within such a brief time—little more than five hours—Franklin was the South's darkest day."[19]

About 1,750 Southern troops were slaughtered. Another 5,500 were wounded or captured. Six Confederate generals died; six more were wounded or captured. Franklin was the last great charge that the Confederates mounted in the war. For this effort absolutely nothing was gained except that 2000 casualties were inflicted upon the Yankees and no one ever again said the Army of the Tennessee would not fight bravely in the open.

Among the prisoners taken that evening was E. McKendree Bounds. This time there was no prison for incarceration. Instead, he and his wounded and stunned compatriots were disarmed and herded into a field. Within a few hours every able-bodied Confederate who had not made it back to regroup and join Hood's retreat was pressed into ambulance duty. All night and for most of the next day prisoners in gray and victors in blue carted the wounded to makeshift hospitals. Not until late on December 1 did they begin to dig mass graves for the dead.

B. F. Haynes, destined to become a Methodist preacher of the Wesleyan holiness persuasion and president of Asbury College, was a firsthand observer of events of the day after the horrible battle. Once the battle began "[We] children were sent to our grandfather's who lived about a mile from town." That night their house was filled with wounded soldiers. "Early the next morning in company with a cousin much older than myself," wrote Haynes, "I hurried to town to visit the battlefield. The scenes my boyish eyes witnessed were simply indescribable. The dead and wounded, the suffering, the piteous cries and moans," were almost too much to see:

> I remained for an hour or two and walked over the battlefield, which was on Carter's farm overlooking the town, and watched them as they carried the dead and wounded from the field. Returning to the town I found that all the public buildings including the churches, and indeed a very large number of private residences were used

as hospitals. This one brief experience of the horrors of war was enough for me and made me an earnest advocate of peace for all time to come.[20]

If these horrors of combat were not enough to demoralize the men captured at Franklin, news came on December 16 that Hood's Army of the Tennessee had moved up to Nashville and suffered another crushing defeat. With less than half of the number of men who marched northward out of Atlanta with him, Hood's decimated ranks fled Tennessee and limped back to the deep South and certain defeat.

The curtain was coming down on the Confederacy. No major force was left to block Sherman or cut his supply lines. Furthermore, everyone knew that General Robert E. Lee's army could not long withstand General Ulysses S. Grant's besieging force with its drive firmly set toward Richmond, the capital of the Confederate States of America. Consequently on December 17, a day after Hood's debacle at Nashville, all of the Confederates captured at Franklin were given an option. They could go to prison or be released to go home if they would sign an oath of loyalty to the United States and promise not to bear arms against the government in the future. Most of the dejected secessionists signed the oath.

Among those battle-scarred troops who stood in line to surrender and take the Oath of Allegiance was E. McKendree Bounds. His clothing tattered, his boots nearly worn through, Bounds owned nothing of material value except the smoke-saturated rags on his back, his Bible, and a little accordion-shaped wallet that carried his ordination papers and his 1859 license to preach. As he stood there surrounded by mass graves, devastated farmhouses and land, and a throng of wounded and weakened fellow warriors, Bounds realized more than ever before that this world is not home.

Before Christmas Bounds made his way back to his birthplace to see family and friends. But he did not stay long. Missouri was not home either. The Confederacy was, for all practical purposes, dead. But many of the people were still alive there. The tasks of recovery, reconstruction, and reconciliation were ahead, and Bounds intended to be involved. Many lost souls needed to be led to Christ, because now in the wake of defeat, more people than before realized they needed forgiveness and healing.

By early spring 1865 Bounds was back in Franklin, Tennessee. He and a number of other veterans joined forces with some local people and agreed to properly bury and memorialize those men who died the previous November. The efforts of Bounds and a few others resulted in a local farmer donating a beautiful piece of land on a little ridge north and east of the city. During the spring and summer of 1865, workers exhumed 1,496 Confederate soldiers' bodies from makeshift mass graves nearer the town and on the field of battle. The remains were identified by name and unit whenever possible. In line with the Confederacy's admiration for state's rights, the bodies were then moved to the memorial cemetery and interred in sections laid out by states.[21]

Bounds supervised the exhumation, identification, and reburial of all those who had served in Missouri units. In all, 130 Missourians were identified and relocated in the new cemetery on the Carter Farm where they remain to this day. The veteran chaplain not only oversaw this morbid task, he raised over seven hundred dollars to pay local men to do the labor. Securing space in Missouri newspapers, he published the names, ranks, and units of each Missourian who fell at Franklin, and thus managed to persuade generous people from that state to send enough money to purchase a large monument bearing the wording:

C.S.A.
130
Killed at
Franklin

MISSOURI

Bounds placed in his wallet a list of the names of all the Missourians he buried at Franklin. These were not just dead soldiers. After all, they were part of his congregation, and that list was still in his wallet when he died nearly half a century later.

As much as the memory of Franklin and dead comrades haunted E. M. Bounds, the living were foremost in his thoughts.

He was always an evangelist, convinced of the folly of life without Christ. Consequently he set out with renewed commitment to point lost souls to Jesus Christ. Bounds realized now, especially after the blood bath at Franklin, that nothing on this earth is lasting.

What is amazing is the way Bounds handled his personal wartime experiences. At the onset of war he had been treated harshly, probably unconstitutionally, and thrown into prison. After eighteen months of incarceration he spent two years with combat regiments locked in a life-and-death struggle. After the war, however, the former chaplain never criticized his captors or other Yankees and northern sympathizers. Even years after the Civil War, when most prisoners of war on both sides of the conflict complained about their adversaries, Bounds refused to comment. He never vilified the Yankees, and he was never overheard to vindicate or defend his own actions or stand. That intensely human need to explain ourselves and make others understand, what St. Augustine called "this lust of always vindicating myself," was overcome by this magnetic preacher of the Gospel.

Bounds learned much during those difficult years of imprisonment and combat. Indeed, this was a time of extremely important spiritual growth. As Alexander Maclaren said a century ago, "If a man considers himself to be an iron pillar, he is of no use to God. God works through broken reeds." Between 1861 and 1865 Bounds became a broken reed. God allowed him to suffer humiliation, total loss of freedom and possessions, and He made him a pilgrim. When Bounds was dragged away from Brunswick and thrown into prison, he was stripped of his personal property and citizenship. When he was banished from his home state in 1862, he became a pilgrim who never again felt at home anywhere. A sojourner who earned little money as a preacher, he was always marginally poor, unable to buy a house, and never in possession of savings, stocks, or bonds.

The five-foot-five-inch preacher with fiery eyes never complained of his lot. From the Civil War era he learned that his life was not his own and that in property there is no ultimate security. He never forgot the lessons.

The Civil War also taught Bounds about the fragility of

life. As he marched with Missouri's Third Volunteer Infantry Regiment, eventually serving Missouri's Fifth Infantry as well, he saw the hell of war as he encountered a constant flood of men suffering wounds from minnie balls, grape shot, and cannon shells. Added to this carnage were the debilitating effects of disease, especially dysentery, pneumonia, and the ravages of blood poisoning that came with surgeries performed under the primitive field conditions.

If the guns of war were silent by May 1865, the wounds of battle were observable for at least a generation to come. Men with arms and legs missing were common, as was the presence of widows, orphans, and destroyed houses and barns. In the midst of the humiliation and pain of defeat, E. M. Bounds, not yet thirty years old by the time of Lee's surrender, devoted his entire energy to reaching out to the devastated postwar South.

He felt a keen attachment to the people of Franklin, Tennessee. Indeed, he filled the pulpit of the Methodist Episcopal Church there while he oversaw the grave transfer project. Because there was no Methodist pastor in Franklin, the veteran remained there and eventually made connection with the Tennessee Conference. In October 1866 Bounds was ordained Elder in the Conference, and he became the regular pastor of the Methodist Episcopal Church at Franklin.

Bounds stayed at Franklin for a little more than two years. During that time important events took place under his ministry. First of all B. F. Haynes, who became the third president of Asbury College (1905–1908) as well as a preacher and author of renown, converted under the former soldier's preaching. Haynes later remembered Bounds's impact this way:

> When I was only a lad there came to Franklin, Tennessee, where we lived, as pastor of our church, the Reverend E. M. Bounds whose preaching and life did more to mould and settle my character and experience than any pastor I ever had. His preaching profoundly impressed me, his prayers linger until today, as one of the holiest and sweetest memories of my life, his reading of hymns was simply inimitable. Nothing was sweeter, tenderer, or more enrapturing to my young heart and mind than the impressive,

unctuous reading of the old Wesleyan hymns by this young pastor. Such hymns as "How Sweet the Name of Jesus Sounds in a Believer's Ear," "Majestic Sweetness Sits Enthroned upon the Saviour's Brow," "O, for a Heart to Praise My God," and many others became engraven on my heart. I never hear these hymns today or think of them that the scene is not reenacted of the little black-eyed, black-haired pastor with voice of ineffable tenderness, and life of immaculate purity, and heart of divine love standing in the pulpit, of the old Methodist Church . . . reading one of these matchless hymns in a spirit, tone and manner that simply poured life, hope, peace and holy longings into my boyish heart.[22]

During Bounds's pastorate, which lasted until December 1868, young Haynes went forward at an altar call, made a "public confession of committal to Christ, was accepted, and on the following Sunday assumed the vows of church membership."[23]

Evidently others besides Haynes were touched by Bounds's powerful ministry. "When Bro. Bounds came to Franklin he found the church in a wretched state," recalled Haynes. "It was near the close of the four years of war. Much of the time we had been without a pastor, our ranks had become depleted, and the world had come into the church through the extreme excitement, acrimony and hatred incident to war."[24] What Bounds immediately did was search out a half dozen men who really believed in the power of prayer. With these fellows the young pastor (he was only twenty-nine or thirty at this time) met every Tuesday night. They got on their knees together and prayed for revival—for themselves, the church, and the town. For over a year this faithful band called upon the Lord "until God finally answered by fire. The revival just came down without any previous announcement or plan, and without the pastor sending for an evangelist to help him." The revival lasted for several weeks. About one hundred and fifty souls "were gloriously converted."[25]

The revival put closure on Bounds's tasks at Franklin. In December 1868 he was transferred to the Alabama Conference. Early in the new year he was assigned to a church at Selma in central Alabama.[26] Leaving Franklin was not easy. He had arrived at the outskirts of that village on November 30, 1864. The regimental banners were flying high; there was even the music of horns and drums in the air. As he left four years later there were no more flags, the music of war was silent, the Confederate Army disbanded, and 130 of his own men were buried in the blood-drenched soil.

As Bounds moved south to Alabama, he traveled with some precious possessions. Besides a flood of wartime memories, he had the names of his dead friends carefully tucked in his wallet so that he could always remember them and pray for their families. Bounds also had a strangely warmed heart. The horrors at Franklin notwithstanding, he had a keen sense of God's presence and sovereignty. Prayer did change things, and revival had come. The future was indeed hopeful.

CHAPTER 3

THE TRANQUIL YEARS

Little is known about E. M. Bounds's years in Selma, Alabama. Nevertheless, evidence that has survived suggests that his years there were unruffled and happy—a refreshing respite after the tribulation of war.

Brother Bounds, as his Alabama friends knew him, conducted his pastoral work with sensitivity and faithfulness. He also did evangelistic work where he concentrated on reaching unconverted people for Jesus Christ and calling backsliders to repent of their sins and rededicate their lives to the Master's service. An increasingly sought-after speaker, the seasoned preacher, now in his thirties, also became a keenly talented writer. Consequently he was often requested to write articles for Methodist-related publications and was in frequent demand as a speaker for revivals and camp meetings.

It was probably to lead one of his evangelistic or camp meetings that Brother Bounds first went to Eufaula, Alabama. Located on Lake Eufaula on the eastern edge of Alabama at the Georgia line, the little town at that time had a permanent population of only several hundred souls. During the summers, on the other hand, this popular resort area where the lake is fed by the Chattahoochee River, always experienced a population explosion of several hundred more. A small railroad, the Montgomery and Eufaula, connected the beautiful region with the state capital, and it was therefore relatively easy for Bounds to travel the 150 miles from Selma to Eufaula. What transpired each time the traveling preacher went to this resort-area camp meeting we do not know, but during one of his visits he broke up a race riot by placing himself in the middle of the fray. Also at

Eufaula Bounds met a prominent Methodist family, the Barnetts. Family correspondence shows that the preacher loved the
Barnett family, and as he put it in one of his letters, "My life has
been sweetly blessed in your home."[27]

Certainly the greatest blessing that came to Bounds from
the Barnett home was Emma Elizabeth Barnett. The daughter of
a minister, Dr. A. W. Barnett, she was born in 1835, the same
year as Bounds. The two had much in common. They were the
same age, they were Methodist Episcopal in religious persuasion, and they both were approaching age forty having never
been married. Their true feelings for each other were put to the
test in 1874. That year Bounds was transferred to the St. Louis,
Missouri, Conference where he took the pastorate of St. Paul's
Methodist Episcopal Church, South.[28] This was a young church
with a new building. Indeed, the following year a volume called
Pictorial St. Louis: The Great Metropolis of the Mississippi Valley
noted that St. Paul's, on St. Louis Avenue and Sixteenth, "is a
new organization, but increasing rapidly in numbers and
influence. Rev. E. E. [*sic*] Bounds is pastor."[29]

The pressures of pastoring a new and growing church
notwithstanding, Bounds could not escape from thoughts of
Emmie. Her sentiments were evidently identical. Therefore, in
September 1876, after a respectably long courtship, Emmie
became Mrs. E. M. Bounds. The newlyweds, now forty-one
years old, set up housekeeping in an established yet booming
city at the juncture of the Missouri and Mississippi rivers.

Bounds's church was located about a mile and a half from
the core of the old city. St. Paul's was an attractive little church
planted in a fast-growing section of the city. The streets in the
neighborhood were unpaved, but the buildings were new and
clean. A few recently planted trees adorned the thoroughfares,
but ultimately the adjustment to urban life must have been
difficult for Emmie. Her home in Alabama was rural and serene,
complete with lovely trees and a beautiful lake. St. Louis, on the
other hand, was a teaming urban complex that accommodated
over 350,000 people who had migrated there from Europe,
especially from Germany, Ireland, and Italy. The newcomers
also came from rural America, particularly from areas east of the
Mississippi.

The culture shock for Mrs. Bounds that resulted from moving from rural Alabama to an urban environment like St. Louis was exacerbated by being hundreds of miles from the family she so dearly loved. Although the pain of the move was severe, she did not complain. To this day family members maintain that she was deeply devoted to her husband and his pastoral ministry.

Life in the Bounds family changed markedly fourteen months after the wedding. In November 1877 a girl named Celeste was born. She was followed by a second daughter, Corneille, born just twenty-six months later. If tending her babies and keeping up with parish work was not enough to keep Emmie Bounds busy, she must have been exhausted by the pressures that accompany household moves. The St. Louis City directories for these years show the Bounds family constantly on the move. From September 1876 until February 1886—not counting the move to St. Louis—the family moved seven times.[30] Edward and Emmie owned no home, and they evidently rented rooms in new quarters when their needs changed.

One change of location occurred when Brother Bounds was called to be pastor of the elegant and massive First Methodist Episcopal Church, South, located in the heart of the city. He was senior pastor there from 1879 to 1881. This was the church attended by the Methodist members of the social elite, and it was one of the most prestigious churches in all of Missouri. In its building designed in the style of the late Middle Ages, annual conferences and other large Methodist festivities were regularly hosted. This was also the church where the body of the famous general Sterling Price rested in state when he died in 1867.[31]

Bounds was sent to First Church in 1879 and stayed there only two years. From the evidence that can be pieced together it seems he was an increasingly well-known preacher who had done a splendid earlier work of building St. Paul's. Indeed, during his years there the young church grew from 70 to 247 members. While Bounds helped build St. Paul's during the late 1870s, he also did itinerant evangelistic work for the Missouri Conference. In fact, it became increasingly apparent that he was gifted in building and reviving the church. Therefore, the bishop, hoping to revitalize old First Church, which had been entrenched in its stately building since 1821 and yet had only 202 members, sent Bounds there to offer new leadership.[32]

It is unlikely that Brother Bounds had much patience with the elitist social views of a few First Church members. Indeed, he abhorred the pew rental system. In concert with his sympathy for the poor, he sent out advertising for the church that read "SEATS FREE. ALL ARE WELCOME IN GOD'S HOUSE." In an effort to reach outside of the ornate walls of the enormous church, especially to the poor and downtrodden, Pastor Bounds gave a document to all the members of the First Methodist Episcopal Church, South:

TO THE MEMBERS OF THE CHURCH
If you would grow in grace give attention to the means of grace in the Church.
Every member of the Church has covenanted to attend upon its ordinances and support its institutions.
Give the Pastor your co-operation and your prayers.
Attend to private devotion: Keep your heart right and your influence will take care of itself.
Be attentive to the sick, the poor and to strangers. Speak to strangers in the congregation, and, if possible, introduce them to the Pastor.
When you change residence notify the Pastor by card.[33]

It is difficult to imagine this document or the abolition of reserved pews for the wealthy sitting well with all members. But here was vintage Bounds, underscoring the devotional life, urging more time in prayer, and advocating outreach to the poor and sick. Such a program was designed either to transform an indolent church or get the pastor moved. Not surprisingly, Bounds was gone from First Church within two years. By 1881 the family moved again, and he was pastor once more at St. Paul's.

The Bounds family faithfully ministered to the growing congregation at St. Paul's until 1883, when the conference called the talented local pastor to become associate editor of the St. Louis Conference's official paper, *The St. Louis Advocate.* He took the position at age forty-seven with hope and enthusiasm. He enjoyed writing. He did it well. And he had some burdens for revival that he hoped to present to the people. This new assignment also allowed him ample time to do evangelistic preaching.

For a season everything was joyous and rewarding. The new position was challenging, and in February 1884 a little boy, named Edward for his father, was born. But nothing remained stable long for the Bounds family. Not only did they pack up and move once more, but Emmie became critically ill (probably cancer) and went South for the early part of the winter in 1886. By going to Alabama she could be with her family and stay in a warmer climate. Change of environment, however, did little to retard her illness. On February 20 the forty-nine-year-old mother of three children, ages eight, six, and two—died. Before her death she called for her beloved husband to come and be with her and the children. Her dying wish was that he marry her first cousin Harriet who lived in Washington, Georgia. Emmie was confident that Harriet Barnett would love Edward and the children—and they would need a faithful wife and mother to help them on the remainder of their pilgrimage. Edward promised to pursue her wish.[34]

For E. M. Bounds, the years from 1874 to 1886 had been tranquil ones. To be sure he moved often, he had no place to call home, and financially he was no better off than before the Civil War. But for years he knew he was called to be a pilgrim and a sojourner. Especially after 1861 he knew that this world was not his home. Since the baptism of the Holy Spirit came to him in 1859, the Missouri-born preacher walked by faith. During this time God removed one support after another, leaving him with nothing to lean on but the grace of Christ. From experience Brother Bounds had been accustomed to the process, but somehow he never expected to lose Emmie. For a time he was convinced that his broken heart would not heal and that it might be impossible to carry on his ministry. Ultimately, though, he knew he must go forward for the children's sake and because God had spared him and called him to preach.

CHAPTER 4

MATTERS OF PAIN, CONSCIENCE, AND CALLING

For the next nineteen months the Reverend E. M. Bounds served as associate editor of *The Advocate*, filled pulpits when local pastors were away, did evangelistic preaching, and took care of three children under age ten. Sometimes his brother Charley's family, who lived two hundred miles north at Kirksville, Missouri, took the children while he attended Annual Conference, traveled, and preached. At other times, especially during holidays and summer, Emmie's family in Alabama watched the children. But mostly it was this faithful father and widower who shouldered the responsibilities of keeping hearth and home together.[35]

One year and nine months after Emmie's body was laid to rest in the red soil of southern Alabama, the fifty-two-year-old widower fulfilled a promise he made at Emmie's deathbed. On October 25, 1887, in a small and simple service, Bounds married his deceased wife's cousin, Harriet Elizabeth Barnett, at Washington, Georgia. The officiant of the quiet little service was Dr. A. W. Barnett, the father of Bounds's late wife and the uncle of the new bride. Dr. Barnett's brother and the bride's father, Samuel Barnett, was a resident of Washington, Georgia, and a banking and railroad investor.[36]

Harriet Elizabeth Barnett was thirty years old at the time of her marriage to Bounds. Never married before, this petite young woman with soft brown hair, warm eyes, and finely-cut features, entered into this union with a man nearly twenty-two years her senior. Despite their age differences, family members maintain that this was an idyllic match. The two were devout Christians of Methodist Holiness persuasion. Furthermore, they had strong and loving family connections, and they were both committed to large families and the Lord's service on a full-time basis.[37]

Soon after the autumn wedding, Brother Bounds, his three children, and their new mother left Georgia and returned to rented quarters in St. Louis. Bounds resumed his duties editing the paper, and he enjoyed the bliss of his family life. Nine months after their marriage, Hattie, as she was called by the family, gave birth to their first child. Born on the Fourth of July, 1888, the baby boy was named Samuel Barnett after Hattie's father.

Joy reigned throughout the Bounds and Barnett extended families. Hattie and her husband were devoted to one another, and they were delighted to have four children. Added to their pleasures came an invitation for Bounds to become the associate editor of the Nashville *Christian Advocate*. The St. Louis paper was the organ of only one conference, whereas the Nashville weekly was the official paper for the entire Methodist Episcopal Church, South, denomination.

The new opportunity did more than place Bounds with a prestigious paper—he would never have accepted the call on that ground alone. Indeed, the associate editor at Nashville was expected to do much writing—even more than the editor who was to devote much of his time traveling and attending to administrative matters. The Nashville paper, then, would give Bounds a much wider audience for teaching on the key issues burdening his heart. Also, living in Nashville would place Hattie and the children over three hundred miles closer to the Barnett family in Georgia.

Early in the new year of 1890 six Boundses boarded the train for Nashville. With very few possessions besides their clothes (they always lived in furnished, rented quarters), they headed south with assurance that they were in God's will, and they had high expectations for the future. As the wheels of the train clicked out its monotonous rhythm on the metal rails, Hattie and Edward basked in the special joy of knowing that her second child was due in midsummer.

Initially 1890 promised to be a good year. Bounds got the family comfortably situated in a modest rental house in

Nashville, and he settled in to enjoy the challenge and routine of the Christian publication. Before the new baby was born, Hattie asked her husband to take her to her parents' home in Washington. She wanted to have the baby in Georgia where she could find comfort with her mother and help with her new baby and the other four children. In any case Harriet's parents resided in a three-story antebellum house that offered six bedrooms on the top floor as well as many spacious rooms on the downstairs two levels. House servants helped with the cooking, laundry, and sundry household chores.[38]

On July 11, 1890, Hattie telegraphed her husband that they had another healthy boy. This child they named Charles Rees after Edward's brother in Kirksville, Missouri. However, before Bounds could finish some writing deadlines, clear his desk, and leave the newspaper to an assistant, another telegram arrived from Georgia. On Wednesday evening, July 23, a wired message came with the shocking news of six-year-old Edward's death. Only a few weeks before, when his father had left him in Georgia with the rest of the family, the boy's health was robust.

A stunned Bounds boarded the next train to Georgia. Five days later he wrote to Dr. Barnett in Alabama:

> Your kindly sympathetic letter was duly received and fulfilled its gracious mission.
>
> I came at once to bury our dear little Edward. My first intimation as to his sickness was the telegram announcing his death on Wednesday. I arrived here Thursday. The rain was so hard and so incessant that we could only deposit his body in a vault expecting to bury him Friday or Saturday but the weather has been so rainy that we will postpone his burial till tomorrow. The point of carrying him to Eufaula was in my mind and raised by the family here. His natural burial place would be beside his dear mother and had he died up the country I would have taken him there. But he was here. Hattie was anxious for him to sleep here. Your family is leaving Eufaula, the visits of the children, Hattie and myself will in the very nature of things be oftener to Washington than to Eufaula and the fact of a long trip and the attachment of the family here and the fact that they had

arranged for his burial here decided me to let the dear body of our precious boy sleep here.

His devotion to Hattie was the most beautiful thing I ever knew. . . . He begged to be carried to her while sick and he did spend one day in her room.

He was almost a perfect boy and he had often talked to me of doing my work when I was gone to Heaven. He said to Hattie, when I think of my mother in heaven I have to shut my eyes.[39]

Bounds did not try to hide his enormous grief from Dr. Barnett. "The blow is heavy on me, my heart seems literally broken." Trying faithfully to surrender the tragedy to God, the devastated father wrote, nevertheless, "I rejoice in the will of God, its wisdom and love but my heart is broken by the blow [and] it seems to spend its full force on me." Bounds confided that Edward "was so dear to me and so full of life, the perfection of a boy." Finally, the wounded evangelist and prayer warrior testified, "I am sure it is a call to me for intense effort and a deeper consecration. I will heal by God's grace."[40]

The wound of Edward's death could only have begun to heal when yet another blow was unleashed on the fifty-six year old preacher. Exactly four days short of the first anniversary of Edward's death, little Charley, just eight days past his first birthday, died as unexpectantly as his brother. The pain was nearly unbearable for Hattie and her husband. They buried Charley near his brother in the Barnett family plot in Washington's cemetery.

No glib words could ease their pain. True, the Boundses were people of enormous faith. But how could they understand what was happening? The truth was that they could not. Once they stopped reeling from the initial numbness, they went on with the business of living because Hattie was two months pregnant and they had three other children to raise.

Ultimately Hattie and Edward got on with parenting and working because, as they expressed it, God's grace carries us through. God's grace did carry them through, but only because they trusted His ultimate love and wisdom. They certainly did not understand.

If they ever compared themselves to Job—and they must have—there was hope for the blessing of other children. This came to pass on February 29, 1892, when little Osborne Stone was born. This strong boy was followed by a healthy baby girl named Elizabeth who entered the world in September 1893.[41]

Despite the pain of burying his first wife and two children during a period of five years, Bounds had confidence in God's love. He had suffered before, after all, burying many men he cared about during the Civil War. These numerous deaths drove him further into the study of the Scriptures as he searched for answers to questions and the assurance of a further hope. During this grievous time Bounds began working on the outlines and texts of what would eventually become two books: *Heaven: A Place—A City—A Home* (published posthumously in 1921) and *The Resurrection* (1907). In *The Resurrection* he wrote:

> [The Resurrection] is a brave and tender statement of a precious and divine truth. Who are sleeping in Christ? We know Who! We folded their hands with tears and kissed the lips and laid them to sleep and wrote on their tombs the words of hope and resurrection. We did not see their spirits and could not follow them in their heavenward flight, but we did bear their bodies, broken-hearted, and lay them to sleep mirrored on our hearts, and Christ shall bring them back to us out of their graves and out of their sleep to our embrace and to our hearts.[42]

A man cannot fabricate this kind of confidence in Christ's promises—at least not for long. With all of his heart and mind, Bounds believed in the resurrection of the body, and he also believed in the reality of heaven. Indeed, Bounds was no idealist who embraced dreams and concepts that were not real. On the contrary, he knew that Jesus Christ had walked this earth. Bounds likewise believed that Jesus' promises were inviolable to those who trusted, loved, and followed Him.

Because of his confidence in Jesus Christ, Bounds had absolute assurance about life after death and a place called heaven. In the book *Heaven*, the author wrote that Jesus said the "earth is unsafe." "People die, and moths, thieves and rust do their work here." But "Heaven is a place, as really as earth is a place, a place of absolute safety." Bounds noted with assurance that Jesus "emphasizes heaven! He wants our hearts to be there. The heart is the soul, the being, the man. Safety is in heaven. Put your values there only, put your heart there." He went on to note that "no tears are there to flood your heart, no sorrows there to break it, no losses there to grieve and embitter."[43]

It was this hope based upon the reality of Jesus and the integrity of His promises that drove Bounds on to faithful service despite the hardships. During the early 1890s he not only worked on his books, he continued his work at the *Christian Advocate*. Although his concerns at the Nashville paper were manifold, it is fair to say that he used his office there to try and block the spread of liberalism in the Methodist Episcopal Church, South. After the Civil War, and most especially by the 1870s and 1880s, the so-called "New Theology" was gaining fashion among seminary professors and modernist clergy. Although this movement was widespread and multifaceted, its major tenets came out of Germany. Theologians there were raising serious questions about the reliability and veracity of the Bible. Consequently reason and experience were given priority over Scripture as guides for God's revelation. In brief, the champions of reason and experience were questioning the biblical revelation for morals, behavior, and the path to salvation.

The liberalism of the late nineteenth century questioned such doctrines as original sin and faith in Christ as the only way to salvation. Many modernists likewise turned their guns on the doctrine of hell, especially on the concepts of eternal damnation and eternal punishment.

Modernists hoped to redirect the Christian faith in still other areas. The Social Gospel, that is, the emphasis upon the Great Commandment to serve and love our neighbor, was given much more emphasis than the Great Commission in which the emphasis is on making converts and disciples of Jesus Christ. Furthermore, the liberals were increasingly disdainful of pietism, mysteries of the faith, entire sanctification, and the deeper-life movements. To the modernist temper the emphasis on the next world, the New Jerusalem, was an erroneous separation of the secular and sacred. Theodore Munger, for example, a leading spokesman for the modernist cause, wrote in 1883:

> The New Theology does indeed regard with question the line often drawn between the sacred and the secular . . . a line that, by its distinction, ignores the very process by which the kingdoms of this world are becoming the Kingdom of the Lord Jesus Christ.[44]

Modernists in the Methodist Episcopal Church had been gaining numerous converts among the clergy and seminaries in the North since the Civil War. Likewise, great inroads were being made within the southern wing of Methodism as well. To E. M. Bounds this movement of liberalism was anathema, so he used all of the force he could muster to repudiate it.

From the pulpit and from the pages of the *Christian Advocate* Bounds urged prayer for revival. In 1890 he wrote, "It is not new truth that the world needs, so much as the constant iteration of old truths, yet ever new truths, of the Bible." He wrote articles upholding the doctrine of original sin, and he advocated biblical preaching with calls for holiness and simplicity of lifestyle. The one-time Confederate chaplain took up the pen as a lance and went after those who advocated "worldly Christianity," and he urged Methodists to study the Bible, read the sermons of John Wesley, and learn the doctrinally sound hymns of the faith—especially those by Charles Wesley.[45]

Bounds urged evangelists and ministers to preach Bible truths not modern ideas. He also urged them to study the lives of earlier Christians such as David Brainerd, John Fletcher, and Louis Harms. Harms, a German, had been in the bonds of "rationalism, a dead orthodoxy, and worldliness," wrote Bounds, "[until] he was mightily converted to God by reading the Bible." Christians needed to be men and women of prayer— "mighty in prayer"—who sought sanctification and holiness as well as salvation.[46]

Bounds was deeply troubled by the liberal and worldly drift of Methodism. The fault, he believed, was love for money and love for this world. In one issue of the *Christian Advocate* he quoted a London reformer who made an observation that Bounds believed applied to North America:

> John Wesley said that if Methodism was ever destroyed, it would be destroyed by the love of money. He wrote his last sermons and spent his last years in warning the Methodist people against the love of money. He knew that the enterprising and hearty genius of Methodism would tend to make our people rich, and he foresaw that unsanctified wealth would [corrupt].[47]

Not only were people growing rich, sleek, and comfortable, many people so enjoyed the world's ways that the doctrine of holiness was being at best discounted, most often ignored, and at worst attacked as an archaic view unfit for sophisticates of modern times. In short, it was increasingly difficult to distinguish a Methodist from anyone else.

According to Bounds, decadent clergy were largely responsible for the church's downward slide. Clergy lifestyles and even their teachings were leading the flock astray. Consequently, as soon as Bounds arrived at Nashville he began a series of long prophetic articles and a number of pungent short pieces where he boldly employed the Scriptures to show how the Lord never called His servants to seek money and employ the ways of the world. "Few men get rich with clean hands," he wrote in 1890. "Fewer still get rich with religious hands. Fewer still hold on to their riches and hold onto Christ with a strong grasp at the same time. Who can serve Christ and money?"[48]

If Bounds the prophet made some preachers uncomfortable with his call for holiness and his attacks on lusting for money, prestige, and power, his constant call for revival annoyed those who believed that the church was essentially sound except for its unfashionable preoccupation with the next world. The extent to which Bounds was standing outside of the growing liberalism within Methodism on these issues was markedly apparent during the Tennessee Annual Conference in 1893. One of the major disputes that year concerned evangelism. For nearly a year a debate had been raging over this ministry. Most regular Methodist ministers were called itinerant or traveling ministers.

That is, they were in full connection with an Annual Conference and were regularly relocated by order of the presiding bishop. A few men who felt called to the office of evangelist were given appointments that freed them to travel and evangelize. This freedom, however, was extended only if the bishop was sympathetic to the belief that evangelists are part of a divinely ordained order of ministry.

The pros and cons of evangelists as legitimate ministers were hotly debated by the 1890s. Certainly the growing heat of the debate was in direct proportion to the rise of liberalism and deprecation of holiness. In 1893 the problem came to a head over the appointment of Samuel Porter Jones. Born in 1847 in Alabama, Sam Jones fought on the Confederate side of the War Between the States. After the war he practiced law in Georgia. Alcoholism had all but destroyed his legal career when he was converted at a revival in 1872. Soon thereafter he sensed a call to the ministry. While serving several pastorates in the North Georgia Conference, he gradually realized that God was calling him to do the work of an evangelist. In 1880, thanks to the good offices of a bishop who believed in evangelism, Jones was assigned as an agent of the Conference at the Orphans' Home in Decatur.

Jones was a powerful preacher with obvious gifts in evangelism. Consequently, he was called to hold revivals all over the nation, especially in the South. A fiery preacher who spoke in the common vernacular, he always gave a large percentage of his revival honoraria to the Decatur orphanage. He likewise took up freewill offerings for the children's facility. As a result of his ministry, effective evangelism went forth, and the orphanage expanded its size and services without debt.[49]

Beginning in 1892 the *Christian Advocate* published letters to the editor that debated the wisdom of allowing a minister to do the work of a traveling evangelist. Some critics of men like Sam Jones, including the senior editor, E. E. Hoss, of the *Christian Advocate*, and the Tennessee Conference presiding Bishop, A. G. Haygood, were ardently opposed to Jones's kind of work. The bishop wrote in the *Advocate* that no official office of "evangelist" existed in the Methodist Episcopal Church, South. Furthermore, he noted that such an office should not be created, on the grounds that too many evangelists were doctrinally unsound. We do not need, he argued, "herds of imitators of noted evangelists in small towns, villages, and country places."[50]

On the other side of the issue, H. R. Withers wrote:

> God is filling us with evangelists and we make no place for them. Evangelism is taking hold of the church with a strong plea for recognition. Here is a clearly defined class of zealous workers springing up and growing in the church, a ministry without place, made to catch and hold on to life. . . . As churches grow large and wealthy and cold and indifferent, the pastoral work also becomes regular, systematic and burdensome. . . . Evangelists are needed and will come. Our church has made no place for one of the established offices of the New Testament.[51]

The battle lines were drawn in what both sides saw as a holy war. Indeed, at the Annual Conference session held at Nashville in 1893, Bishop Haygood argued that if Jones were reappointed to his position at the Decatur Orphans' Home, this would be tantamount to appointing him to the office of evangelist. Inasmuch as no such office existed, the bishop said that siding with Jones was a violation of Methodist polity. Jones responded by saying he must be free to accept calls to do revivals, whenever and wherever they be.

Finally, after much debate, the Conference voted to support the bishop. When the count was tallied, Jones "located," or, in official Methodist language, he left the itinerant ministry of the Annual Conference.[52]

The Conference was in tears when Jones stood up and delivered his farewell address to his fellow Methodists. One bishop who looked back from the vantage point of 1906, said at Jones's funeral:

> His life of almost unexampled activity was dominated by one high and holy purpose—to do good to his fellow men and faithfully serve his generation by the will of God. To that high aim every ambition was subjugated and every energy put into commission. Believing that providence had

clearly indicated his field of largest usefulness to be unconfined by the narrow limits of a local pastorate, he retired from the regular itinerant ministry and made the nation his parish. Whatever the judgment of others as to the wisdom of that course, he never doubted that God had ordered it and would approve it.[53]

Sam Jones declined opportunities to join other denominations. He likewise refused to criticize his mother church. Nevertheless, in candid moments he confided that if Bishop Haygood had been sympathetic to evangelism he would have interpreted the law in another light. In any case, Jones went forward in his evangelist work and became an active lay member of a North Georgia congregation.

To E. M. Bounds, Jones's decision to locate became a matter of crisis and conscience. Called to the biblical office of evangelist himself, Bounds had always valued freedom to travel and do evangelistic work. In fact, throughout his ministry since the late 1860s he had found congregations and bishops who encouraged him in itinerant work. But now the evangelist-editor was at odds with his immediate superior, Editor E. E. Hoss, and he was wholeheartedly on Jones's side against Tennessee's bishop.

Suffering great agony of soul, Bounds prayed for direction about his future with the church. Truly he feared no man and no amount of deprivation, but he did not want to do anything impetuous that would snare him out of God's will. Therefore, he waited until the General Conference of 1894 to see which way Southern Methodism would go.

The tide of modernism began to roll in at General Conference. While liberalism would not reach high tide until the new century, its powerful impact was already evident at this meeting in 1894. A solid stand was taken against recognizing the office of evangelist. One bishop summarized the majority position this way:

> The signal success of a few evangelists of burning zeal, effective speech and skill in leadership has given great popular favor and impulse to this movement. A notion

spreads that in order to have a wide and mighty awakening, evangelists must be employed; that they are the only class on whom we can rely to rebuke sin fearlessly and to attract the unconverted.

The offering of the regular army is more important than any guerrilla warfare, however brilliant. We do not want an order with pastors to keep up a routine or a higher, freer, bolder order of prophets to bring down fire from heaven.[54]

This stand by the denomination settled the issue for Bounds. In his heart he believed evangelism to be a divinely ordained ministry. The office was biblical, and Bounds himself had been called to it. He had known of this call since 1859, and God had used him in revival harvests among soldiers during the war and at Franklin, Tennessee, immediately after the great conflict. Bounds had done the work of an evangelist concurrently with his various pastorates in Selma and St. Louis. Likewise his associate editorships in St. Louis and Nashville had complemented his evangelistic work equally well.

In late May 1894, without fanfare or rancor, Bounds gave notice to both the editor and the bishop of his decision to take "voluntary location." In effect, to demonstrate how far he believed the church to be drifting from biblical guidelines, Bounds gave up his salary, benefits, and future pension. This was no modest protest, considering that he was an evangelist who had responsibilities for a wife and five children. Furthermore, this sojourner and pilgrim owned no home and had virtually no material assets.

According to Brother Bounds's granddaughter, his wife was loyal and supportive. Nevertheless, she did say, "Now that you have left the church, how do you propose to feed all of us?" Bounds's response was succinct: "My dear, if we are in the Lord's will, the ravens will feed us if necessary."[55]

CHAPTER 5

EVANGELIST, WRITER, AND PRAYER WARRIOR

Years later some of the Bounds children maintained that "the ravens were Mama and Papa Barnett."[56] If the remark was meant reverently, Bounds would have agreed. Soon after his resignation from the *Advocate*, he, Hattie, and the children packed up their clothes and few belongings and moved to Georgia to live with her parents.

The Barnett family had always been kind and generous to their daughter and son-in-law. At least once a year since the wedding Hattie made a pilgrimage to Washington to enjoy the company of her kin. She also went there each time she was ready to deliver her babies. These visits were usually joyous occasions because the family was genuinely close. They seemed to enjoy one another's company. Truly this was a family that somehow escaped the awkwardness of families that have nothing in common except ties of marriage or circumstances of birth.

One reason the Barnetts could be so generous to the Bounds clan was that they had the resources and facilities to accommodate all seven of them. Samuel Barnett, Hattie's father, had purchased an 1830s-vintage home in 1857, complete with a hundred acres of choice Georgia land. Before his daughter married Bounds, this railroad promoter and investor greatly expanded the house by adding many rooms, a hallway, and a new staircase. Before the Civil War the lovely antebellum home with about fifteen spacious rooms, wide halls, a massive brick-floored kitchen, verandas, and graceful shade trees was remodeled by Barnett and made ready for guests.[57]

Although the Barnetts were pleased to have their daughter's family move in, the relocation must have been somewhat painful for Edward McKendree Bounds. To be sure, he was confident that God was leading him out from under ecclesiastical authorities who were moving the church in a modernist direction. He was also certain of God's call to preach repentance, salvation through faith in Jesus Christ, the witness of the Spirit, and entire sanctification. Likewise Bounds felt assured of God's leading toward a deeper life of spending more time in prayer and helping others learn the joys of a life of fellowship with the Holy Spirit that leads to holiness, prayer, and sacrificial service. In brief, the call to preach, pray, and write was clear; but how God would provide food and shelter was a mystery.

Moving to Georgia was at once a blessing and a humiliating experience for Bounds. He was grateful for the hospitality, but no nineteenth-century man enjoyed living off the charity of his wife's parents. Bounds, however, laid aside his pride and trusted that this was the Lord's guidance. He did his utmost to preach revivals and fill temporarily vacant pulpits. As a result, a modest but sporadic income was forthcoming. In any case, everyone assumed that their living in the Barnett home was only a short-term arrangement. In fact, it was not. The truth was that Bounds had left a prestigious and secure position in Nashville, for, as Willis Irvin put it, a life "hindered by poverty, obscurity, loss of prestige."[58]

When the Boundses arrived in Washington, approximately three thousand people lived there, with another fifteen thousand in surrounding Wilkes County. Of the total county population of eighteen thousand, nearly six thousand were white and more than twelve thousand were black. Washington itself was an attractive town that boasted a new public school, a railroad depot, several thriving agricultural service businesses, and all the county offices. Although the streets were not paved and horse droppings dotted the thoroughfares, Washington was adorned by several magnificent antebellum homes—including the handsome mansion owned by Senator Robert C. Toombs.[59]

Wilbur J. Cash, one of the South's most perceptive historians, wrote in his classic, *The Mind of the South*, that property and wealth were the pillars of the power base on which the planter class stood. The Barnetts, of course, had property and wealth. Bounds, by comparison, was a pauper. Not only was the down-at-the-heels evangelist and holiness preacher without the badges of status so venerated in the South and elsewhere in America, he was decidedly on the outside. The 1890 manuscript census documents show that the vast bulk of Wilkes County residents were Georgia-born. Indeed, skimming through the list of thousands of names one finds a monotonous refrain of "Georgia" listed in the Place-of-Birth column. The jolt to the eyes when suddenly coming upon "Missouri" in this census column merely symbolizes what it was like for this border-state dweller to live among Georgia-born citizens of the deep South.

Brother Bounds might have been a Confederate chaplain and combat veteran of the War Between the States, but he still had a Missouri accent. To the residents of Georgia a Missourian sounded like a northerner. As soon as two words uttered forth from Bounds's mouth, a red flag appeared in the minds of the southerners who still chafed from the burden of losing a war and suffering the twin indignities of Yankee occupation and carpet-bagger economic schemes.

The evidence indicates that Bounds was at once loved and welcomed by the Barnetts but viewed as an outsider by the local community. Congregations were not large when he preached in Washington, and to this day little remains there to satisfy those who come seeking information about his life. It is significant that when Mr. and Mrs. Barnett died a few years after the Boundses arrived, and Hattie inherited the house as the result of a family lottery, everyone merely viewed E. M. Bounds as the husband of Harriet Barnett. To this day the brochure of the Washington-Wilkes Historical Museum surveys the history of the house and mentions that it was Samuel Barnett's house after 1857. "His descendants lived here," according to the sketch, "until the death of his daughter, Mrs. Edward McKendree Bounds, in 1913." The preacher himself is not mentioned in the literature, and his seventeen-year residency is ignored at the museum, despite the fact that over a dozen books were written there and eight of these are still in print.[60]

Apparently E. M. Bounds took his inferior status at Washington in stride and turned his attention to his work. When he and Hattie inherited the large beautiful house, he must have rejoiced and thanked God for this unexpected and most generous provision. Nevertheless, the grey-haired preacher's head was not turned by property. He went right on with his work of preaching, writing, and intercessory prayer. Furthermore, despite the coolness of his welcome by Washingtonians, he developed a great love for the guarded community. When he was away preaching in cities like Nashville, Atlanta, or St. Louis, he complained of the incessant traffic noise that assaulted his ears both day and night. "I am getting a little restless for home," he wrote at one time, because of the "unceasing noise" and "the hurrying, eager crowds intent on this life. Thought, hope and effort for the eternal life all seem gone in the struggles and hopes of this life. This saddens me."[61]

Life in the Bounds's Georgia household was always warm and loving, but it was unceasingly busy. Two more children arrived soon after the move—Mary Willis in 1895 and Emmie in 1897. In 1901 Corneille and Celeste, the two oldest daughters, moved out of the house and made more room for the other five children. Aged twenty-three and twenty-one respectively, these daughters of Edward's first wife were married by their father in a double ceremony at the Washington First Methodist Episcopal Church, South.[62]

Family correspondence, as well as stories handed down through children and grandchildren, portray vivid pictures of life in the Bounds household during the late 1890s and early 1900s. Bounds himself was up at four o'clock every morning to be alone with the Lord in prayer. His routine was to pray until seven o'clock. Then he would eat breakfast, spend the day studying Scripture and writing sermons and books—with periodic intermissions for more prayer. Usually the entire family would join him for prayer and songs of praise at 4:00 a.m. After an hour he went off for more prayer while Hattie and the children ate and got on with their day's schedule. This agenda evidently varied little unless Brother Bounds was preaching out of town. In fact, the family still laughs about the shock that came to some girls spending the night at a slumber party in the Bounds's home. It seems the preteen celebrants stayed up late talking. Nevertheless, they were rousted out early by the patriarch-preacher who herded them all into the parlor for prayer and praise. Bounds's granddaughter said that her grandfather's success that day in getting others to join him in prayer was similar to the success Jesus experienced at Gethsemane. Everyone else fell asleep while the one who convened the meeting prayed on.[63]

Bounds's behavior was eccentric in more than his early morning prayer program; he often worked so intently that he forgot to come to dinner. Even after being called he might forget the summons and continue working, oblivious to the ordinary life carried on in the house.

Bounds also appeared singular to outsiders because of his absolute confidence in God's ability to provide for the family's needs. His trust is a remarkable testimony to God's faithfulness and power, but it evidently struck more earth-bound people as downright strange. On one occasion when cash was short, Bounds was invited to preach a revival in Atlanta. After praying to learn God's will, the evangelist was not only confident he was to go, he believed he should take his son Osborne along. With bags in hand they climbed aboard the West-bound train at Washington. When the conductor came by, the bearded preacher reached his hand in a deep pocket and pulled out a fistful of coins. "My son and I are going to Atlanta," explained Bounds. "I know this is not enough money to get us all the way there, but put us off whenever this fare runs out." The incredulous railroad man counted the coins and said, "Brother Bounds, this is not nearly enough to get you and the boy there. Why, I'll have to put you out in the middle of a field somewhere." Bounds replied that if they were put out in the middle of a field that is precisely where God would want them to be.

Young Osborne trembled in fear as he heard the fate predicted by the conductor. However, the boy soon came to appreciate his father's trust in God. Within a few minutes a well-groomed man approached the pair. "I understand you are Reverend Bounds and you and the boy don't have quite enough to get to your destination."

"So we are told," replied Bounds.

"Well, your fare is covered Brother Bounds. Have a blessed meeting in Atlanta."[64]

This event was just one of a lifetime of God's dealings with

E. M. Bounds. Ever since God stirred a Tennessee farmer to give the penniless Confederate chaplain a mule to ride back to Missouri in 1865, the awestruck preacher unswervingly trusted the literalness of Jesus' exhortation to seek first the kingdom and trust that the necessities of life will be forthcoming. Bounds had not only experienced the fulfillment of this promise in 1865, he realized similar provisions through every step of his ministry. God took his wife, Emmie, but gave him another bride who was equally loving and loyal. Two children died, but many more came to gladden his heart and warm his home. A secure position as associate editor was surrendered in Nashville, but an antebellum mansion on a hundred lovely acres was provided in place of rented quarters in the Tennessee city.

Because God always supplied their needs, E. M. Bounds's faith grew with each passing year. He came to believe that all earthly resources were to be used to glorify God and further His kingdom—never were they given to us to stockpile and hoard. Such a view of stewardship, which Bounds gleaned from Scripture and observed in lives he admired, led the Bounds family to share generously of their resources. Even though they never had much money because of the evangelist's meager earnings, they willingly gave to those less fortunate. It is still recalled in the family that whenever a needy person called at the home, Brother Bounds instructed his wife to meet their needs. Even if the family pantry or purse held little, he insisted that they share. If they ran out, God would provide for them in the way He was providing for the unfortunate person at their door.

There must have been times when it was difficult to live with a man like E. M. Bounds. Even if Hattie adored him—and the family maintains that she did—the children often felt the tug of society pulling them toward a more mainstream lifestyle. However, Osborne so adored his father that he changed his middle name from Stone to McKendree at age ten. Celeste and Corneille greatly admired their father, too. Indeed, Celeste named one of her children after him. But not all of the other children loved their father so unconditionally.[65] It was embarrassing to have slumber-party guests ushered into the parlor for devotions at four in the morning. Likewise some of the children found it difficult to believe it was more blessed to give money to poor people and missions rather than to dress in the latest fashion. As a result, two of the children quietly but decidedly rebelled. Although they did not openly break with their father, they denied his faith and lived out their lives as agnostics.[66]

These problems notwithstanding, E. M. Bounds had a close and loving relationship with most of the children. Family correspondence and reminiscences show that he wrote thoughtful and endearing letters to his children when he was away from them. He was neither the sort of person who believed it was unmanly for a father to demonstrate affection nor was he the kind of man who left all the letter writing to women. He communicated with his children in love, and he occasionally sent them money and helpful advice about travel.

Being a faithful correspondent enabled Bounds to remain in close contact with his family, despite the frequency of his travel. However, it would be incorrect to say that he was in great demand as a speaker. In fact, C. F. Wimberly, who knew Bounds and had him preach at his church, remembered that he had limited engagements as an evangelist because "his ministry was so rare and so sublime, that few congregations could breathe in the heavenlies where he would lead them. He was so quiet, so modest, so unassuming, that one felt something akin to awe in his presence." Wimberly went on to note that Bounds was one of the most "unearthly men we ever saw." No other word was sufficient to describe him.[67]

Nevertheless, he did receive some invitations to travel and speak. The local pulpit supply did not take him away from home overnight, but regular camp meeting appearances put him back on the road most summers during the late 1890s and the early twentieth century. He spoke also at Georgia's Indian Springs Holiness Camp Meeting on more than one occasion, and also led services at many holiness camps in Tennessee and Alabama.

Mainline Methodists increasingly found his deeper life too radical for their urbane tastes. Holiness Wesleyans, on the other hand, invited the slight little man to their gatherings. Asbury College in Wilmore, Kentucky, a center for the Wesleyan Holiness movement, brought Bounds to campus in the 1890s for a revival. He also preached at the Central Holiness Camp Meeting in Wilmore, and preached at a revival in the Wilmore

Methodist Episcopal Church, South.[68] A Methodist school, Birmingham Southern College, in Alabama, brought the independent evangelist to Birmingham for a meeting in the late nineteenth century. While he was there they awarded him an honorary Doctor of Divinity degree in recognition of his years of faithful service as a preacher and writer.[69]

Occasionally a Methodist Conference invited the prayer warrior to speak at Annual Conference or annual retreat. This was especially the case after he published his first two books, *Preacher and Prayer* and *The Resurrection* with the publishing house of the Methodist Episcopal Church, South, in 1907. By then the zealous evangelist had snow-white hair, was in his early seventies, and no longer enjoyed travel. Indeed, the seventy-five-year-old wrote from Missouri in July 1910, "The Methodist preachers have a kind of Camp Meeting. They have invited me and say I shall have a chance to address them. But I fear the recreation will swallow up the more serious ends of the meeting." He went on most candidly, "I can't say I am enjoying myself. All is pleasant and agreeable but I am too far away from home to be happy."[70]

During the last decade of his life, Dr. Bounds accepted a few invitations to preach. However, no decision to preach was accepted without ardent prayerful consideration. Age and infirmity were not the principal factors in his decisions, rather he felt God was calling him to a daily effort of prayer—what he termed the "Business of Prayerside." Requiring daily intercession for the sanctification of preachers, revival of the church in North America, and the spread of holiness among professing Christians, this "work" of prayer consumed a minimum of three to four hours a day. Sometimes the venerable mystic would lie flat on his back and talk to God; but many hours were spent on his knees, or lying face down in a prone posture where he could be heard weeping for the conversion of sinners and sanctification of preachers.[71]

Bounds stayed in Washington, Georgia, to engage in the Business of Prayerside—usually in a little cabin near their big house—but he also stayed at home to write. By the beginning of the new century he was convinced that God was calling him to a special writing ministry. The Holy Spirit burdened Bounds to prepare guidebooks on prayer as well as major works on Satan, heaven, and the resurrection of the body. The author's goal was not to publish for money. On the contrary, Bounds, like Jesus and John Wesley, was keenly aware of the corrupting influence of money. Dr. Bounds did concede that "God sometimes uses money to further Kingdom work, but it is very low on His list of priorities for how He gets things done."[72] Instead, Dr. Bounds eagerly desired to publish little books that would fit into the pocket with ease, and sell for a dollar or less. He even offered the copyright free to anyone who would disseminate his writings for ministry rather than profit.[73]

Bounds was able to publish some of his thoughts in the *Christian Advocate* before he left Nashville in 1894. But that paper had a modest circulation and, like all newspapers, a very limited life. Now he felt certain that God wished him to write little books. So the man of enormous faith asked God to open avenues for publication because his personal resources were entirely inadequate for the task.

His granite-like faith convinced him that if God calls, He will provide the way. Therefore, he set out to do the writing, assuming that the books would appear when and where God wanted them to.

The Lord did provide, but in a variety of ways. First of all Bounds published *Preacher and Prayer* with Marshall Brothers in England in 1902. Two years later he found enough money to hire a private printer in Atlanta to bring out the same book in America. Then in 1907 he acquired resources to bring out another printing with the Chicago Bible Institute Colportage Association. That same year Bounds borrowed funds to pay the Methodist Episcopal Church, South, in Nashville to publish *The Resurrection*.

Although Dr. Bounds lived to see only *Preacher and Prayer* (subsequently slightly altered and given the title *Power Through Prayer*) and *The Resurrection* in print, God led him to a man who would oversee the printing of everything else that the aged evangelist hoped to print.

CHAPTER 6

DISCIPLESHIP AND DEATH

In 1905 Homer W. Hodge, a Methodist preacher attached to a fashionable Atlanta church, received a letter from a Gainesville, Georgia, man. Robert O. Smith, the author of the letter, was a Wesleyan Holiness preacher with a word of advice. "Get Dr. Edward McKendree Bounds of Washington, Georgia, to speak at your ministerial conference. He will bless all of you."[74]

Hodge acted on the suggestion and invited Bounds to speak. The Washington-based evangelist accepted the call and arrived in Atlanta by train. When Hodge met the five-foot-five septuagenarian at the station, his heart sank. Evidently the urban preacher expected a giant of a man given the resounding build up from Smith. Instead "a small man with gray hair and an eye like an eagle came along. His stature and little handbag were against him."[75]

"It was a ten days' convention," recalled Hodge, and Bounds had been asked to speak at three o'clock on the first afternoon. "He spoke the first day to a small crowd with little effect and I recall the subject was prayer." That night Hodge provided lodging in his house for several of the ministers. Bounds and one other preacher shared Hodge's room. Hodge remembered this about the next two days:

> I was surprised early the next morning to see a man bathing and rubbing himself before day and then see him get down and begin to pray. I said to myself, "He will not disturb us, but will soon finish." He kept on softly for hours, interceding and weeping softly, for me and my indifference,

and for all ministers of God. He spoke again the next day at three p.m., on the same subject, viz: "Prayer." I became interested, for I was young in the ministry, and had often desired to meet with a man of God that prayed like the old saints of the apostolic age. Next morning he was up early praying for hours. I became intensely interested, and thanked God for sending him.[76]

Hodge also recalled that Bounds spoke on prayer for the next eight days, but only after beginning each day at four o'clock with fervent, tearful yet quiet intercession to the heavenly Father.

This conference proved a turning point for both Hodge and Bounds. The younger man was forty-six years old and relatively new to full-time ministry. He had been looking for a man to disciple him ever since his mid-life conversion that came as a result of "a little pilgrim band singing on the streets and preaching holiness, 'without which no man shall see the Lord.'"[77] Yet the mentor Hodge sought failed to appear until his encounter with E. M. Bounds. Indeed, for the next eight years, until Bounds died, Homer W. Hodge annually spent as much fruitful time with this God-sent teacher as each of their schedules allowed.

For Dr. Bounds this 1905 meeting was equally providential. Despite a ministry that spanned four and a half decades and included residency in four states, this diminutive man never attracted a large personal following. Certainly many people admired Bounds and some called on him to speak in churches, revivals, camp meetings, or an occasional conference. Nevertheless, after forty-six years in ministry no clergyman and only one layman ever asked Bounds to be his spiritual guide.[78] To be sure he led many to the Lord over the years, and he had a profound impact on many others along the way. But in the last analysis few wanted to be tutored by a man who pressed them to join a life of early morning prayer, humble service, and purposeful austerity.

This failure to attract a disciple disappointed Brother Bounds. He sorrowed not because he craved the adulation of people, but because he wanted so much to pass on to others the joys and riches he had found in the Business of Prayerside and the walk of holiness and service.

Homer W. Hodge was cut from similar cloth. He found Bounds's personality, ministry, and lifestyle to be enormously captivating. "He drew me to him with hooks of steel," Hodge confessed.[79] Consequently, the Atlanta pastor eagerly anticipated his time with Bounds. He learned all he could from the old prayer warrior about preaching, praying, and devotional reading. Hodge also grew committed to Bounds's book-writing project. Indeed, when Bounds died with only two of his books in print, Hodge undertook the task of seeing nine more books published as well as the reprinting of one more.

Hodge's eight-year relationship with Bounds is both fascinating and instructive.[80] Brother Bounds delighted in his association because he viewed the younger man as an answer to years of prayer. Bounds yearned for men to covenant with him to be at prayer by four o'clock in the morning—during the "Great While Before Day Hour," which he gleaned from Jesus' early prayer time recorded in Mark 1:35. Bounds also wanted an ally to encourage others to join in this same ministry and "business" of prayer. Hodge not only willingly joined the old evangelist in rising by four, he also promised to launch an all-out effort to enlist others in the work as well.

Bounds, for his part, prayed daily and fervently for Hodge, asking the Lord to give him unction and to enable him to do the work of an evangelist and pastor. The venerable Civil War veteran spent weeks and eventually months instructing the student in the ways of holiness and the deeper life. Bounds taught him to pray early and earnestly, asking God to give him the essential ingredients for a meaningful prayer life. These essentials included faith, trust, desire, fervency, persistence, good character and conduct, obedience, and vigilance. Beyond these Bounds taught Hodge how to study the Bible more effectively, and he gave him instruction on how to preach with power.

The elder prayer warrior taught the younger man through lengthy conversations at least once a year, and then through letters while they were apart. Of all the methods and mediums, however, Bounds's example proved the most effective. The young disciple was awestruck by what he quietly observed when the older man was not aware of his presence. "No man could have made more melting appeals for lost souls and backslidden ministers than did Bounds." Hodge recalled that "tears ran down his face" as he interceded for indolent preachers and people without Christ.

"We were constantly with him, in prayer and preaching, for eight precious years." He never uttered foolish words, and he eschewed gossip as well as criticism of those he disagreed with or who had wronged him in the past. He had his eyes on the New Jerusalem. "He was one of the most intense eagles of God that ever penetrated the spiritual ether."

In 1911, after six years of visitation and correspondence between Atlanta and Washington, Pastor Hodge was appointed to a congregation in Brooklyn, New York. Not long after Hodge felt settled with his new congregation, he wrote to his mentor and asked him to come to New York, pray with him, and instruct the church in the practical theology of prayer. Bounds replied, "I am thinking more of going to Heaven than to New York. . . . But it is in God's will. I would enjoy being with you. God seems to have opened the way."

God did open the way, and the former Confederate soldier found himself on Yankee soil by early autumn 1912. Already seventy-six years old, Bounds wore out his younger colleague by announcing that he now arose at three o'clock for an even lengthier session of prayer! Hodge suggested that four would do just as well, but Bounds would not budge. Indeed, the Brooklyn pastor reported, "So intense was [Bounds] that he awoke up at 3 o'clock . . . praying and weeping over the lost of the earth." Then after breakfast, "all during the day he would go into the church next door and be found on his knees until called for his meals."

His sermons during that two-month visit were brief, usually about twenty minutes in length. Although he presented a fervent message, his voice was not strong and his little frame trembled from the strain.

Hodge said that their eight weeks together were spent in "sweet fellowship and mighty prevailing prayer." They also took a side trip to Northampton, Massachusetts. Bounds was a great admirer of David Brainerd, and next to the Bible and Wesley's sermons he probably reread nothing so much as Jonathan Edwards's edition of Brainerd's diary. Years before, Hodge had heard Bounds say that he would love to see Brainerd's grave before he died. Now Hodge delighted in taking his teacher the 175 miles to Northampton. "We went at once," wrote Hodge, "to the cemetery ... sat down by the side of the graves of Brainerd and Jerusha and Jonathan Edwards. There we knelt and prayed; thanked God for those lives; thanked God for the eminent saints; and we also partook of the blessed communion."

In late October 1912, Hodge bade his dear friend farewell. "I took that dear, sweet, wrinkled face in my hands, and kissed him for the last time." Both of them knew they would not meet again this side of glory. For a few months more, however, they did correspond. Bounds asked Hodge to pray that he would have the strength and vision to finish the book manuscripts. The evangelist was running out of energy and time, and he wrote in December, "I am turning to you and [our friend C. L.] Chilton. One of you must help me to do the work on my manuscripts. . . . Keep them if necessary until I die—until God's fitting time to publish."

A few notes came in early 1913. "Dearly beloved: A good time praying for you." In another letter, "Let your mind live in the spirit of prayer. . . . I am right feeble, but will strive to work on and wait for God's time for *heaven*." In late April he reminded Hodge, "God will manage our affairs if we will be filled with His affairs." In May he said he was still up early and keeping Hodge in prayer. Then on June 26, a postcard: "Hold to the old truths—double distilled."

The last direct message Hodge received from Edward McKendree Bounds came dated August 9, 1913, in Hattie's hand: "Tell him he is on the right line; press it. Have a high standard and hold to it."

On August 24, 1913, Reverend Hodge received the telegram that he knew must come:

"Doctor Bounds went home this afternoon; funeral here tomorrow afternoon. —Hattie Bounds."

CHAPTER 7

LEGACY

August 24 fell on Sunday in 1913. That morning at Washington's First Methodist Episcopal Church, South, prayers no doubt were offered for the congregation's sick and shut in. Certainly a petition was raised heavenward for Dr. Edward McKendree Bounds, who had been bed-ridden for several weeks. The white-haired evangelist, who just nine days before celebrated his seventy-eighth birthday, was growing weaker by the hour. Obviously he and his family needed the Lord's blessing.

During that Sabbath afternoon, still a few hours before the sun's heat was broken by late summer twilight, Brother Bounds took his final breath. With Hattie at his side he slipped quietly from her presence into full view of the One he had longed to see.

The following Thursday the town's weekly newspaper ran a lead article on the front page with this headline: CHRISTIAN SOLDIER ANSWERS LAST CALL. The obituary noted that "as a minister, a Christian gentleman and an author he was well known in Southern Methodism. . . ." The journalist observed that Bounds's "passing not only carried the sense of a deep personal loss to all who knew him here but was the occasion of deep sorrow to countless friends, particularly in Georgia, Tennessee, and Missouri. . . ."[81]

The sorrow and grief were most keenly felt in the Bounds home on East Main Street. Indeed, Hattie so grieved over her husband's death that her health broke, and she died less than four months later at age fifty-six.

Bounds's death did not totally devastate anyone but Hattie, yet plenty of Methodists felt an enormous sense of loss. Those who knew Bounds realized that a great warrior had departed. It seemed that he alone had the courage to write and say what many others believed but feared to express. For many years Bounds stood in the gap attempting to stem the growing tide of Methodist liberalism. An old-school Wesleyan, Bounds staunchly maintained that the Bible was written "directly under the superintendency of the Holy Spirit. . . . We hold definitely without compromise in the least to the plenary inspiration of the Scriptures."[82]

The Methodist-ordained evangelist not only embraced the primacy of Scripture, he embraced the doctrine of holiness wherein a justified and regenerated person is baptized by the Holy Spirit in a second work of grace that brings death to the regenerated person's sin nature. This "entire sanctification" leads to a path of holiness, according to Bounds, that is guided by the Holy Spirit and nurtured on ceaseless prayer.

This deeper life—this wholly sanctified life—is not only marked by victory over known and willful sin, it is recognizable by increasing likeness to Christ. The disciple, then, is called to pursue a life that glorifies God as it takes on more Christlikeness and simultaneously sheds its worldliness. Indeed, sanctified believers will care less and less about this world as they increasingly long for the one to come. Money, worldly power, and status among people should not simply be guarded against, they should be repudiated. In truth everything that binds us to this life must be "put away." We are, he always insisted, in the manner of Hebrews 11 and 13, only "pilgrims and sojourners" here. "This world is not our home. We are seeking another city—the New Jerusalem." In this vein Bounds often expressed his disdain for earthlings who called themselves Christians. He was especially outspoken in one Conference-wide message that was reported in the *Christian Advocate* in 1890. In his typical refreshing, prophetic posture, Bounds wrote that the "greatest danger" facing the church is "found in the ambition of the preachers and the covetousness of the laymen." He was not slandering Zion or overlooking other problems. On the contrary, he was convinced that ambition for office or for honor is, in a preacher, nothing short of sin. Covetousness in a layman is the refinement of idolatry. The worship of money, which is too absorbing to give time for the claims of conscience, is not half so worthy of toleration as was the worship of the sun and moon. God made these. Human hands fashioned that. The push for place in the clergy is next, in disloyalty to Christ, to a denial of the faith.[83]

Bounds's pronouncements—especially his ability to cut sharply to the heart of spiritual matters without the usual gentle qualifiers—infuriated the modernists but endeared him to genuine Wesleyans. It was from this latter group of conservatives that some men stepped forward to keep Bounds's voice alive even after his body was buried in Washington, Georgia.

Homer W. Hodge did more than any human to keep the evangelist's legacy alive. Hodge, fifty-four years old and living in New York when his mentor died, immediately proceeded to form the "Great While Before Day Prayer Band" in Brooklyn on New Year's Day, 1914. Within a few months this zealot for prayer had enrolled nearly one hundred people. Included were men and women from twenty-six states representing both sea coasts, the Gulf states, and every region in between. These people agreed to pray for three hours every morning from four to seven o'clock for lost souls and the revival of the church. They were also pledged to pray "as the Spirit leads me to adoration, intercession, thanksgiving, praise, meditation, the study of God's Word." Furthermore, they promised "to pray for a deeper spiritual life in my soul." Beyond this they interceded for the church and all ministers, for missionaries in foreign lands, and for members of The Prayer Band. Finally they covenanted to pray "for the spread of scriptural 'holiness' in the earth" and "for the early appearing of the great God and our Savior Jesus Christ."[84]

Hodge's commitment to the work Bounds began was not a temporary commitment out of the moment's grief. On the contrary, nearly twenty years after the Prayer Band was founded, Hodge, by then over seventy years old, was still sending personal notes to people and enrolling them in "the business of prayer." In 1931, for example, he wrote to H. Blair Ward, a Long Island, New York, Nazarene pastor, and sent him a copy of Bounds's *Power Through Prayer*. "This book is sweeping over England," he wrote. "I can buy 1000 for $30.00. Pls. read it over and over. Pray for me. I am trying to carry out the life of prayer and rising again. Early. Let us Pray."[85]

Urging Christians into purposeful, early prayer represented only part of Homer Hodge's efforts to keep Bounds's influence alive. This dedicated friend of the late author also saw to it that *Preacher and Prayer* or *Power Through Prayer* remained in print. Furthermore, he found money to reprint *The Resurrection*, (sometimes retitled *The Ineffable Glory*). Hodge likewise published Bounds's unpublished books on *Heaven* and *Satan*, plus seven more on the subject of prayer.

This effort on Hodge's part was herculean in scale. With some assistance from another close friend of Bounds, C. L. Chilton, he edited and prepared nine unpublished books for the printer, and he oversaw the reprinting of two more. Not only did some of the volumes require extensive editing, money had to be raised to subvent each volume.

By the middle 1920s, eleven of Bounds's books were in print. Yet it is ironic that Bounds earned no royalties from his books, and Hodge could not have realized even enough to pay his expenses. What does matter is that the eight books on prayer are still in print in English, and one of these, *Power Through Prayer*, can be found in several other languages.

It is now nearly eighty years since Edward McKendree Bounds died. Yet his books on prayer, in particular *Power Through Prayer*, continue to sell, continue to be read, and, most important, continue to change lives. As soon as they appeared in the 1920s, testimonies came forth praising God for the influence of E. M. Bounds and his books. Witnesses to the impact of Bounds's writings were heard in the decades that followed, and they are echoing to this day. For example, Dr. Robert E. Coleman, well-known evangelist and author of nearly a score of books on evangelism, testifies to Bounds's impact on his life. Coleman is so keen on Bounds that he edited a pocket-sized edition of *Preacher and Prayer* to make available to students and preachers whom he has the opportunity to teach. Also Dr.

Wesley Duewel, in *OMS Outreach* (Volume 87, September/October 1988), listed the five books that have most influenced his ministry. Dr. Duewel, former OMS president and author of *Mighty Prevailing Prayer* and the best-selling *Touch the World Through Prayer*,[86] listed *Power Through Prayer* as one of the five and the one that "opened my mind to the possibilities of prayer more than any other one book."

It is impossible to measure the extent of Dr. Bounds's legacy. Testimonies about the powerful impact of his prayer books are legion, but we know less about the influence of such books as *Satan*, *Heaven*, and *The Resurrection*. Evidence does exist to show that Billy Sunday, to take one example, was markedly influenced by *Satan*. Bounds's 156-page work on the biblical portrait of the Evil One's personality, power, and overthrow helped the famous baseball player turned evangelist to understand some of the vast opposition to his ministry. Sunday also incorporated material from the book in his sermons beginning in 1922.[87]

The eight volumes on prayer that are easily accessible in paperback will continue to edify serious disciples of the Lord Jesus Christ. These volumes are Christ-centered, Bible-based works that in their entirety comprise a veritable course on the theology, practice, and history of prayer. These popularly written textbooks—and texts is what they are—are thoughtfully crafted. They are replete with evidence and illustrations presented by a man thoroughly and lovingly acquainted with the Scriptures.

These little volumes speak to the mind of any intelligent and reflective disciple, but they do even more—they speak directly to the heart as well. Indeed, Bounds sometimes expressed his sadness over the state of theological education in the western world. So much emphasis was placed on head knowledge that the heart was often ignored. Bounds recognized that a heartless ministry—regardless of how orthodox it may be—is ultimately deadly:

> The true ministry is God-touched, God-enabled, and God-made. The Spirit of God is on the preacher in anointing power, the fruit of the Spirit is in his heart, the Spirit of

God has vitalized the man and the word; his preaching gives life, gives life as the spring gives life; gives life as the resurrection gives life; gives ardent life as the summer gives ardent life; gives fruitful life as the autumn gives fruitful life.

Bounds concluded with his often-repeated heart-life theme, "The life-giving preacher is a man of God, whose heart is ever athirst for God."[88]

Besides these classic volumes on prayer, E. M. Bounds bequeathed a rich legacy that has been long ignored. His editorials in the *Christian Advocate* have not been read for a century, just as his books *Satan, Heaven,* and *The Resurrection* have been too long out of print for people to find. Part Two of this book is comprised largely of selections from this rich storehouse of Bounds's writing. Most of the material reprinted here was written while he was on the editorial staff of the *Christian Advocate* in Nashville (1890–1894), or it was the product of his prayer-drenched efforts during his more reclusive years in the big house in Washington, Georgia (1894–1913).

It is my prayer that the selections that follow will bless you as much as they have blessed me. May Brother Bounds's legacy enrich you, edify your spirit, and drive you on to the work we are all called to do. As he wrote to Homer Hodge from Georgia on May 22, 1913, so he writes to us today: "Go out into the highways and hedges and compel them to come in. Bear your boys [those whom you are discipling] on your prayers to the doors of heaven."[89]

END NOTES

[1]Ruth T. Dryden, *The Boundless Bounds Family* (San Diego: no publisher, privately printed, 1989), 29.

[2]Dryden, *Bounds Family*, 29; *History of Monroe and Shelby Counties, Mo.* (St. Louis, 1884), Chap. 3; *General History of Shelby County* (Chicago, 1911), 25–50.

[3]*History of Monroe and Shelby*, Chap. 3; *History of Shelby*, 25–50.

[4]Dryden, *Bounds Family*, 29.

[5]Walter Williams, ed., *History of Northeast Missouri* (Chicago, 1911). See the section in this volume written by M. L. Gray entitled "Methodism and Methodists." See also Matthew Simpson, ed., *Cyclopaedia of Methodism* (Philadelphia, 1878), 577, 807–8; Frank C. Tucker, *The Methodist Church in Missouri, 1798–1939* (Missouri East & Missouri West Annual Conferences, no city cited, 1966), 23.

[6]*History of Monroe and Shelby Counties*, Chap. IV.

[7]*History of Shelby County*, 688.

[8]Dryden, *Bounds Family*, 29.

[9]Photocopy of Legal Documents dated June 9, 1854, signed by A. Reese, Judge, "4th Judicial Cirt. Mo." Original owned by Mrs. Rosemary Bounds Reynolds, Washington, Georgia.

[10]Issues of the Methodist Episcopal Church, South, newspaper, *Christian Advocate*, especially those from 1890–1894, show Bounds's background and reading interests. I also consulted the Bounds Family Papers in the possession of Rosemary Reynolds, Washington, Georgia.

[11]See J. A. Merchant, *Methodism in Brunswick, Mo.* (no city and no publisher cited, 1903); William Warren Sweet, *The Methodist Episcopal Church and the Civil War* (Cincinnati: Methodist Book Concern Press, 1912); Robert E. Shalhope, *Sterling Price: Portrait of a Southerner* (Columbia, Mo.: University of Missouri Press, 1971); W. M. Leftwich, *Martyrdom in Missouri* (St. Louis: privately published, 1870).

[12]Bounds Family Papers relate to this incident. See also Leftwich, *Martyrdom in Missouri*, 89–91; 123–56; 249; 344–50.

[13]Special Order No. 163 in the Bounds Family Papers.

[14]See documents in Bounds Family Papers, including enlistment papers, pay vouchers, and special orders.

[15]Pay vouchers in Bounds Family Papers.

[16]Charles F. Pitts, *Chaplains in Gray* (Nashville: Broadman, 1957). See also

Gardiner H. Shattuck, Jr., *A Shield and Hiding Place: The Religious Life of the Civil War Armies* (Macon, Ga.: Mercerle Press, 1987), and Roy J. Honeywell, *Chaplains of the United States Army* (Washington, D.C.: Dept. of the Army, U.S. Government Printing Office, 1958).

[17]My sources regarding the battle of Franklin come from a personal tour of the historic battlefield and Carter House Museum. I also relied upon *Battles and Leaders of the Civil War*, Vol. 4 (New York: Yoselof rep. ed., 1956); Bruce Catton, *This Hallowed Ground* (New York: Pocket Books, 1956); James M. McPherson, *Battle Cry of Freedom: The Civil War Era* (New York: Oxford University Press, 1988); and James Lee McDonough and Thomas L. Connelly, *Five Tragic Hours: The Battle of Franklin* (Knoxville: University of Tennessee Press, 1983).

[18]This story was related to me by a relative of Dr. Bounds, Mrs. Rosemary Bounds Reynolds.

[19]McDonough and Connelly, *Five Tragic Hours: The Battle of Franklin*, xii.

[20]B. F. Haynes, *Tempest-Tossed on Methodist Seas: Or, A Sketch of My Life* (Louisville: Pentecostal Publishing Co., 1921), 20–21.

[21]Evidence for this burial project is from the markers at the cemetery and information in the Franklin Civil War Museum. Also Bounds's papers have material on this subject as well.

[22]Haynes, *Tempest-Tossed on Methodist Seas*, 22–23.

[23]Ibid., 23.

[24]Ibid.

[25]Ibid.

[26]Marion Elias Lazenby, *History of Methodism in Alabama and West Florida* (Alabama and West Florida Conference, no city, 1960), 355–56.

[27]Bounds Papers, E. M. B. to Dr. A. W. Barnett, September 5, 1887. The story about the riot was given to me by the Reverend Willis Irvin, August 21, 1989.

[28]Lazenby, *History*, 390.

[29]*Pictorial St. Louis* (St. Louis, 1875), 98.

[30]Gould's *St. Louis Directory*. A complete set is at the Missouri Historical Society, Jefferson Memorial, St. Louis.

[31]Shalhope, *Sterling Price*, 289–90.

[32]See the paperback pamphlet published in 1879 in St. Louis entitled *Condensed History of the First M. E. Church, South*. A copy of this rare item is in the Missouri Historical Society, St. Louis. See also *Ninety-Eighth Anniversary 1841–1939* (St. Louis: privately printed, 1939).

[33]This document is printed on the first page of the 1879–1880 church pamphlet. "Rev. E. M. Bounds, Pastor" is on the cover.

[34]Interview with the Reverend Willis Irvin and Mrs. Rosemary Bounds Reynolds, August 21 and 22, 1989, respectively.

[35]Bounds Papers, especially a letter from E. M. Bounds to Dr. Barnett, September 7, 1887, reveal some of these patterns.

[36]Bounds Papers, including marriage certificate and correspondence.

[37]Interviews with the Reverend Willis Irvin and Mrs. Rosemary Reynolds. A photograph helped me with the physical description of Harriet Barnett.

³⁸This house is now the Washington-Wilkes Historical Museum. It is open to the public.

³⁹Bounds Papers. E. M. Bounds to A. W. Barnett, July 28, 1890.

⁴⁰Ibid.

⁴¹Dryden, *The Boundless Bounds*, 29, is useful here. However, it should be noted that two errors are in this genealogy. Charles Rees was born of Hattie, not Emmie. He was born in 1890. Also, Dryden omits Edward born of Emmie.

⁴²*The Resurrection* (Nashville: Publishing House of the Methodist Episcopal Church, South, 1907), 144.

⁴³*Heaven: A Place—A City—A Home* (New York: Revell, 1921), 28–29.

⁴⁴Quoted in William R. Hutchison, *The Modernist Impulse in American Protestantism* (New York: Oxford University Press, 1982), 76.

⁴⁵For example, see *Christian Advocate*, December 20, 1890; December 27, 1890; December 13, 1890; and an undated article entitled "A Needed Revival" in the author's personal Bounds collection.

⁴⁶*Christian Advocate*, July 26, 1890; October 4, 1890.

⁴⁷Ibid., December 13, 1890.

⁴⁸Ibid., December 27, 1890.

⁴⁹The material on Sam Jones and the evangelism controversy is gleaned from an important M.A. thesis by Harold Ivan Smith: "An Analysis and Evaluation of the Evangelistic Work of Samuel Porter Jones in Nashville, 1885–1906," unpublished M.A. thesis, Scarritt College for Christian Workers, Nashville, 1971.

⁵⁰Ibid., 129.

⁵¹Ibid., 129–30.

⁵²Ibid.

⁵³Ibid., 130–31.

⁵⁴Ibid., 132.

⁵⁵Interview with Rosemary Bounds Reynolds, August 22, 1989.

⁵⁶This family lore was passed to me by Rosemary Reynolds.

⁵⁷Information about this house and its history is available on site and in the Washington-Wilkes Historical Museum brochure. The home is now a museum.

⁵⁸Willis Irvin, Jr., *The Prayer Warrior: A Mini-Biography of E. M. Bounds* (privately printed, no city and no publisher cited, 1983), 12.

⁵⁹The 1890 manuscript census, photographs of old Wilkes County and Washington, and *The Story of Washington-Wilkes* (Athens: University of Georgia Press, Federal Writers Project, 1941)—all located in the Mary Willis Library, Washington, Ga.—were useful for this data.

⁶⁰Mrs. Reynolds told me that Bounds's children were saddened by the small congregations that came out in Washington to hear him speak.

⁶¹Letter to Celeste, July 20, 1910, from E. M. Bounds. Bounds Papers.

⁶²Clippings on this wedding are in the Mary Willis Library.

⁶³Bounds Papers and interview with Willis Irvin and Rosemary Bounds Reynolds.

[64]This story recounted to me by Mrs. Reynolds. Her father, Osborne, told it to her.

[65]Interview with Mrs. Reynolds. See also Bounds Papers, especially E. M. Bounds to Celeste, July 20, 1910.

[66]Ibid.

[67]C. F. Wimberly, "Modern Apostles of Faith," *Pentecostal Herald*, September 14, 1927.

[68]Joseph A. Thacker, Jr., *Asbury College: Vision and Miracle* (Nappanee, Ind.: Evangel Press, 1990), 34–35.

[69]Irvin, *Bounds*, 11.

[70]Bounds Papers, E. M. Bounds to Celeste, July 20, 1910.

[71]Wimberly, "Modern Apostles of the Faith," and Irvin, *Bounds*, 8.

[72]This quotation is from the *Christian Advocate*, 1890.

[73]Irvin, *Bounds*, 2.

[74]Homer W. Hodge, "Foreword" to Edward M. Bounds, *Satan: His Personality, Power and Overthrow* (New York: Revell, 1922), 5.

[75]Homer W. Hodge, *Prayer: "The Forgotten Secret of the Church"* (no city and no publisher cited, n.d.), 11.

[76]Ibid., 12.

[77]Ibid., 11.

[78]Ibid., 16.

[79]Ibid., 12.

[80]Homer Hodge's reminiscences, which comprise the next few paragraphs, are drawn from several sources. First, the booklet by him cited above called *Prayer*. Also, I used his forewords to the following Bounds books: *Satan, Heaven, The Possibilities of Prayer*, and *Purpose in Prayer*.

[81]*The Washington Report*, August 28, 1913.

[82]Bounds expressed this view of the primacy of Scripture on many occasions and in many places. This particular quotation is from p. 112 of his book, *Prayer and Praying Men*. The George Doran edition was published in 1921.

[83]*Christian Advocate*, May 24, 1890.

[84]A membership sheet on the "Great While Before Day Prayer Band" is in the E. M. Bounds file in the Mary Willis Library, Washington, Georgia. Also the elaborated pledge is in Hodge's booklet, *Prayer: "The Forgotten Secret of the Church,"* p. 23.

[85]Dr. Patricia Ward, Dean of Arts and Sciences at Wheaton College, Illinois, gave me two books from her father's library. The Reverend H. Blair Ward was a Nazarene pastor. His copy of Bounds's *Power Through Prayer* was sent to him with a note typed on the title page. The note is by Homer Hodge, and it is dated 2/9/31. The text is what I have quoted above. The other book from Reverend Ward's library is Hodge's *Prayer*.

[86]Both published by Zondervan.

[87]Lyle W. Dorsett, *Billy Sunday and the Redemption of Urban America* (Grand Rapids: Eerdmans, 1991), 125.

[88]*Power Through Prayer*, chap. 2.

[89]Quoted in Hodge's Foreword to *Heaven*.

PART TWO

The Message
of
E. M. Bounds

In the following pages twenty-six categories of the writings of E. M. Bounds are arranged in alphabetical order. Most entries are gleaned from *The Christian Advocate* (1890–1894) and are identified by date. If the entry comes from another source, it is indicated by title and chapter number. Pagination is omitted because the editions vary so much that such citations are not useful.

Bible

The Old Truths. It is not new truth that the world needs, so much as the constant iteration of old truths, yet ever new truths, of the Bible.

Christian Advocate, December 20, 1890

The doctrine of original sin is one of the old-time ideas. Man, in other days, was held to be depraved—that there was in him original and strong tendencies to wrong, his nature corrupted, and contrary to the law of God; or, as the Creed has it, "that man is far gone from original righteousness, and is of his own nature inclined to evil." All this seems changed in the current of modern thought and action. This age does not accept this doctrine. It is very proud of man's material and mental success, and refuses to see the ruins of the moral edifice. It is very jealous of man's reputation, and will not tolerate the attributing of any original badness to him. If men are in any way to be charged as sinners, it must not be in an original or radical way. Sin must be attributed to them in a mild form as the result of certain outward and irresponsible conditions, or to some amiable weakness which has a leaning to virtue's side. The item of the Creed declaring man's original sinfulness did but voice the public sentiment of that day, and did but formulate Bible truth. The Creed affirmed it because the Bible taught it, and the age gave credence to the Creed and to the Bible. But a great change has been wrought in the public sentiment and the floating faith of these times in regard to this fundamental item of the old Creed and the old way of thinking about it. This change is not evidenced by the violent breaking up of the old view or by the creation of new parties. But it has soaked public sentiment and seeped into church life until the religiousness of the age is saturated with views in direct conflict with their creeds and traditions. . . .

This change, whatever may be the cause does not have its source in a change of the facts. Observation and experience of the daily recurring facts give no support to the changed sentiment. The daily record flowing from individual action goes to confirm the old truth that something is sadly out of joint with man. The out of joint is not with the times, for the times are bettered, and if it were not for man the times would have many gleams of the halcyon. . . .

This age has lost, in a large measure, its faith in the word of God, and the atmosphere once created by the popular and almost universal credence in the Bible does not now pervade society as it did once. In the heart of faith the Bible may be held as sacred as ever, but public sentiment outside of the generation of the faithful do not accord to the truths of the Bible, or the statement of creeds that weight that they once gave is certain. The outside public sentiment has been captured by the heterodox thought of the past, and the force and dust of its surging columns are felt in the very strongholds of faith.

The Bible is not to us what it was to our fathers. It is the exception to find a theological work these days that treats the Bible with the reverence of the past or which accepts its statements as the men of another generation did. The whole range of rejected heresies and outlawed heterodoxies have massed themselves, and, while the foundations have not been destroyed or removed, they have been submerged. The sun still shines, but the clouds and fogs have shorn him of his rays, and eclipsed, in a measure and for a moment, his brightness.

This doctrine of original sin is dependent for its reception on a hearty and full faith in the Bible. It can have no place in a surface faith—a faith that is eclectic about the truths of the Bible. Original sin is the breaking up of man's moral nature in a way that harmony with God's will in his word is destroyed. Man's natural spirit and foundations are all crooked and warped when the straight edge of God's law is laid to them. But to a generation who have in a measure lost their faith in the Bible, or lost the inclination or ability to apply its spiritual rightness to their spiritual . . . standard to test the inward spiritual defection. Man, to them, has no original sin, because they have no original perfect standard by which to judge of this original condition. In literature, theology, books on the Bible, the doctrine has been caricatured, denied, or ignored till a quasi-rationalism has swept over the land, and for a while hidden the truth. We admit the changed attitude toward this doctrine, but the change is no greater in regard to original sin than it is toward the inspiration of the Bible, the Atonement, the resurrection of the body, or the eternal punishment of the wicked. All these doctrines, for the time being, are weakened, perverted, obscured, or denied.

The main cause of this change is found in the fact that this doctrine that underlies and solves all the mysterious facts of revelation is not declared and fought for by those in whose creed it is written, and who ought to be its fearless and aggressive defenders. The great truths of revelation are neither able to preach nor defend themselves. They must have soldier preachers who proclaim and defend them. They have never conquered as silent forces, they have never won as a reserve corps. They are not only to be declared, but put in the front as veteran legions on whose action are staked the empire of God's truth, not as an occasional force, but in the fiercest and most decisive conflict. These are the trained legions that win on every field God's victories. It is the failure, in season and out of season, to proclaim these great doctrines that accounts for their fading from sight and from faith. Every doctrine of the Bible that is not continually preached dies out of the faith of the people. Our fathers had to fight for every inch of ground on which they advanced these great truths, and this age requires a loyal and militant campaign for God's great truths. An unsheathed sword is the only preserver and defender of God's truth.

Literature, science, popular sentiment, heterodoxy, may do their worst, and occupy all their strongholds, but the truth of God will flourish and conquer if its preachers have faith to boldly proclaim and courage to fight for it without compromise or wavering. A militant ministry, aggressive at every point, with holy boldness, is the only conserving force for God's revealed truth. A generation of orthodox captain-generals in the pulpit will reissue these wasted and obscured creeds with more force than emperors' rescripts, or the deliverances of ecumenical councils.

Christian Advocate, December 20, 1890

† † †

Let it be noted before we go any further that Paul wrote directly under the superintendency of the Holy Spirit, who guarded Paul against error, and who suggested the truths which Paul taught. We hold definitely without compromise in the least to the plenary inspiration of the Scriptures, and as Paul's writings are part and parcel of those Sacred Writings, then Paul's epistles are portions of the Scriptures or the Word of God. This being true, the doctrine of prayer which Paul affirmed is the doctrine of the Holy Spirit. His epistles are of the Word of God, inspired, authentic and of Divine authority.

Prayer and Praying Men, Chap. 12

† † †

It is said that Mr. Moody, at a time when no other place was available, kept his morning watch in the coal shed, pouring out his heart to God, and finding in his precious Bible a true "feast of fat things."

George Müller also combined Bible study with prayer in the quiet morning hours. At one time his practice was to give himself to prayer, after having dressed, in the morning. Then his plan underwent a change. As he himself put it: "I saw the most important thing I had to do was to give myself to the reading of the Word of God, and to meditation on it, that thus my heart might be comforted, encouraged, warned, reproved, instructed; and that thus, by means of the Word of God, whilst meditating on it, my heart might be brought into experimental communion with the Lord. I began, therefore, to meditate on the New Testament early in the morning. The first thing I did, after having asked in a few words for the Lord's blessing upon his precious Word, was to begin to meditate on the Word of God, searching, as it were, into every verse to get blessing out of it; not for the sake of the public ministry of the Word, not for the sake of preaching on what I had meditated on, but for the sake of obtaining food for my own soul. The result I have found to be almost invariably thus, that after a very few minutes my soul has been led to confession, or to thanksgiving, or to intercession, or to supplication; so that, though I did not, as it were, give myself to prayer, but to meditation, yet it turned almost immediately more or less into prayer."

The study of the Word and prayer go together, and where we find the one truly practised, the other is sure to be seen in close alliance.

Purpose in Prayer, Chap. 7

Christ and Heaven

What is the description as thus given by Paul? It has passion, but neither envy nor jealousy have any place in that pure flame. It is clothed with humility, so that neither vanity nor pride inflate its heart, nor speak from its lips. Unseemly conduct never mars its beauty, nor casts reproach nor suspicion on its fidelity. Self renders his scepter, and claims his rights with modesty, and meekness. It is never provoked to peevish irritation, not insulted to bitterness, and wrath. It does not suspect ill nor avenge wrongs. It is saddened by the triumphs of evil, but rejoicing in the success of truth. It is akin to God in its freedom from hasty and angry excitements, long-suffering, self-restrained to evil but to the good mobile, and everflowing in kindness, usefulness, beneficence.

It has strength to bear, is credulous for good, full of hope and cheer for the best, and waits patiently, serene and gentle, when faith and fortitude and hope have almost failed.

Such is the divine portraiture of this divine love. Such are the principles on which Christ proposes to reconstruct human nature—sublime principles, sublimer purposes of the Son of God. Out of no other material does He propose to begin and complete His fair and costly building and make His heaven.

Religion is shut up to this one principle. All else is foreign or false. It is the capsheaf, the commandment which completes, aggregates and dominates the whole; burnished, emphatic and pregnant with His life and death. The summary of that life and death is: "Love one another." This is the decalogue revised and completed—the Sinai of Calvary—the law of the Gospel.

Love is the regenerating principle implanted in man's heart by the Holy Ghost, and its perfection is the end for which he is to labor with incessant effort and incessant prayer.

This love to Jesus implanted in the renewed heart has retired earth's most sacred attachments and become the animating force and crown of our earthly lives. "Where I am there ye may be also." "To be at home with the Lord." "To be with Christ which is far better." "Father, I will that those whom thou hast given me be with me where I am."

To love Jesus is to long to be with Him. To love Jesus is to think about Him. To love Jesus is to obey Him, to obey Him readily and implicitly, not feebly and reluctantly. The certainty of heaven is assured when we keep Jesus in the center of our hearts, in the center of our lives. He is to be the author of impulse and desire, of effort and action. "Whatsoever ye do in word or deed, do all in the name of the Lord Jesus."

Will you get to heaven? What is Jesus to you? Does He charm you? Does He draw you heavenward? Is it to be with Him that you seek heaven? Is He the fairest flower in all its garden? Is He the rarest and most precious of all its jewels? Is He sweeter than all its songs?

Does He beget the longings for its blissful abodes? Does

the desire to see and be with Him stir the profoundest ambition of your soul? Jesus and heaven are bound up together. To love Him with an untold passionate devotion is heaven begun, heaven continued, and heaven ended. Paul says: "I am now ready to be offered, and the time of my departure is at hand. I have fought a good fight, I have finished my course, I have kept the faith. Henceforth there is laid up for me a crown of righteousness, which the Lord, the righteous judge, shall give me at that day: and not to me only, but onto all them also that love his appearing."

The crown is not only personal to him, but universal, only limited "unto all them that love his appearing." Here it is not simply love for Jesus personally, but love for the great fact which is to culminate in the great glory of Jesus. To "love his appearing" there is the absolute necessity for loving His Person. The loving His coming is the test of loving His Person. We love the fact because we love the Person. We are not charged to love any theory or opinion about the manner of His coming, or the time, but the fact. Let Him come when He will, how He will, and for what purpose He will. We love His coming because we love Him. "Even so, come quickly, Lord Jesus," and bring Thy heaven with Thee.

The overcomers, the victorious ones, the conquerors, they are the heaven-crowned ones. Their valorous strength, their undaunted courage, their dire conflicts, their unyielding stead-fastness, their holding fast even unto death; they who, by their Christian constancy and courage, keep themselves unharmed and spotless from all the devices, assaults, solicitations of the world, the flesh and the devil—these are crowned to the heavenly life.

They have gained the victory over the devil; conquerors they are of him. "I write unto you young men because ye have overcome the wicked one." The spirit of antichrist they have overcome. "For whatsoever is born of God overcometh the world; and this is the victory that overcometh the world, even our faith. Who is he that overcometh the world but he that believeth that Jesus is the Son of God." "He that overcometh shall inherit all things; and I will be his God, and he shall be my son." Blessed company! "They all are robed in spotless white.

And conquering palms they bear." They are the victors. The conflict is past, the battle has been fought, and the victory has been won and won forever. They are "more than conquerors through him that loved them." The blessed Jesus has always led them in triumph, and now they are with Him upon His throne in their last and great triumph.

This love is born of the Spirit of God and is centered on Jesus Christ. Heaven depends on our love to the Saviour of sinners. We love heaven only as we love Him and as we seek for Him. This love is to be ardent and supreme. Jesus is the joy and glory of heaven.

The Christian's attitude to heaven is one of desire. Paul puts it thus: "I am in a strait betwixt two, having the desire to depart and be with Christ, which is far better." To set one's heart upon, longing for heaven, a great desire for Jesus, to be with Him—that was Paul's attitude. The very best Jesus has is for His disciples. God gives Jesus the key to everything, and Jesus turns everything over to His followers. This ought to kindle and inflame desire.

Heaven, Chaps. 9–10

Christ and Prayer

The example of our Lord in the matter of prayer is one which His followers might well copy. Christ prayed much and He taught much about prayer. His life and His works, as well as His teaching, are illustrations of the nature and necessity of prayer. He lived and labored to answer prayer. But the necessity of importunity in prayer was the emphasized point in His teaching about prayer. He taught not only that men must pray, but that they must persevere in prayer.

He taught in command and precept the idea of energy and earnestness in praying. He gives to our efforts gradation and climax. We are to ask, but to the asking we must add seeking, and seeking must pass into the full force of effort in knocking. The pleading soul must be aroused to effort by God's silence. Denial, instead of abating or abashing, must arouse its latent energies and kindle anew its highest ardor.

In the Sermon on the Mount, in which He lays down the cardinal duties of His religion, He not only gives prominence to prayer in general and secret prayer in particular, but He sets apart a distinct and different section to give weight to importunate prayer. To prevent any discouragement in praying He lays as a basic principle the fact of God's great fatherly willingness— that God's willingness to answer our prayers exceeds our willingness to give good and necessary things to our children, just as far as God's ability, goodness and perfection exceed our infirmities and evil. As a further assurance and stimulant to prayer Christ gives the most positive and iterated assurance of answer to prayers. He declares: "Ask and it shall be given you; seek and ye shall find; knock and it shall be opened unto you." And to make assurance doubly sure, He adds: "For every one that asketh, receiveth; and he that seeketh, findeth; and to him that knocketh it shall be opened."

Why does He unfold to us the Father's loving readiness to answer the prayer of His children? Why does He asseverate so strongly that prayer will be answered? Why does He repeat that positive asseveration six times? Why does Christ on two distinct occasions go over the same strong promises, iterations, and reiterations in regard to the certainty of prayer being answered? Because He knew that there would be delay in many an answer which would call for importunate pressing, and that if our faith did not have the strongest assurance of God's willingness to answer, delay would break it down. And that our spiritual sloth would come in, under the guise of submission and say it is not God's will to give what we ask, and so cease praying and lose our case. After Christ had put God's willingness to answer prayer in a very clear and strong light, He then urges to importunity, and that every unanswered prayer, instead of abating our pressure should only increase intensity and energy. If asking does not get, let asking pass into the settled attitude and spirit of seeking. If seeking does not secure the answer, let seeking pass on to the more energetic and clamorous pleas of knocking. We must persevere till we get it. No failure here if our faith does not break down.

As our great example in prayer, our Lord puts love as a primary condition—a love that has purified the heart from all the elements of hate, revenge, and ill will. Love is the supreme condition of prayer, a life inspired by love. First Corinthians 13 is the law of prayer as well as the law of love. The law of love is the law of prayer, and to master this chapter from the epistle of St. Paul is to learn the first and fullest condition of prayer.

Christ taught us also to approach the Father in His name. That is our passport. It is in His name that we are to make our petitions known. "Verily, verily, I say unto you, He that believeth on Me, the works that I do shall he do also; and greater *works* than these shall he do; because I go unto the Father. And whatsoever ye shall ask in My name, that will I do, that the Father may be glorified in the Son. If ye shall ask Me anything in My name, that will I do."

How wide and comprehensive is that "whatsoever." There is no limit to the power of that name. "Whatsoever ye shall ask." That is the Divine declaration, and it opens up to every praying child a vista of infinite resource and possibility.

And that is our heritage. All that Christ has may become ours if we obey the conditions. The one secret is prayer. The place of revealing and of equipment, of grace and of power, is the prayer chamber, and as we meet there with God we shall not only win our triumphs but we shall also grow in the likeness of our Lord and become His living witnesses to men.

Purpose in Prayer, Chap. 13

Jesus Christ was the Divine Teacher of prayer. Its power and nature had been illustrated by many a saint and prophet in olden times, but modern sainthood and modern teachers of prayer had lost their inspiration and life. Religiously dead, teachers and superficial ecclesiastics had forgotten what it was to pray. They did much of saying prayers, on state occasions, in public, with much ostentation and parade, but pray they did not. To them it was almost a lost practice. In the multiplicity of saying prayers they had lost the art of praying.

The history of the disciples during the earthly life of our Lord was not marked with much devotion. They were much enamored by their personal association with Christ. They were charmed by His words, excited by His miracles, and were entertained and concerned by the hopes which a selfish interest aroused in His person and mission. Taken up with the superficial and worldly views of His character, they neglected and overlooked the deeper and weightier things which belonged to Him and His mission. The neglect of the most obliging and ordinary duties by them was a noticeable feature in their conduct. So evident and singular was their conduct in this regard, that it became a matter of grave inquiry on one occasion and severe chiding on another.

"They said unto him, Why do the disciples of John fast often, and make prayers, and likewise the disciples of the Pharisees; but thine eat and drink? And he said unto them, Can ye make the children of the bridechamber fast, while the bridegroom is with them? But the days will come, when the bridegroom shall be taken away from them, and then shall they fast in those days."

In the example and the teaching of Jesus Christ, prayer assumes its normal relation to God's person, God's movements and God's Son. Jesus Christ was essentially the Teacher of prayer by precept and example. We have glimpses of His praying which, like indices, tell how full of prayer the pages, chapters and volumes of His life were. The epitome which covers not one segment only, but the whole circle of His life, and character, is preeminently that of prayer! "In the days of his flesh," the divine record reads, "when he had offered up prayers and supplications, with strong crying and tears." The suppliant of all suppliants He was, the intercessor of all intercessors. In lowliest form He approached God, and with strongest pleas He prayed and supplicated.

Jesus Christ teaches the importance of prayer by His urgency to His disciples to pray. But He shows us more than that. He shows how far prayer enters into the purposes of God. We must ever keep in mind that the relation of Jesus Christ to

God is the relation of asking and giving, the Son ever asking, the Father ever giving. We must never forget that God has put the conquering, inheriting and expanding forces of Christ's cause in prayer. "Ask of me, and I will give thee the heathen for thy inheritance, and the uttermost part of the earth for thy possession."

This was the clause embodying the royal proclamation and the universal condition when the Son was enthroned as the world's Mediator, and when He was sent on His mission of receiving grace and power. We very naturally learn from this how Jesus would stress praying as the one sole condition of His receiving His possession and inheritance.

Necessarily in this study on prayer, lines of thought will cross each other, and the same Scripture passage or incident will be mentioned more than once, simply because a passage may teach one or more truths. This is the case when we speak of the vast comprehensiveness of prayer. How all-inclusive Jesus Christ makes prayer! It has no limitations in extent or things! The promises to prayer are Godlike in their magnificence, wideness and universality. In their nature these promises have to do with God—with Him in their inspiration, creation and results. Who but God could say, "All things whatsoever ye ask in prayer, believing, ye shall receive?" Who can command and direct "All things whatsoever" but God? Neither man nor chance nor the law of results are so far lifted above change, limitations or condition, nor have in them mighty forces which can direct and result all things, as to promise the bestowment and direction of all things.

Whole sections, parables and incidents were used by Christ to enforce the necessity and importance of prayer. His miracles are but parables of prayer. In nearly all of them prayer figures distinctly, and some features of it are illustrated. The Syrophœnician woman is a preeminent illustration of the ability and success of importunity in prayer. The case of blind Bartimæus has points of suggestion along the same line. Jairus and the centurion illustrate and impress phases of prayer. The parable of the Pharisee and the publican enforce humility in prayer, declare the wondrous results of praying, and show the vanity and worthlessness of wrong praying. The failure to enforce church discipline and the readiness of violating the brotherhood, are all used to make an exhibit of far-reaching results of agreed praying, a record of which we have in Matthew 18:19.

It is of prayer in concert that Christ is speaking. Two agreed ones, two whose hearts have been keyed into perfect symphony by the Holy Spirit. Anything that they shall ask, it shall be done. Christ had been speaking of discipline in the church, how things were to be kept in unity, and how the fellowship of the brethren was to be maintained, by the restoration of the offender or by his exclusion. Members who had been true to the brotherhood of Christ, and who were laboring to preserve that brotherhood unbroken, would be the agreed ones to make appeals to God in united prayer.

In the Sermon on the Mount, Christ lays down constitutional principles. Types and shadows are retired, and the law of spiritual life is declared. In this foundation law of the Christian system prayer assumes a conspicuous, if not a paramount, position. It is not only wide, all-commanding, and comprehensive in its own sphere of action and relief, but it is ancillary to all duties. Even the one demanding kindly and discriminating judgment toward others, and also the royal injunction, the Golden Rule of action, these owe their being to prayer.

Christ puts prayer among the statutory promises. He does not leave it to natural law. The law of need, demand and supply, of helplessness, of natural instincts, or the law of sweet, high attractive privilege—these howsoever strong as motives of action, are not the basis of praying. Christ puts it as spiritual law. Men must pray. Not to pray is not simply a privation, an omission, but a positive violation of law, of spiritual life, a crime, bringing disorder and ruin. Prayer is law worldwide and eternity-reaching.

In the Sermon on the Mount many important utterances are dismissed with a line or a verse, while the subject of prayer occupies a large space. To it Christ returns again and again. He bases the possibilities and necessities of prayer on the relation of father and child, the child crying for bread, and the father giving that for which the child asks. Prayer and its answer are in the relation of a father to his child. The teaching of Jesus Christ on the nature and necessity of prayer as recorded in His life, is remarkable. He sends men to their closets. Prayer must be a holy exercise, untainted by vanity, or pride. It must be in secret. The disciple must live in secret. God lives there, is sought there and is found there. The command of Christ as to prayer is that pride and publicity should be shunned. Prayer is to be in private. "But thou when thou prayest, enter into thy closet, and shut thy door, and pray to thy Father in secret. And thy Father, which seeth in secret, shall reward thee openly."

The Beatitudes are not only to enrich and adorn, but they are the material out of which spiritual character is built. The very first one of these fixes prayer in the very foundation of spiritual character, not simply to adorn, but to compose. "Blessed are the poor in spirit." The word "poor" means a pauper, one who lives by begging. The real Christian lives on the bounties of another, whose bounties he gets by asking. Prayer then becomes the basis of Christian character, the Christian's business, his life and his living. This is Christ's law of prayer, putting it into the very being of the Christian. It is his first step, and his first breath, which is to color and to form all his afterlife. Blessed are the poor ones, for they only can pray.

> *Prayer is the Christian's vital breath,*
> *The Christian's native air;*
> *His watchword at the gates of death;*
> *He enters heaven with prayer.*

From praying Christ eliminates all self-sufficiency, all pride, and all spiritual values. The poor in spirit are the praying ones. Beggars are God's princes. They are God's heirs. Christ removes the rubbish of Jewish traditions and glosses from the regulations of the prayer altar.

Ye have heard that it was said by them of old time, Thou shalt not kill; and whosoever shall kill shall be in danger of the judgment:

But I say unto you, that whosoever is angry with his brother shall be in danger of the judgment: and whosoever shall say to his brother, Raca, shall be in danger of the council: but whosoever shall say, thou fool, shall be in danger of hell fire.

Therefore if thou bring thy gift to the altar and there rememberest that thy brother has aught against thee:

Leave there thy gift before the altar, and go thy way; first, be reconciled to thy brother, and then come and offer thy gift."

He who essays to pray to God with an angry spirit, with loose and irreverent lips, with an irreconciled heart, and with unsettled neighborly scores, spends his labor for that which is worse than naught, violates the law of prayer, and adds to his sin.

How rigidly exacting is Christ's law of prayer! It goes to the heart, and demands that love be enthroned there, love to the brotherhood. The sacrifice of prayer must be seasoned and perfumed with love, by love in the inward parts. The law of prayer, its creator and inspirer, is love.

Praying must be done. God wants it done. He commands it. Man needs it and man must do it. Something must surely come of praying, for God engages that something shall come out of it, if men are in earnest and are persevering in prayer.

After Jesus teaches "Ask and it shall be given you," etc., He encourages real praying, and more praying. He repeats and avers with redoubled assurance, "For every one that asketh receiveth." No exception. "Every one." "He that seeketh, findeth." Here it is again, sealed and stamped with infinite veracity. Then closed and signed, as well as sealed, with divine attestation, "To him that knocketh it shall be opened." Note how we are encouraged to pray by our relation to God!

If ye then, being evil, know how to give good gifts unto your children, how much more shall your Father which is in Heaven give good things to them that ask him?

The relation of prayer to God's work and God's rule in this world is most fully illustrated by Jesus Christ in both His teaching and His practice. He is first in every way and in everything. Among the rulers of the church He is primary in a preeminent way. He has the throne. The golden crown is His in eminent preciousness. The white garments enrobe Him in preeminent whiteness and beauty. In the ministry of prayer He is a divine example as well as the Divine Teacher. His example is affluent, and His prayer teaching abounds. How imperative the teaching of our Lord when He affirms that "men ought always to pray and not to faint!" and then presents a striking parable of an unjust judge and a poor widow to illustrate and enforce His teaching. It is a necessity to pray. It is exacting and binding for men always to be in prayer. Courage, endurance and perseverance are demanded that men may never faint in prayer. "And shall not God avenge his own elect that cry day and night unto him?"

This is His strong and indignant questioning and affirmation. Men must pray according to Christ's teaching. They must not get tired nor grow weary in praying. God's character is the assured surety that much will come of the persistent praying of true men.

Doubtless the praying of our Lord had much to do with the revelation made to Peter and the confession he made to Christ, "Thou art the Christ, the Son of the Living God." Prayer mightily affects and molds the circle of our associates. Christ made disciples and kept them disciples by praying. His twelve disciples were much impressed by His praying. Never man prayed like this man. How different His praying from the cold, proud, self-righteous praying which they heard and saw on the streets, in the synagogue, and in the temple.

———

Let it not be forgotten that prayer was one of the great truths which He came into the world to teach and illustrate. It was worth a trip from Heaven to earth to teach men this great lesson of prayer. A great lesson it was, a very difficult lesson for men to learn. Men are naturally averse to learning this lesson of prayer. The lesson is a very lowly one. None but God can teach it. It is a despised beggary, a sublime and heavenly vocation. The disciples were very stupid scholars, but were quickened to prayer by hearing Him pray and talk about prayer.

The dispensation of Christ's personality, while it was not and could not be the dispensation in its fullest and highest sense of need and dependence, yet Christ did try to impress on His disciples not alone a deep necessity of the necessity of prayer in general, but the importance of prayer to them in their personal and spiritual needs. And there came moments to them when they felt the need of a deeper and more thorough schooling in prayer and of their grave neglect in this regard. One of these hours of deep conviction on their part and of eager inquiry was when He was praying at a certain place and time, and they saw Him, and they said to Him, "Lord, teach us to pray, as John also taught his disciples."

As they listened to Him praying, they felt very keenly their ignorance and deficiency in praying. Who has not felt the same deficiency and ignorance? Who has not longed for a teacher in the divine art of praying?

The conviction which these twelve men had of their defect in prayer arose from hearing their Lord and Master pray, but likewise from a sense of serious defect even when compared with John the Baptist's training of his disciples in prayer. As they listened to their Lord pray (for unquestionably He must have been seen and heard by them as He prayed, who prayed with marvelous simplicity, and power, so human and so divine) such praying had a stimulating charm for them. In the presence and hearing of His praying, very keenly they felt their ignorance and deficiency in prayer. Who has not felt the same ignorance and deficiency?

We do not regret the schooling our Lord gave these twelve men, for in schooling them He schools us. The lesson is one already learned in the law of Christ. But so dull were they, that many a patient iteration and reiteration was required to instruct them in this divine art of prayer. And likewise so dull are we and inapt that many a wearying patient repetition must be given us before we will learn any important lesson in the all-important school of prayer.

This Divine Teacher of prayer lays Himself out to make it clear and strong that God answers prayer, assuredly, certainly, inevitably; that it is the duty of the child to ask, and to press, and that the Father is obliged to answer, and to give for the asking. In Christ's teaching, prayer is no sterile, vain performance, not a mere rite, a form, but a request for an answer, a plea to gain, the seeking of a great good from God. It is a lesson of getting that for which we ask, of finding that for which we seek, and of entering the door at which we knock.

A notable occasion we have as Jesus comes down from the Mount of Transfiguration. He finds His disciples defeated, humiliated and confused in the presence of their enemies. A father has brought his child possessed with a demon to have the demon cast out. They essayed to do it but failed. They had been commissioned by Jesus and sent to do that very work, but had signally failed. "And when he was come into the house, his disciples asked him privately, saying, Why could not we cast him out? And he said unto them, This kind can come forth by nothing but by prayer and fasting." Their faith had not been cultured by prayer. They failed in prayer before they failed in ability to do their work. They failed in faith because they had failed in prayer. That one thing which was necessary to do God's work was prayer. The work which God sends us to do cannot be done without prayer.

In Christ's teaching on prayer we have another pertinent statement. It was in connection with the cursing of the barren fig tree:

> Jesus answered and said unto them, Verily I say unto you, if ye have faith, and doubt not, ye shall not only do this which is done to the fig tree, but also if ye shall say unto this mountain, Be thou removed and be thou cast into the sea; it shall be done.
> And all things whatsoever ye shall ask in prayer, believing, ye shall receive.

In this passage we have faith and prayer, their possibilities and powers conjoined. A fig tree had been blasted to the roots by the word of the Lord Jesus. The power and quickness of the result surprised the disciples. Jesus says to them that it need be no surprise to them or such a difficult work to be done. "If ye have faith" its possibilities to affect will not be confined to the little fig tree, but the gigantic, rock-ribbed, rock-founded mountains can be uprooted and moved into the sea. Prayer is leverage of this great power of faith.

It is well to refer again to the occasion when the heart of our Lord was so deeply moved with compassion as he beheld the multitudes because they fainted and were scattered as having no shepherd. Then it was He urged upon His disciples the injunction, "Pray ye the Lord of the harvest that he would send forth labourers into his harvest," clearly teaching them that it belonged to God to call into the ministry men whom He will, and that in answer to prayer the Holy Spirit does this very work.

Prayer is as necessary now as it was then to secure the needed laborers to reap earthly harvests for the heavenly garners. Has the church of God ever learned this lesson of so vital and exacting import? God alone can choose the laborers and thrust them out, and this choosing He does not delegate to man, or church, convocation or synod, association or conference. And God is moved to this great work of calling men into the ministry by prayer. Earthly fields are rotting. They are untilled because prayer is silent. The laborers are few. Fields are unworked because prayer has not worked with God.

We have the prayer promise and the prayer ability put in a distinct form in the higher teachings of prayer by our Lord: "If ye abide in me, and my words abide in you, ye shall ask what ye will, and it shall be done unto you."

Here we have a fixed attitude of life as the condition of prayer. Not simply a fixed attitude of life toward some great principles or purposes, but the fixed attitude and unity of life with Jesus Christ. To live in Him, to dwell there, to be one with Him, to draw all life from Him, to let all life from Him flow through us—this is the attitude of prayer and the ability to pray. No abiding in Him can be separated from His Word abiding in us. It must live in us to give birth to and food for prayer. The attitude of the Person of Christ is the condition of prayer.

The Old Testament saints had been taught that "God had magnified his word above all his name." New Testament saints must learn fully how to exalt by perfect obedience that Word issuing from the lips of Him who is the Word. Praying ones under Christ must learn what praying ones under Moses had already learned, that "man shall not live by bread alone, but by every word that proceedeth out of the mouth of God." The life of Christ flowing through us and the words of Christ living in us, these give potency to prayer. They breathe the spirit of prayer, and make the body, blood and bones of prayer. Then it is Christ praying in me and through me, and all things which "I will" are the will of God. My will becomes the law and the answer, for it is written "Ye shall ask what ye will, and it shall be done unto you."

Fruit bearing our Lord puts to the front in our praying:

> Ye have not chosen me, but I have chosen you, and ordained you, that ye shall go and bring forth fruit and that your fruit shall remain, that whatsoever ye shall ask of the Father in my name, he may give it you.

Barrenness cannot pray. Fruit-bearing capacity and reality only can pray. It is not past fruitfulness, but present: "That your fruit should remain." Fruit, the product of life, is the condition of praying. A life vigorous enough to bear fruit, much fruit, is the condition and the source of prayer. "And in that day ye shall ask me nothing. Verily, verily, I say unto you, Whatsoever ye shall ask the Father in my name, he will give it you. Hitherto have ye asked nothing in my name: ask and ye shall receive, that your joy may be full." "In that day ye shall ask me nothing." It is not solving riddles, not revealing mysteries, not curious questionings. This is not our attitude, not our business under the dispensation of the Spirit, but to pray, and to pray largely. Much true praying increases man's joy and God's glory.

"Whatsoever ye shall ask in my name, I will give," says Christ, and the Father will give. Both Father and Son are pledged to give the very things for which we ask. But the condition is "in His name." This does not mean that His name is talismanic, to give value by magic. It does not mean that His name in beautiful settings of pearl will give value to prayer. It is not that His name perfumed with sentiment and larded in and closing up our prayers and doings will do the deed. How fearful the statement: "Many will say unto me in that day, Lord, Lord, have we not prophesied in thy name? and in thy name cast out devils? and in thy name done many wonderful works? And then will I profess unto them, I never knew you. Depart from me, ye that work iniquity." How blasting the doom of these great workers and doers who claim to work in His name!

It means far more than sentiment, verbiage, and nomenclature. It means to stand in His stead, to bear His nature, to stand for all for which He stood, for righteousness, truth, holiness and zeal. It means to be one with God as He was, one in spirit, in will and in purpose. It means that our praying is singly and solely for God's glory through His Son. It means that we abide in Him, that Christ prays through us, lives in us and shines out of us; that we pray by the Holy Spirit according to the will of God.

Even amid the darkness of Gethsemane, with the stupor which had settled upon the disciples, we have the sharp warning from Christ to His sluggish disciples, "Watch and pray lest ye enter into temptation. The spirit truly is willing, but the flesh is weak." How needful to hear such a warning, to awaken all our powers, not simply for the great crises of our lives, but as the inseparable and constant attendants of a career marked with perils and dangers on every hand.

As Christ nears the close of His earthly mission, nearer to the greater and more powerful dispensation of the Spirit, His teaching about prayer takes on a more absorbing and higher form. It has now become a graduating school. His connection with prayer becomes more intimate and more absolute. He becomes in prayer what He is in all else pertaining to our salvation, the beginning and the end, the first and the last. His name becomes all potent. Mighty works are to be done by the faith which can pray in His name. Like His nature, His name covers all needs, embraces all worlds, and gets all good.

Believest thou not that I am in the Father and the Father in me? The words that I speak unto you I speak not of myself: but the Father that dwelleth in me, he doeth the works.

Believe me that I am in the Father and the Father in me: or else believe me for the very works' sake.

Verily, verily, I say unto you, He that believeth on me, the works that I do shall he do also; and greater works than these shall he do; because I go unto my Father.

And whatsoever ye shall ask in my name, that will I do, that the Father may be glorified in the Son.

If ye shall ask anything in my name I will do it.

The Father, the Son and the praying one are all bound up together. All things are in Christ, and all things are in prayer in His name. "If ye shall ask anything in my name." The key which unlocks the vast storehouse of God is prayer. The power to do greater works than Christ did lies in the faith which can grasp His name truly and in true praying.

In the last of His life, note how He urges prayer as a preventive of the many evils to which they were exposed. In view of the temporal and fearful terrors of the destruction of Jerusalem, He charges them to this effect: "Pray ye that your flight be not in winter."

How many evils in this life which can be escaped by prayer! How many fearful temporal calamities can be mitigated, if not wholly relieved, by prayer! Notice how, amid the excesses and stupefying influences to which we are exposed in this world, Christ charges us to pray:

And take heed to yourselves, lest at any time your hearts be overcharged with surfeiting, and drunkenness, and cares of this life, and so that day come upon you unawares.

For as a snare shall it come on all them that dwell on the face of the whole earth.

Watch ye therefore and pray always, that ye may be accounted worthy to escape all these things that shall come to pass, and to stand before the Son of man.

In view of the uncertainty of Christ's coming to judgment, and the uncertainty of our going out of this world, He says: "But of that day and that hour knoweth no man, no, not the angels which are in Heaven, neither the Son, but the Father. Take ye heed, watch and pray, for ye know not when the time is."

We have the words of Jesus as given in His last interview with His twelve disciples, found in John 14–17. These are true, solemn parting words. The disciples were to move out into the regions of toil, and peril, bereft of the personal presence of their Lord and Master. They were to be impressed that prayer would serve them in everything, and its use, and unlimited possibilities would in some measure supply their loss, and by it they would be able to command all the possibilities of Jesus Christ and God the Father.

It was the occasion of momentous interest to Jesus Christ. His work was to receive its climax and crown in His death and His resurrection. His glory and the success of His work and of its execution, under the mastery and direction of the Holy Spirit, was to be committed to His apostles. To them it was an hour of strange wonderment and of peculiar, mysterious sorrow, only too well assured of the fact that Jesus was to leave them. All else was dark and impalpable.

He was to give them His parting words and pray His parting prayer. Solemn, vital truths were to be the weight and counsel of that hour. He speaks to them of heaven. Young men, strong though they were, yet they could not meet the duties of their preaching life and their apostolic life, without the fact, the thought, the hope and the relish of heaven. These things were to be present constantly in all sweetness, in all their vigor, in all freshness, in all brightness. He spoke to them about their spiritual and conscious connection with Himself, an abiding indwelling, so close and continuous that His own life would flow into them, as the life of the vine flows into the branches. Their lives and their fruitfulness were dependent upon this. Then praying was urged upon them as one of the vital, essential forces. This was the one thing upon which all the divine force depended, and this was the avenue and agency through which the divine life and power were to be secured and continued in their ministry.

He spake to them about prayer. He had taught them many lessons upon this all-important subject as they had been together. This solemn hour he seizes to perfect his teaching. They must be made to realize that they have an illimitable and exhaustless storehouse of good in God and that they can draw on Him at all times and for all things without stint, as Paul said in after years to the Philippians, "My God shall supply all your need according to His riches in glory by Christ Jesus."

———————

The Bible record of the life of Jesus Christ gives but a glance of His busy doing, a small selection of His many words, and only a brief record of His great works. But even in this record we see Him as being much in prayer. Even though busy and exhausted by the severe strain and toils of His life, "in the morning a great while before day, he rose up and went out and departed into a desert place, and there prayed." Alone in the desert and in the darkness with God! Prayer filled the life of our Lord while on earth. His life was a constant stream of incense sweet and perfumed by prayer. When we see how the life of Jesus was but one of prayer, then we must conclude that to be like Jesus is to pray like Jesus and is to live like Jesus. A serious life it is to pray as Jesus prayed.

We cannot follow any chronological order in the praying of Jesus Christ. What were His steps of advance and skill in the Divine art of praying we know not. He is in the act of prayer when we find Him at the fords of the Jordan, when the waters of baptism, at the hands of John the Baptist, are upon Him. So passing over the three years of His ministry, when closing the drama of His life in that terrible baptism of fear, pain, suffering, and shame, we find Him in the spirit, and also in the very act of praying. The baptism of the Cross, as well as the baptism of the Jordan, are sanctified by prayer. With the breath of prayer in His last sigh, He commits His spirit to God. In His first recorded utterances, as well as His first acts, we find Him teaching His disciples how to pray as His first lesson, and as their first duty. Under the shadow of the Cross, in the urgency and importance of His last interview with His chosen disciples, He is at the same all-important business, teaching the world's teachers how to pray, trying to make prayerful those lips and hearts out of which were to flow the divine deposits of truth.

The great eras of His life were created and crowned with

prayer. What were His habits of prayer during His stay at home and His toil as a carpenter in Nazareth, we have no means of knowing. God has veiled it, and guess and speculation are not only vain and misleading, but proud and prurient. It would be presumptuous searching into that which God has hidden, which would make us seek to be wise above that which was written, trying to lift up the veil with which God has covered His own revelation.

We find Christ in the presence of the famed, the prophet and the preacher. He has left His Nazareth home and His carpenter shop by God's call. He is now at a transitional point. He has moved out to His great work. John's baptism and the baptism of the Holy Ghost are prefatory and are to qualify Him for that work. This epochal and transitional period is marked by prayer.

> Now when all the people were baptized, it came to pass that Jesus, being also baptized, and praying, the heaven was opened.
> And the Holy Ghost descended in a bodily shape like a dove upon him, and a voice came from heaven, which said, Thou art my beloved Son; in thee I am well pleased.

It is a supreme hour in His history, different and in striking contrast with, but not in opposition to, the past. The descent and abiding of the Holy Spirit in all His fullness, the opening heavens, and the attesting voice which involved God's recognition of His only Son—all of these are the result, if not the direct creation and response to His praying on that occasion.

"As He was praying," so we are to be praying. If we would pray as Christ prayed, we must be as Christ was, and must live as Christ lived. The Christ character, the Christ life, and the Christ spirit, must be ours if we would do the Christ praying, and would have our prayers answered as He had His prayers answered. The business of Christ even now in Heaven at His Father's right hand is to pray. Certainly if we are His, if we love Him, if we live for Him, and if we live close to Him, we will catch the contagion of His praying life, both on earth and in

Heaven. We will learn His trade and carry on His business on earth.

Jesus Christ loved all men, He tasted death for all men, He intercedes for all men. Let us ask then, are we the imitators, the representatives, and the executors of Jesus Christ? Then must we in our prayers run parallel with His atonement in its extent. The atoning blood of Jesus Christ gives sanctity and efficiency to our prayers. As worldwide, as broad, and as human as the man Christ Jesus was, so must be our prayers. The intercessions of Christ's people must give currency and expedition to the work of Christ, carry the atoning blood to its benignant ends, and help to strike off the chains of sin from every ransomed soul. We must be as praying, as tearful, and as compassionate as was Christ.

Prayer affects all things. God blesses the person who prays. He who prays goes out on a long voyage for God and is enriched himself while enriching others, and is blessed himself while the world is blessed by his praying. To "live a quiet and peaceable life in all godliness and honesty" is the wealthiest wealth.

The praying of Christ was real. No man prayed as He prayed. Prayer pressed upon Him as a solemn, all-imperative, all-commanding duty, as well as a royal privilege in which all sweetness was condensed, alluring and absorbing. Prayer was the secret of His power, the law of His life, the inspiration of His toil and the source of His wealth, His joy, His communion and His strength.

To Christ Jesus prayer occupied no secondary place, but was exacting and paramount, a necessity, a life, the satisfying of a restless yearning and a preparation for heavy responsibilities.

Closeting with His Father in counsel and fellowship, with vigor and in deep joy, all this was His praying. Present trials, future glory, the history of His Church, and the struggles and perils of His disciples in all times and to the very end of time— all these things were born and shaped by His praying.

Nothing is more conspicuous in the life of our Lord than prayer. His campaigns were arranged and His victories were gained in the struggles and communion of His all night praying. By prayer He rent the heavens. Moses and Elijah and the transfiguration glory wait on his praying. His miracles and teaching had their power from the same source. Gethsemane's praying crimsoned Calvary with serenity and glory. His sacerdotal prayer makes the history and hastens the triumph of His Church on earth. What an inspiration and command to pray is the prayer life of Jesus Christ while in this world! What a comment it is on the value, the nature and the necessity of prayer!

The dispensation of the Person of Jesus Christ was a dispensation of prayer. A synopsis of His teaching and practice of prayer was that "Men ought always to pray and not to faint."

As the Jews prayed in the name of their patriarchs and invoked the privileges granted to them by covenant with God; as we have a new Name and a new covenant, more privileged and more powerful and more all-comprehensive, more authoritative and more divine; and as far as the Son of God is lifted above the patriarchs in divinity, glory and power, by so much should our praying exceed theirs in range of largeness, glory and power of results.

Jesus Christ prayed to God as Father. Simply and directly did He approach God in the charmed and revered circle of the Father. The awful, repelling fear was entirely absent, lost in the supreme confidence of a child.

Jesus Christ crowns His life, His works and His teaching with prayer. How His Father attests His relationship and puts on Him the glory of answered prayer at His baptism and transfiguration when all other glories are growing dim in the night which settles on Him! What almighty potencies are in prayer when we are charged and surcharged with but one inspiration and aim! "Father, glorify thy name." This sweetens all, brightens all, conquers all and gets all. "Father, glorify thy name." That guiding star will illumine the darkest night and calm the wildest storm and will make us brave and true. An imperial principle it is. It will make an imperial Christian.

The range and potencies of prayer, so clearly shown by Jesus in life and teaching, but reveal the great purposes of God. They not only reveal the Son in the reality and fullness of His humanity, but also reveal the Father.

Christ prayed as a child. The spirit of a child was found in

Him. At the grave of Lazarus "Jesus lifted up His eyes and said, Father." Again we hear Him begin His prayer after this fashion: "In that hour Jesus rejoiced in spirit, and said, I thank thee, O Father." So also on other occasions we find Him in praying addressing God as His Father, assuming the attitude of the child asking something of the Father. What confidence, simplicity and artlessness! What readiness, freeness and fullness of approach are all involved in the spirit of a child! What confiding trust, what assurance, what tender interest! What profound solicitudes, and tender sympathy on the Father's part! What respect deepening into reverence! What loving obedience and grateful emotions glow in the child's heart! What divine fellowship and royal intimacy! What sacred and sweet emotions! All these meet in the hour of prayer when the child of God meets His Father in heaven, and when the Father meets His child! We must live as children if we would ask as children. We must act as children if we would pray as children. The spirit of prayer is born of the child spirit.

The profound reverence in this relation of paternity must forever exclude all lightness, frivolity and pertness, as well as all undue familiarity. Solemnity and gravity become the hour of prayer. It has been well said: "The worshipper who invokes God under the name of Father and realises the gracious and beneficent love of God, must at the same time remember and recognise God's glorious majesty, which is neither annulled nor impaired, but rather supremely intensified through His fatherly love. An appeal to God as Father, if not associated with reverence and homage before the divine Majesty, would betray a want of understanding of the character of God." And, we might add, would show a lack of the attributes of a child.

Patriarchs and prophets knew something of the doctrine of the Fatherhood of God to God's family. They "saw it afar off, were persuaded of it, and embraced it," but understood it not, in all its fullness, "God having provided some better thing for us, that they without us should not be made perfect."

"Behold he prayeth!" was God's statement of wonderment and surprise to the timid Ananias in regard to Saul of Tarsus. "Behold he prayeth!" applied to Christ has in it far more of wonderment and mystery and surprise. He, the Maker of all worlds, the Lord of angels and of men, co-equal and co-eternal with the Everlasting God; the "brightness of the Father's glory and the express image of his person"; "fresh from his Father's glory and from his Father's throne."—"Behold he prayeth!" To find Him in lowly, dependent attitude of prayer, the suppliant of all suppliants, His richest legacy and His royal privilege to pray—this is the mystery of all mysteries, the wonder of all wonders.

Paul gives in brief and comprehensive statement the habit of our Lord in prayer in Hebrews 5:7—"Who, in the days of his flesh, when he had offered up prayers and supplications, with strong crying and tears, unto him that was able to save him from death, and was heard in that he feared." We have in this description of our Lord's praying the outgoing of great spiritual forces. He prayed with "prayers and supplications." It was no formal, tentative effort. He was intense, personal and real. He was a pleader for God's good. He was in great need and He must cry with "strong cryings," made stronger still by His tears. In an agony the Son of God wrestled. His praying was no playing a mere part. His soul was engaged, and all His powers were taxed to a strain. Let us pause and look at Him and learn how to pray in earnest. Let us learn how to win in an agony of prayer that which seems to be withholden from us. A beautiful word is that, "feared," which occurs only twice in the New Testament, the fear of God.

Jesus Christ was always a busy man with His work, but never too busy to pray. "The divinest of business filled His heart and filled His hands, consumed His time, exhausted His nerves. But with Him even God's work must not crowd out God's praying. Saving people from sin or suffering must not, even with Christ, be substituted for praying, nor abate in the least the time or the intensity of these holiest of seasons. He filled the day with working for God; He employed the night with praying to God. The day-working made the night-praying a necessity. The night-praying sanctified and made successful the day-working. Too busy to pray gives religion Christian burial, it is true, but kills it nevertheless.

In many cases only the bare fact, yet important and suggestive fact, is stated that He prayed. In other cases the very words which came out of His heart and fell from His lips are recorded. The man of prayer by preeminence was Jesus Christ. The epochs of His life were created by prayer, and all the minor details outlines and inlines of His life were inspired, colored and impregnated by prayer.

The prayer words of Jesus were sacred words. By them God speaks to God, and by them God is revealed and prayer is illustrated and enforced. Here is prayer in its purest form and in its mightiest potencies. It would seem that earth and heaven would uncover head and open ears most wide to catch the words of His praying who was truest God and truest man, and divinest of suppliants, who prayed as never man prayed. His prayers are our inspiration and pattern to pray.

Reality of Prayer, Chaps. 5–7

Crazy for God

No man does much for God who does not rise above the age in which he lives. But to do this is the most intolerable crime that one can commit against any age. It is this that makes him the sport of the multitude, and fixes on him the stigma of being singular or eccentric, this defames him by the terms fanatic or crank. Ardor is the only intemperance a worldly religion knows. Zeal the only mortal sin on its list.

We boast of our liberality. We flaunt our charity on our sleeves, but an illiberal and almost savage cruelty is felt and often exercised toward those who dare rise above the worldly drift, or go faster than the sluggish religious current that sickens the truly religious heart by its stagnancy or sloth. We know men who in a truer age, one less boastful of its charity than this, would be called geniuses, but who are now called cranks. We instance a man who came out of the Civil War paralyzed by the honorable wounds received in his brave and patriotic career, crippled for life, and in a lowly condition every way. He chose, at God's call, the vocation of an itinerant Methodist preacher. By the force of his genius, by his resolute and fearless heart, he became the author of books, wrote the lives of bishops; the religious press has teemed with the productions of his prolific and exhaustless pen. A happier and more tolerant age would have exalted the heroic elements in him, and enrolled him on the list of its geniuses, but he has been dubbed a crank, and under this ban all his nobility is buried.

We instance a man, comparatively young, whose preaching ability is of the highest order, the productions of whose pen are often classic, brilliant, always forceful; generous, and without the taint of self, who would sever his right arm before he would go in the popular ways to place and position. Yet this man, with his gifts of genius, with the elements of a hero and a saint in him, is classed as a crank by men who can lay no claim to either, simply because he gives himself to God in a way that shames the selfishness in them and in their age.

We know women, who for their illustrious piety would have been canonized as saints in an age when saints were canonized, who are denominated fanatics, and shunned as though their touch were poison, by a worldly church and worldly preachers.

The Christ-life is no more in favor with the world now than when it was manifest in the Son of Mary and Joseph, and paid the penalty of the Cross for its holy eccentricity.

This age so vauntful of its charity and liberality is as jealous of the men who rise above its selfish code as any other. But these decried men are the ones who are doing the most for God. There must be in the man the great force of an eccentric movement if he works God's work. The very intensity that projects God's work, singles its possessor out as erratic. The unity of his purpose makes him singular. The world cannot understand these men who are narrow and one-ideaed for God. They do not measure up to their standard; they are a misfit to their pattern.

The men who are crazy for God, who have a weakness at that point, are the ones who have left God's footprints, and moved God's revolutions among men. The glorious summary of the olden saints, who "had trial of cruel mockings and scourgings, yea, moreover, of bonds and imprisonment: they were stoned, they were sawn asunder, were tempted, were slain with the sword: they wandered about in sheepskins and goatskins; being destitute, afflicted, tormented; of whom the world was not worthy; they wandered in deserts, and in mountains, and in dens and caves of the earth."

What is it? This noble, and divine summary according to our modern exquisite but the summary of tramps, but these are the heroes of God, "who through faith subdued kingdoms, wrought righteousness, obtained promises, stopped the mouths of lions, quenched the violence of fire, escaped the edge of the sword, out of weakness were made strong, waxed valiant in fight, turned to flight the armies of the aliens. Women received their dead raised to life again; and others were tortured, not accepting deliverance that they might obtain a better resurrection."

Was not Christ charged with being beside himself? Did not Paul share in the same charge? The force, unity, and fire that the true worker puts into his toil for God seems to these worldly saints as the aberrations of lunacy. This despising and leaving the pursuits of earth for those of heaven seems intangible and visionary.

Luther and Wesley shared the same odium. Fletcher, Harms, Brainerd, were crazed by the world's estimate. It makes us smile to read of Wesley's father urging him to retirement and cessation because he was dishonored, shunned, and disgraced by the charge of fanaticism. Henry Martyn, suffering and dying for Christ and India, is called by England's purest if not most brilliant statesman, "a mild and benevolent enthusiast."

Fletcher, at five, Sabbath morning, going through the town and ringing his bell to awaken the people for church seems much off. His intercourse and visits smack much of this which the world calls beside himself. A friend relates his manner of visits: He came to a smith's shop, to one who was hammering upon the anvil, "O," says he, "pray to God that he may hammer that hard heart of yours." To another that was heating the iron, "Ah! thus it is that God tries his people in the furnace of affliction." To another when a furnace was drawing, "See, Thomas, if *you* can make such a furnace as that; think what a furnace God can make for ungodly souls." Fletcher's going about calls to mind the talks of the Athenian sage, who was voted by his age not only as being a crank but a criminal ripe for the hemlock.

The deliberate rejection, by Moses, of the crown of Egypt, and linking his destiny to enslaved Israel, has in it much that looks to the world like absolute madness. Paul's career, counting all things but loss for the excellency of Christ, is nonsense to the world's most sober view.

There are many crazy people in the world, cranks innumerable, fanatics who mar all religious beauty by their extremes, but the world doesn't know its crazy people. Its commission on insanity puts the straitjacket on the sanest of people. They mistake the earnestness and severity of conviction, which concentrates all the forces to a given object, and the energy of will holding these convictions to one object as being beside one's self. It was no lunacy that decided Luther to go to the Diet of Worms. "I am called," he said, "in the name of God to go, and I would go though I were certain to meet as many devils in Worms as there are tiles on the houses." "Daniel braving in calm devotion the decree which virtually consigned him to the den of lions. Or Shadrach, Meshach, and Abednego, saying to the tyrant, 'We are not careful to answer thee in this matter,' when the fiery furnace was in sight." Or Stephen charging the infuriated and bloodthirsty mob with being the betrayers and murderers of Christ. This divine intoxication of spirit, the indignant calmness and resolute purpose at the cost of life, and all beside to sacrifice and serve God, the world can see nothing in it but a distempered mind. It is a craziness, but it is a craziness for God. It is the craziness that made David so vile and offensive in the eyes of his worldly wife. The craziness that subjected the disciples on the day of Pentecost to the charge of intoxication.

Christian Advocate, October 11, 1890

Devotions

The irregularity of our modern life is one of the greatest foes to deep spirituality. Men are so much away from home; they eat, sleep, and travel at such unseasonable hours that it is often almost impossible for them to have fixed times and places for devotion. The more is the reason why they should be careful to omit no duty, and to neglect no means of grace.

Christian Advocate, July 26, 1890

Books of devotion are not in favor with this age. Even the Bible is read by many persons by way of habit, or as a mixture of habit and task. Its life does not penetrate our inner being, neither do we assimilate its essence. Devotional reading is necessary to the culture of a devotional spirit. Devotional reading aids in nurturing the affections for God, and puts us in frames of thought and feeling that kindle and enliven all the nature for heaven. Frederick Robertson said: "I perceive more than ever the necessity of devotional reading. I mean the works of eminently holy persons, whose tone was not merely uprightness of character and high-mindedness, but communion with God—a strong sense of ever-personal, and ever-living communion with God. I recollect how far more peaceful my mind used to be when I was in the regular habit of reading daily, with scrupulous adherence to a plan, works of this kind." *The Imitation of Christ*, by à Kempis; Archbishop Leighton's *Works*; the *Lives* of Fletcher, Brainerd, Martyn, McCheyne, and the range of biographies of the eminently pious men and women of early Methodism, afford a wide and edifying range of literature that is too much neglected.

Christian Advocate, September 6, 1890

Evangelism and The Gospel

Go out into the highways and hedges and compel them to come in. . . . Pray God to open the way for it to His glory.
Letter to H. M. Hodge, quoted in the Introduction to Heaven

Bringing the Masses to the Gospel. *The Congregationalist* reminds us of the fact that the Holy Ghost is the only drawing power that draws to save—a fact that the church is ever prone to forget and ever has to learn anew. Members of city churches in many states, who shared in the revival scenes of 1857–58, will well remember what throngs of people, apparently self-moved, but really drawn by the Holy Spirit, crowded places of prayer, which they could not be persuaded before to enter, and there found Christ as their Saviour. They who most effectually labor and pray for the reviving power of the Holy Spirit in our cities will do most toward bringing the masses to the gospel.

Christian Advocate, December 13, 1890

The unseen and feeble forces by worldly estimates are the mighty forces in the advance of the gospel. The power of the gospel is in ratio to the seeming impotency of the seen forces. God delights to honor the unshowy and hidden spiritual forces. Nothing so disgusts him as a great parade of agencies or results. Worldly wisdom is accounted as foolishness, and worldly power esteemed as weakness by God in the march of his work. The lesson the hardest for the Church to learn, and when learned the soonest forgotten is this: "God hath chosen the foolish things of the world to confound the wise; and God hath chosen the weak things of the world to confound the things which are mighty; and base things of the world, and things which are despised, hath God chosen, yea, and things which are not, to bring to nought things that are: that no flesh should glory in his presence." "At that time Jesus answered and said, I thank thee, O Father, Lord of heaven and earth, because thou hast hid these things from the wise and prudent, and hast revealed them unto babes. Even so, Father, for so it seemed good in thy sight." This is God's way. It is strange to our eyes.

Christian Advocate, September 6, 1890

Family and Home

The injunction given by Paul to the widows, that they were first to learn to show piety at home, is an injunction of first importance not only in the specific application given it by the apostle, but as a general direction to all in the home life. Home religion is the truest religion, the most beautiful, the most lasting, and the most difficult.

Family worship ought to be performed in a reverent and deliberate way. All the household present, God's word read distinctly, a hymn of praise sung, and a prayer, straight from the heart, surcharged with fatherly benediction, and solicitudes offered.

Family worship focalizes and aids home piety very much. While it sanctifies the home it trains the home circle in the idea of worship, and associates religion with all that is most tender, enduring, and impressive.

Christian Advocate, September 27, 1890

† † †

Are you looking after the salvation of your children? No matter what else you may do, your life is a failure if you neglect this. Do you think of your children? Do you pray for them, and with them? Do you instruct them? Do you set a right example before them?

Christian Advocate, July 26, 1890

Heaven

One of the efforts of modern progressive religion is to center Christian thought and hope mainly on this life, and to make as little as possible of the life to come. Heaven in the new creed is to have little or no place as an inspiration, a solace, or an end. It talks glibly with force and much truth of the necessity of work for humanity and earth and of the Christian demands of this life. All this has a show of good, but the tendency, if not the aim, is to materialize religion, and so harden and deform it that it will be fit neither for earth nor heaven.

A large leaven of the spirit of heaven, of the hopes of heaven, its purity and inspiration, must permeate our service for earth. The full force of this heavenly stimulant must replenish our souls and sublime them, or our labors for earth and men will exhaust and vitiate all solid principles.

The idea of heaven and its prospect kept constantly before the mind are necessary to hold men to religion. God is in heaven, Christ is there enthroned and glorious, and our affections must be fixed on that center. He that has but little of heaven in his religion will have but little of God and Christ in it, for Christ and God and heaven in this are one. Heaven has always been to the pious the most alluring and powerful motive. The earnest of heaven, its foretaste and promise, are put into the heart by the Holy Ghost at conversion, and its presence and realization grows stronger and more engaging as the years increase the piety and add to faith and works. This motive was prominent in the piety of Abraham, who during the whole pilgrimage of his faith, looked for a city that hath foundations, whose maker and builder is God. Heaven threw its weight in the scale and decided Moses when he was balancing Egypt's crown with the reproach of Christ, its vision relieved the present desperate conditions and decided him in his choice and nerved him for the sacrifice and its conflict. Paul labored under the constant inspiration of heaven. The visions he had of it made him restless for its fruition, and he died supported and enlivened by its crown. Christ braved the cross, endured its shame with the prospect of heaven in full view. At points heaven has come into the faith and thought of God's people with increased force and brightness to soothe their sorrows or increase their fortitude. When sorrow and despair were oppressing the disciples, Christ pointed to his Father's house with its many mansions, and their entrance into it as a solace and strength for their trouble and fainting. Of the saints of old it is said, "they took joyfully the spoiling of their goods, knowing that in heaven they had a more enduring substance." What relief and ecstasy those words from Christ, "today thou shalt be with me in paradise," carried to the dying thief! How the incorruptible crown and the house not made with hands, which the apostle brought before the gaze of the Corinthian saints, served to allure, to inspire, to strengthen for trial, for denial, and for the most strenuous efforts!

The fact of heaven is an imperishable element in Christian character, an ever-increasing stimulant to Christian exertion, an indispensable and vital part of Christian experience. Our hearts must be in heaven, our eyes fixed there, our citizenship enrolled there; we must own its allegiance. Its language must be on our lips, its music on our ears, its purity in our hearts, our hands busy about its work, our feet ready and eager to enter its gate and press its soil. We cannot make too much of heaven, cannot think too often of it, cannot long too greatly for it, cannot labor too hard for it. We must away with this songless, heartless materialism that earthens every sentiment and blots out heaven in the name of religion—ostensibly in the interest of piety, but really stabbing piety to the heart.

The truth is, the Christian cannot do his full duty to man till heaven is imaged in his heart; he is not ready to work well for earth till his name is written on its jeweled columns and the visions of the third heaven are in his heart and oppress his tongue. No man can work for God in true measure whose longings do not reach to heaven. No man can be truly loyal to Christ on earth till his desires are inflamed to depart and be with Christ in heaven.

Instead of eliminating heaven from our creed and work and life, we need a greater infusion of its power, a clearer experience of its reality, a more confident apprehension and a growing appreciation of our title to its incorruptible and fadeless inheritance. Instead of expunging it, we need a fuller inflow.

Christian Advocate, November 22, 1890

Heaven is a place. Out of the region of all fancy it is taken and put into the realm of the actual, the local. The revelations of the bare fact that death does not end all, death cannot end all; that man *must* exist to all eternity, that the future may be one of unutterable bliss—that is the fact. This fact may have many colorings, many symbols, but these are not the main things, nor of the main thing. Heaven does not float around. It is not made of air, thin air. It is real, a country, a clime, a home sacred affinities draw to the spot. Divine assurance settles and fixes the fact.

Heaven might be a reality, but simply a state. In its location and grasp it might be airy, volatile. The Bible statement is of a place. One of the main ideas contained in the heavenly symbol, of a city, is place, location, a settled place, in contrast with a pilgrim state, unsettled and temporary.

The strong argument for heaven as a place centers in, and clusters about Jesus. The man Jesus, bearing a man's form, the body He wore on earth, has a place assigned Him—a high place.

Wherefore God also hath highly exalted him, and given him a name which is above every name: That at the name of Jesus every knee should bow, of things in heaven, and things in earth, and things under the earth; And that every tongue should confess that Jesus Christ is Lord, to the glory of God the Father (Phil. 2:9–11).

Whom he raised from the dead and set him at his right hand in the heavenly places, Far above all principality, and power, and might, and dominion, and every name that is named, not only in this world, but also in that which is to come: And hath put all things under his feet, and gave him to be head over all things to the church, which is his body, the fulness of him that filleth all in all (Eph. 1:20–23).

This excellence and dignity is all conclusive of a place of high honor, the best, the most royal in the heavenly world.

God who at sundry times and in divers manners spake in time past unto the fathers by the prophets, Hath in these last days spoken unto us by his Son, whom he hath appointed heir to all things, by whom also he made the worlds; Who being the brightness of his glory, and the express image of his person, and upholding all things by the word of his power, when he had by himself purged our sins, sat down on the right hand of the Majesty on high (Heb. 1:1–3).

These all bespeak His place among the home places of God's many-mansioned country. "Who is gone into heaven, and is on the right hand of God; angels and authorities and powers being made subject unto him."

These are figures of Christ's exaltation and location. They are figures of a place. Jesus wants us with Him. To see and share His glory. He dwells in a place. A place which honors and glorifies His person and presence. His business is not to be enthroned and receive honor, but He is there for us, to prepare a place for us.

Father, I will that they also, whom thou hast given me, be with me where I am; that they may behold my glory, which thou hast given me (John 17:24).

Heaven in the Bible is represented as a place in contrast with earth. The earth is a place, but unstable, insecure, fleeting. Heaven is stable, secure, eternal.

> For here have we no continuing city, but we seek one to come (Heb. 13:14).

How marked the contrast between earth and heaven! Earth is but a pilgrim's stay, a pilgrim's journey, a pilgrim's tent. Heaven is a city, permanent, God-planned, God-built, whose foundations are as stable as God's throne.

> By faith Abraham, when he was called to go out into a place which he should after receive for an inheritance, obeyed; and he went out not knowing whither he went. By faith, he sojourned in the land of promise, as in a strange country, dwelling in tabernacles with Isaac and Jacob, the heirs with him of the same promise: For he looked for a city which hath foundations, whose builder and maker is God (Heb. 11:8–9).

The Bible reveals heaven as a place. It is measured off, has its appointed metes and bounds, as definite place as a city, a walled city. It has its inside and its outside. Heaven is within the city, hell is without.

> For without are dogs, and sorcerers, and whoremongers, and murderers, and idolaters, and whosoever loveth and maketh a lie (Rev. 22:15).

Heaven is a *place*. Not airy, impalpable, delocalized, is heaven. "I go," said Jesus, "to prepare a *place* for you." That means locality, something settled. Heaven has its deep, strong colorings, its metes and bounds on God's map.

Heaven: A Place—A City—A Home

Holiness

Archbishop Leighton's summary of a holy life is perhaps as complete as any statement out of the Bible. First. Remember always the presence of God. Second. Rejoice always in the will of God. Third. Direct all to the glory of God. We cannot exceed this in statement, but we can come up to it in practice, and this is much better. It is much wiser to be able to do the truth than to be able to state the truth.

Christian Advocate, November 29, 1890

Holy Spirit

The affluence of life in the apostolic church is one of its marked features. The life was too strong for programme, too overflowing for ruts, too fresh and full for stiffness, too ardent to be chilled or checked by formality. The opulence of the spiritual life burst out spontaneously, joyously. The Holy Ghost was on them in power, and every thing was full and quickened and mightily stirred by his presence. The fullness of life, a stirring, talking, working life, was theirs. Silence and deadness were strangers to their assemblies. Every one brought a personal contribution of spiritual gifts to bless the occasion.

Christian Advocate, December 27, 1890

† † †

There is force in organization. Unity, directness, and energy are secured by organization. The waste and weakness in individual effort are prevented. But organization beyond certain limits, in religious efforts, is weakness and not strength. There must be full play for individual effort, individual sympathies, and freedom. To reduce the church life to the control of machinery is to make it automatic. Organization does not always betoken life, neither does it always quicken life. The measure of the aggregated force in the church is simply the measure of the Holy Ghost on each individual member, placing him in his appropriate place in the body, giving coherence, unity, and content.

Christian Advocate, October 27, 1890

Holy Spirit and Prayer

Our divine example in praying is the Son of God. Our Divine Helper in praying is the Holy Spirit. He quickens us to pray and helps us in praying. Acceptable prayer must be begun and carried on by His presence and inspiration. We are enjoined in the Holy Scriptures to "pray in the Holy Ghost." We are charged to "pray always with all prayer and supplication in the Spirit." We are reminded for our encouragement, that "Likewise the Spirit also helpeth our infirmities; for we know not what we should pray for as we ought; but the Spirit itself maketh intercession for us with groanings which cannot be uttered." "And he that searcheth the hearts knoweth what is the mind of the Spirit, because he maketh intercession for the saints according to the will of God."

So ignorant are we in this matter of prayer; so impotent are all other teachers to impart its lessons to our understanding and heart, that the Holy Spirit comes as the infallible and all-wise teacher to instruct us in this divine art. "To pray with all your heart and all your strength, with the reason and the will, this is the greatest achievement of the Christian warfare on earth." This is what we are taught to do and enabled to do by the Holy Spirit. If no man can say that Jesus is the Christ but by the Spirit's help; for the much greater reason can no man pray save by the aid of God's Spirit. Our mother's lips, now sealed by death, taught us many sweet lessons of prayer; prayers which have bound and held our hearts like golden threads; but these prayers, flowing through the natural channel of a mother's love, can not serve the purposes of our manhood's warring, stormy life. These maternal lessons are but the A B C of praying. For the higher and graduating lessons in prayer we must have the Holy Spirit. He only can unfold to us the mysteries of the prayer life, its duty and its service.

To pray by the Holy Spirit we must have Him always. He does not, like earthly teachers, teach us the lesson and then withdraw. He stays to help us practise the lesson He has taught. We pray, not by the precepts and lessons He has taught, but we pray by Him. He is both teacher and lesson. We can only know the lesson because He is ever with us to inspire, to illumine, to explain, to help us to do. We pray not by the truth the Holy Spirit reveals to us but we pray by the actual presence of the Holy Spirit. He puts the desire in our hearts; kindles that desire by His own flame. We simply give lip and voice and heart to His unutterable groanings. Our prayers are taken up by Him and energised and sanctified by His intercession. He prays for us, through us and in us. We pray by Him, through Him and in Him. He puts the prayer in us and we give it utterance and heart.

We always pray according to the will of God when the Holy Spirit helps our praying. He prays through us only "according to the will of God." If our prayers are not according to the will of God they die in the presence of the Holy Spirit. He gives such prayers no countenance, no help. Discountenanced and unhelped by Him, prayers, not according to God's will, soon die out of every heart where the Holy Spirit dwells.

We must, as Jude says, "Pray in the Holy Ghost." As Paul says, "with all prayer and supplication in the Spirit." Never forgetting that "the Spirit also helpeth our infirmities; for we know not what we should pray for as we ought: but the Spirit itself maketh intercession for us with groanings which cannot be uttered." Above all, over all, and through all our praying there must be the Name of Christ, which includes the power of His blood, the energy of His intercession, the fullness of the enthroned Christ. "Whatsoever ye ask in my name that will I do."

Reality of Prayer, Chap. 14

Hymns

The hymn book we use will have much to do with training our people in Methodist doctrine and experience. Next in influence to what the preacher says will be the words of the songs we sing. These song words ought to be the embodiment of some great religious truth that will live in the memory and heart and life after the cadence has died. Use the Methodist Hymn book in all the song service. Sing the standard Methodist hymns much.

Christian Advocate, September 27, 1890

Among the revivals needed just now is the revival of the use of the Methodist hymn book; the revival of the singing of Methodist hymns. In some Methodist churches the Methodist hymn book has been banished or is a retired, neglected guest. In not a few Methodist churches the Methodist hymns are strangers. The average Methodist choir can be dumbfounded quicker by announcing an old hymn than by any other method; praise then or something worse sits silent on their lips. When a Methodist church sings itself away from Methodist hymns, it sings itself away from Methodist experience and doctrine.

I would not ban all hymns outside of our hymn book by any means. Some of them are good and may come in occasionally or as dessert after the substantials are solidly laid. But to make the whole meal of dessert will vitiate appetite and break down constitution.

That we sing is very important. Song belongs to the first and last principles of religion, is an element of the new birth, the employment of the heavenly life. What we sing is all important. It is not the fact of singing, not the tune, the melody, or the sentiment of song; but the message which the song bears to the soul that gives enduring, spiritual value to the song. It was not the singing of the songs of Thales that prepared Sparta for the reforms of Lykingus, but the political and unifying principles which were veiled under his poetry. It was not the poetic worth of Charles Wesley's hymns only which made them the efficient handmaid to John Wesley's preaching, but the body and life of God's word which by these hymns were wrought into melody and song.

Our religious songs teach, train and implant spiritual truths. "Teaching" says the apostle "and admonishing one another in psalms, hymns, and spiritual songs." If the hymns are defective or wrong in their statements, the poison of error is infused, only the more deadly because set to music and inhaled in the sweets of song. The hymns which have been substituted for the old ones are often surcharged with deadly error. They have been mutilated, the verbiage changed to suit phases of doctrine with which Methodism has always been at war. I heard Mr. Moody, in a manner, arraign the Methodist church for not putting in its revised hymnal Mr. Bliss' song, "Free from the law," that hymn having in it the seeds of all antinomianism, against which Methodism has always set its face like a flint. I heard him say, He did not believe in "wrestling prayer" and his songs are set to that keynote. How antagonistic such views are to Methodism; the throes of whose birth, and the signs and spoils of whose victories are those of "Wrestling Jacob"!

Hymns may not be defective or perverse in statement and yet so light and chaffy in sentiment, so vapory, or frivolous, or worldly in air, so gay and popular in tune as to dissipate all serious and spiritual frames. The right impressions of a soul seeking after God or in holy communion with him could scarcely be more seriously offended or more readily dissipated than by many of these songs with their lusty gush and machine made poetry or merely human sentiments.

The true object of song in worship cannot be better set

forth than by Mr. Wesley in the preface to his hymn book. "Full account of scriptural Christianity—A declaration of the heights and depths of religion, speculative and practical. Strong cautions against the most plausible errors. Clear directions for making our calling and election sure: for perfecting holiness in the fear of the Lord. Raising and quickening the spirit of devotion: confirming faith, enlivening hope; kindling and increasing love to God and man." All these belong to the province of the service of song. These standard hymns are fitted to secure these lofty ends. Of them it may be said as it was said of their chief composer, Charles Wesley; "Christian experience from the deeps of affliction through all the gradations of doubt, fear, desire, faith, hope, expectation to the transports of perfect love in the very beams of the beatific vision—Christian experience furnishes him with everlasting and inexhaustible themes: and it must be confessed that he has celebrated them with an affluence of dictim: and a splendor of coloring, rarely surpassed. At the same time he has invested them with a power of truth and endeared them both to the imagination and the affections with a pathos which makes feeling conviction and leaves the understanding but little to do but to acquiesce in the decisions of the heart."

For Methodists to think or read themselves out of sympathy with Wesley's sermons (They can never pray themselves out of sympathy) is a great spiritual discount. For Methodists to sing themselves out of sympathy with Methodist hymnology is to be on the same spiritual downgrade.

I find everywhere I have been a great falling off from the radiancy, reality, purity and joy of Methodist experience, which is due in part to the falling off from sympathy, knowledge and use of these Methodist hymns.

Not a few preachers are wholly and seemingly blissfully ignorant of the contents of their hymn book: to put it in the course of study might force the committees as well as the under growth of preachers to study it.

Not a few congregations use the supplement almost wholly, taking their whole meal in syllabub and sweatmeats. Others use the standard hymn book for the state and dignity of the Sabbath Service; but in the social meetings use some other book. A stranger and damaging process this. Our social meetings are the ones where the song power has its greatest effects. If our training songs are to be used any where, it ought to be where they will do the best service. I fear that popular clauses, worldly views, and low spirituality have much to do with our change and surrender along this line. Vital religion begins to decay and the world makes its first and insidious advances under the guise of church music. It seems to me if Methodist preachers and people would relearn the object of singing nothing could induce them to allow this spiritually depraving substitute: that our standard hymn book would be placed in every pew and in the hands of every worshipper and every one exhorted to sing; exhorted not once or twice in a decent casual way but strongly, sharply, insistently till each realized that they had not only a personal and glorious privilege in singing but a solemn duty personal and imperative to perform, that silence evoked sin, and dumbness, death.

Bounds Family Papers

Missions

This is a missionary age. Protestant Christianity is stirred as it never was stirred before in the line of aggression on pagan lands. The missionary movement has taken on proportions that awaken hope, kindle enthusiasm, and demands the attention, if not the interest, of the coldest and most listless. Our own church has caught the contagion, and the sails of her missionary movement are spread wide to catch the favoring breeze. The danger is imminent that the missionary movement will go ahead of the missionary spirit. This has been the peril of the church; losing the substance and spirit in the shell and parade of the movement, putting the force of effort in the movement and not in the spirit. The magnificence of the movement may not only blind us to the spirit, but the spirit that should give life and shape to the movement may be lost in the wealth of the movement, as the ship, borne by favoring winds, may be lost when these winds swell to a storm.

Dr. Olin, a Methodist missionary secretary of over forty years ago, a man who had the rare and matchless combination of great intellectual ability with the profoundest apprehension and grasp of great spiritual principles, said in regard to this danger, as to "whether the offerings of the church to the missionary treasury, inadequate and scanty as they have been, have not yet been greater than their faith—more numerous than their prayers—whether the missionary movement is not far in advance of the missionary spirit." "I do not hesitate to declare," he said, "that this is my most solemn and mature conviction, and that it is the true and chief source of our difficulties. The novelty and even sublimity of the enterprise—the new and strange facts brought to light in missionary reports—the stirring appeals of the press and platform—the extent and glitter of our machinery, stretching out through all the land, have one and all had the effect of waking up an interest in this cause widely different from a true Christian sympathy for perishing sinners, or a pious concern for the honor and will of the Saviour." If these words were true and these principles applicable at that time, with double force are they applicable at that time, with double force are they applicable to us.

The spirit of missions is the spirit of prayer. Prayer is the chief factor in the genuine missionary movement. Prevalent, united prayer is the agent that moves the world toward God and moves God toward the world. Jacob's wily shrewdness of invention and schemes failed him in the presence of Esau's revenge, but he reached and changed Esau when he reached God by prayer.

What we need in our missionary movement now more than any thing else, more than all things else, is the spirit of fervent and effectual prayer.

The inquiry is made at our Conferences: "Are the collections for missions full?" A more pertinent inquiry would be, Are our prayers for missions full? Do we pray up to the full measure of gospel privilege, ardor, and agony? The inquiry is going the rounds in regard to our new secretaries, are they platform men? A more important inquiry would be: Are they closet men? Men's words for this cause will be feeble, their effects ephemeral, if their words are not surcharged with power and permanency by much closet work as well as by much study work.

As much as we need men and money in this work we need God more, and prayer brings God into it, and he never comes alone, but always brings the men and money with him. When God comes there are mighty quickenings, purse strings are loosened, and men are willing and prepared to go.

However we may magnify other conditions, God magnifies one condition, and bases the whole results of the conquest of the world to Christ on the one of prayer. "Ask of me," says God, "and I shall give thee the heathen for thine inheritance, and the uttermost parts of the earth for thy possession." God as a sovereign has original rights, and the power of disposal in this matter, and we ask and importune of God in the name of Christ and for Christ's glory—this is irresistible. Prayer is mighty because it links itself to Christ and shuts its plea up to the power of His Name and the merits of His death and intercession. Prayer is mighty because it is the action of faith in God's word, in God's oath to His Son.

Prayer projects God into our affairs in full force. He does not intrude himself. He does not come unasked into our holiest efforts, nor into the work that so greatly concerns him. His presence must be sought, importuned. Our plans, to have God in them, must be inspired, sustained, and ended in unceasing prayer.

The fervent, effectual prayers of God's people would exalt and purify the motives of those who go. A short-lived enthusiasm would play no part in this call. The force of movement would not propel, but stronger and holier influences than these would decide. Low, questionable motives would be lost in the constraining love of Christ. The church on her knees, with tearful, outstretched hearts to God, would secure the right kind of men and implant the right kind of motives to move them in their going, for God would elect the men and kindle in them the irrepressible desire to go.

A church mighty in prayer would secure the money. God only can break the love of money which restrains the giving of the church. If the church would set its heart on God by mighty prayer he would scatter these Methodist fortunes and pour them through a thousand rills to carry the water of life to the perishing nations.

Prayer will not only secure the men and money, not only secure the right kind of men, but it will make the men and money efficacious. Without the men who go are backed by the faith of a praying church, their going will be but a feint, the marching up the hill with ten thousand men and the marching down again. The money given will be as sterile in saving, fructifying results as the granite, if it be not fertilized by prayer. The church has been fixing her eye and heart so strongly on her growing material resources that she has forgotten, in a measure, the nature, the secret and the power of prayer. To forget these is to forget God. To restrain prayer is to restrain God. The history of the church, the marvelous career of the saints, the word of God, all declare the praying Church to be the aggressive missionary church.

Christian Advocate, September 13, 1890

Money and Materialism

Few men get rich with clean hands. Fewer still get rich with religious hands. Fewer still hold on to their riches and hold on to Christ with a strong grasp at the same time. Who can serve Christ and money?

Christian Advocate, December 27, 1890

† † †

To be rich in gold and poor in spirit is the most difficult of all religious combinations. The only process which will combine the two is found in the man who seeks for poverty of spirit with the same ardor, care, and desire that he seeks money.

Christian Advocate, July 26, 1890

The greatest danger to the church is found in the ambition of the preachers and the covetousness of the laymen.... Ambition for office or for honor is, in a preacher, nothing short of sin. Covetousness in a layman is the refinement of idolatry. The worship of money, which is too absorbing to give time for the claims of conscience, is not half so worthy of toleration as was the worship of the sun and moon. God made these. Human hands fashioned that. The push for place in the clergy is next, in disloyalty to Christ, to a denial of the faith.

Christian Advocate, May 24, 1890

†   †   †

If it be true, as this editor states, that for twenty-five years the proportion of men in the church, as compared with the women, has been growing less, this is a suggestive fact, and it is not a favorable indication. The gospel that does not save the men has some way become emasculated. A church reduced in its membership to women and children will not represent in its virile or divine force the gospel of Christ.

There must be a cause for this condition of things; to discover and locate the disease is the first and great step to a cure.

One cause of the failing hold the church has on the men is found in the increased and strong materiality of the age—a materiality which affects the men in an essential way. Increased wealth, the splendid fortunes built up, the fame and influence connected with these. The material advance of the age, its diversity, magnificence, and munificence have shut out the view and interests of the other world. All the forces of our civilization tend to materialize the men in a way which cannot be arrested or broken by feeble spiritual forces.

Business success demands more intensity and absorbs more greatly. Its results are more stimulating and engaging than in simpler times. That the material forces which bind to the earth are far stronger and more bewildering and alluring; and that the attractions of business, money, and worldly success are more engaging than half a century ago cannot be denied.

The church instead of raising her voice and authority against this worldly tendency, is not infrequently its ally, if not its open advocate; it is often seduced or imposed on by the glory of these kingdoms of the world. The church measures her successes by her material resources, and clothes her authority and prosperity by the parade and aggregate of the earthly. Heaven and the unseen are not always to the church the potent and inspiring objects they ought to be.

Christian Advocate, November 12, 1890

Money: The Hindrance

One of our bishops writes to the missionary secretary's office that we are on record as a missionary church, that the secretary's office must be a missionary bureau, and that the practical results must be in keeping with the advanced movement. This is well, but no mere movement, no General Conference advance can bring the church to the front afire with the missionary spirit. There are hindrances untold to the advance of the gospel outside of the church, but the chief hindrance, at present, is in the church.

We are embarrassed for the lack of money to send men to the mission fields and support them there. Why is this the case? Is the supply of money short? Has a financial panic blasted the kingdom of God? Is there not an abundant supply of money for the uses of trade? Are there not millions of money locked up in vaults and banks and stocks? Is the church made up of the poor and beggarly? Are not her members merchant princes? Are they not the kings on change? Are not bankers her counselors? Does she not count and parade the millionaires on her roll? Are not her communions filled from the houses of wealth and thrift? Are not the honorable and lucrative professions filled with church-men? Are not the titles to millions of real estate in her preachers and people? Why, then, is the church so sadly straitened for money to do her work? Why is she so poor and so many of her members so rich? Why does the mission business languish when the real estate and other businesses run by the same men are so flush? What is the cause of this unseemly condition? It is found in one word, the church is materialized. With it earth outrivals heaven; to be good financiers is better than to be goodly saints; earthly stocks sell better than heavenly stocks in her market.

Money has materialized the church. The money she does not give has earthened her. Money-loving, money-making, money-keeping, is the rock on which the spiritual movements of the church are stranded; it is the Capua that dissolves the strength of her brave legions, and brings effeminacy and disaster on her aggressive campaigns. The church is making earth her home instead of her battlefields; her members are demoralized by palaces instead of being hardened by tents. Her sighs and longings and struggles for the homeland are hushed in the embraces of a foreign love. Money has won on the church, and holds it to earth in a more engaging and tasteful form than the memory of the onions and garlic held apostate Israel to Egypt. Public sentiment and church sentiment have fixed the worth of money so high that we hold it above the price of souls.

This covetousness which has materialized the church, and this material spirit which has rooted covetousness so thoroughly in the church, have arrested and almost destroyed the *grace* of giving, for our giving is too poor to dignify it by the name of a grace. If the grace of giving were the only grace arrested by covetousness, the case would not be so malignant and gravely apprehensive, but it arrests all the other graces, prayer, faith, self-denial, zeal, all are poisoned or perish by the same deadly influence.

This material attitude, induced by our estimate of money, is the baneful source of our financial distress; what money we get is drawn, often, from unwilling purses, by the strong hand of a legal assessment, and comes not as the spontaneous product of a glad faith, giving according to ability, and devoutly thankful for the ability to give.

This state of things can be remedied. The remedy is found, in the first place, in the genuine preaching of the genuine gospel. This age is too intent. Money and its allied forces are too strong to be impressed by a gospel of song, sentiment, or sham. Nothing but the unadulterated gospel—rock-founded, rock-ribbed, iron-cemented—will work this miraculous work. Nothing but God's real forceful gospel can reach this forceful earth-bent age; a gospel bathed in the blood of God, which finds all its mysteries solved, and all its results summed up in heaven and hell.

No gospel of pseudo emasculating love can meet the case, but the whole of God's word must be declared, the full force of all its terrific revelations must be poured on the church like a tempest of shot and shell. The church must be deluged and impregnated with the truth that no man can have two heavens, that he who would gain eternal life must pay the price of this life.

It is not the telling of the old, old story, that is a feeble way to put it, and a childish way to do it, but the gospel of the Son of God preached with the Holy Ghost sent down from heaven; this gospel solid with its adamantine truths is to be iterated and reiterated with all the tremendous consequences attending their rejection, with all the sublime and ineffable results of their acceptance. These are to be set forth, not in feeble accents or with bated breath, but driven with all the melting tenderness of broken hearts, and all the brawny strength of the smith's sleeveless arm on the consciences of the people.

This unabridged gospel, pressed with all the fervor of impassioned exhortation, with all the sharpness, authority, and conviction of reproof, backed by all the solemnities of the judgment, declared by a soul overwhelmed with the interests involved, softened into exhaustless sweetness, patience, and tears, by the compassionate demands of his difficult and delicate work. This, and nothing else, is the unfailing remedy for our disease. These, and nothing but these, mighty truths of God flowing from hearts which have experienced all their mightiness, will break the seductive and hardening spell which money has thrown around the church; nothing but these will arouse her from her fatal lethargy, infatuation, and earthliness, and arm her for the mighty conflict and glorious victory.

The church began its new Pentecostal history by breaking into pieces the greed and selfishness of the money-spirit, and selling out its real estate for God. A mighty baptism of the Holy Ghost will repeat this history, and calcine to ask this strong materiality in the church.

A Pentecost that will break up the great deep, and convulse and excite from center to circumference. A Pentecost that will sell out real estate for God's cause is the second ingredient in the remedy. As surely as real estate is sold out for money so surely God's forces, when given fair and full play, will command title-deeds and bank accounts for God. When real estate passes title because God's cause needs it something will be done. The day of our earthliness and shame will be past, the day of God's power come.

How God's elect ones should be praying day and night for this incoming flood to set the church afloat from her moorings in an enemy's port.

The preachers must quit lauding the money-making talent; must quit following the money-making business. This element must be compounded with the others as the third essential. One rich preacher will fix covetousness in a thousand hearts.

The preachers, by a self-denying, independent, heavenly example, must set their faces like flint against this evil, and shame it at every point. No Methodist preacher can afford to live or die rich; better for us to die penniless and be buried in potter's field than to make money in this money-ruled and money-cursed time.

If every Methodist preacher held the same attitude to money that Mr. Wesley did we would not be straitened in every department of church work for money, and have to lament the parsimony of our giving. He says: "Gold and silver I count dung and dross; I trample it under my feet; I desire it not; I seek it not. None of the accursed thing shall be found in my tent, when the Lord cometh. If I leave behind ten pounds (above my debts and my books, or what may happen to be due on account of them) you and all mankind bear witness against me that I have lived and died a thief and robber."

This sentiment, lived and worked out among the preachers, and going from them in fiery streams of holy utterance and holy living, is the only cure for our condition.

The missionary movement may be a flush movement, but it will be a very shallow one unless our materialized money tendencies are broken up.

Christian Advocate, July 19, 1890

Praise

The distinction between church music and God's praise is of vital importance. They are two things separable, and may be wholly distinct. There may be the finest music, faultless in its taste, and execution, sacred in its character, with not one element of praise. Praise means to think highly of God, and express through the lips the heart's exalted estimate of him. The musician may have his soul in the music and render it with all the grace and influence of art and genius, and God be far away. Praise puts God in the heart, and its songs flow out in melody to him. Many are making the serious mistake of substituting church music, for God's praises. Praise is of first importance in God's service. Its virtue cannot be magnified. Church music serves the purpose of flowers at a funeral.

Christian Advocate, January 7, 1892

Praise means to set a high value on God, and to express this value in words. Praise is an essential as well as an initial element in religion. When God converts a soul he puts in it, as a germinal and organic principle, the spirit of praise. A conversion that does not clothe in the garment of praise in exchange for the spirit of heaviness is but a half-conversion, lame and impotent, of little, if any, worth. The presence or absence of praise marks the depth and intensity, or the beggary of our spiritual life. Prayer and praise are joined as the sun and its light are joined, as the flower and its sweetness are joined. If prayer be the life of religion, praise is the wing by which that life soars to heaven. Prayer brings God down to the soul and praise lifts the soul up to God. Prayer has much to do with our sins and ourselves and God; praise has much to do with grace, gratitude, and God.

The high esteem of God in the heart is the fountain and force of praise. To have this high esteem, luminous views of sin and salvation must be gained. A definite and powerful realization of sin and salvation is the prerequisite of praise. An Almighty rescue from an infinite and imminent peril lays the foundation of praise deep and broad.

God was of such priceless value to many of the saints of old, his revelation of himself to them so glorious and transporting, their consciousness of his being, his presence, and his power, so vivid and profound that they shouted out his praises. Our spiritual strength would scarcely bear the strain of such lofty and strenuous spiritual exercise, even if our low spiritual tastes were not offended by such exhibitions. In our estimate and action we must be careful to distinguish between church music and praise. To confuse the two will be exceedingly damaging. In not a few congregations praise has been wholly substituted by church music. These two are distinct in their inspiration and aims. A great deal of church music has no reference to the high price set on God by the grateful, adoring heart, nor of the expression of that estimate by holy, thankful lips.

The spirit of praise was once the boast of Methodism; it abode on our tabernacles as a cloud of glory out of which God shined and spoke. It filled our temples with the perfume of costly, flaming incense. That this spirit of praise is sadly deficient in our congregations now must be evident to every one. That it is a mighty force in projecting the gospel, and that its decay is the decay of vital forces must be equally evident. To restore the spirit of praise to our congregations should be one of the main points with every pastor.

Singing is one method of praise—not the highest, but the ordinary and usual form.

The apostle puts the whole matter in a small compass: "Let the word of Christ," he says, "dwell in you richly in all wisdom, teaching and admonishing one another in psalms and hymns and spiritual songs, singing with grace in your hearts to the Lord." To do this the nature and quality of the preaching is all-important. The song of praise is the outflow of the strong, inner spiritual principles. No songs exist where the word of God does not dwell richly in the heart. The word of God is the material out of which these songs are manufactured. The preacher lays the foundation on which the beautiful temple of song is built. The word of God implanted in the heart is the overflowing fountain from which this sparkling, musical, and refreshing stream flows. The real song-praise is not the product of a song drill under scientific leaders, not a forced or manufactured thing, the result of outward or natural forces, but the spontaneous outgoing of mighty internal forces implanted by the ever-potent and ever-vitalizing word of God. The homely, earnest preaching of God's word by a preacher filled with the Holy Ghost is the prerequisite to the existence of the spirit of praise in the hearts and lips of the hearers.

One great object of praise is mutual edification; the telling of God of his wondrous works, exalting these with our hearts and lips, is good to the use of edification. To this end the words that are sung are of prime importance. The benefit does not lie in the melody, this gives aroma, but the melody must have body. The tune and poetry may make it tasteful, but the nourishing qualities must come from the solid parts. These songs are to teach. They are to be the depositaries and channels of revealed truth. Poetry and music are used to give a high polish to the rich, hard dogmas of religion. Song-praise is but experience set to tune, and experience is but the solid parts of the gospel reduced to liquid form.

Methodist songs are but Methodist experience and Methodist doctrine stereotyped and beautifully illustrated. We are more indebted to the songs of Charles Wesley for the dissemination and triumph of our doctrines than to the Institutes of Richard Watson.

Charles Wesley's hymns are John Wesley's sermons in rhyme. We have lost immensely in all the stable as well as in the costlier and more beautiful parts of Methodism by allowing the popular, inane melodies to substitute our standard hymns. By this process the spiritual taste has been almost destroyed, the spiritual appetite and digestion vitiated. It is a fatal mistake to aim at getting the people, old or young, to sing *any thing* they can sing with a gush, or whatever strikes the popular ear, but to sing *something*—something that invigorates and instructs. Blank cartridges may have the noise and show of a full charge, but it leaves nothing but emptiness and smoke. Teaching, says the apostle, in psalms and hymns and spiritual songs. The whole system of gospel truth is to flow along the current of song, and flood our souls, and deposit the rich sediment which will remain and fructify when the song-wave has ebbed into silence.

These songs are for admonition; they must be edged to cut. There is to be a touch of censure, an element of warning in them. Everybody, saint or sinner, is imperiled and weak; everybody, saint or sinner, needs to be admonished; and even our songs are to be charged with this necessary and saving element. They must admonish as well as teach—show us our danger as well as our duty. How deficient in this element are the popular songs which we have substituted for Methodist hymnology. That many of them are gotten up with the deliberate aim to eliminate these features we believe. That they are almost wholly destitute of this scriptural, salutary element cannot be denied. It seems to us that if Methodist preachers and people would relearn the lesson of the object of singing, nothing could induce them to allow this vicious, piety-destroying substitution; our standard hymn book would be placed in every pew and in the hands of every worshiper and every one exhorted from the pulpit to sing; exhorted not once or twice, in a decent, casual way, but strongly, sharply, constantly, till they realized they had not only a glorious privilege to exercise, but a solemn duty to perform, and that they dare not be silent while the saints on earth were struggling to fill earth with God's glory by sounding his praise abroad. The heart must have grace in it to sing. It is not to be done by musical taste or talent, but by grace. Nothing helps the singing so mightily as a gracious revival. The presence of God inspires song. The angels and the glorified ones do not need precentors, choirs, or singing schools. God is present in their glorious assemblies, and his glorious presence creates the song and teaches the singer. It is so on earth. God's absence is the death of song. His presence, in power, in our churches, would bring back the full chorus of song.

Where grace abounds, song abounds. When God is in the heart heaven and melody are there, and the lips overflow out of the abundance of the heart.

The aim of it all is for God, "to the Lord"—for his glory— not for the pleasure of the music, not to glorify the choir, not to draw the people, but to the Lord. It is sacrilege for any but sanctified hearts and lips to direct this service. Let all the people praise God. Praise is comely, it glorifies God.

Christian Advocate, November 8, 1890

Prayer

Brethren, pray for us. This is the cry that Paul set in motion. It has been the cry of the spiritual in all the succeeding ages. No condition of success or reverse must abate the cry. It voices the need of humanity. It is the cry of want that God awakens in the heart of his people. It is the increasing cry of foreign missionaries. A hopeful sign of their success is their growing hopelessness in the mere machinery of missions, the adjuncts of the gospel, or worldly-wise plans . . . their hope and cry in God, and as the home church, by their prayers, second this appeal, the work will take on forms of greater power and increased prosperity.

Christian Advocate, December 27, 1890

† † †

The surest way to kill religion is not to murder it outright, but to kill it by piecemeal. Neglect, more surely than the dagger, stabs religion to the heart. To give religion no set or sacred times is to starve it. Other interests, even the most pressing and benevolent, to crowd religious duties out, or into a corner, kill it slowly but surely. A busy mother was asked how she got time to pray, replied: "I am up one hour every morning before my family stirs." This is the secret of growth in grace, of calmness and strength for the day's duties. The busy ones who have prefaced the engaging duties of the day by their hours of holy and ardent communion with God are the strong ones. Daniel was a very busy man, the cares of a great empire were on him, but he found time to pray three times every day—and this praying was of more benefit to the prime minister than all his diplomacy. Christ was a very busy man. The divinest of business filled his heart and filled his hands, exhausted his time, exhausted his nerves. But with him even God's work must not crowd out God's praying. Saving people from sin or suffering must not even with Christ, be made substitutes for praying, nor abate in the least the time or the intensity of these holiest of seasons. He filled the day with working for God; he filled the night with praying to God. The day working made the night praying a necessity. The night praying sanctified and made successful the day working. Too busy to pray gives religion Christian burial, it is true, but kills it, nevertheless.

Christian Advocate, December 27, 1890

Some Methodist preachers pray too short in private and too long in public. As a rule, private prayers ought to be long and public ones short. "I once carefully noted the time actually occupied in praying by one of whom I complain in this respect, and found it less than five minutes; the remaining twenty minutes were devoted to superfluous information given to God about the congregation and a variety of other subjects; a short essay, evidently intended for the congregation, about the character and attributes of God; and the repetition of a few verses from the hymn book." The above is not an exaggerated statement of some prayers we have heard. It is absolute crucifixion to stay on the knees during one of these long, lifeless prayers. To follow them is like going through the catacombs. Devotion is not kindled to relieve the tedium, and the spirit as well as the flesh cry out against the torture. In these long, sapless prayers is found one cause contributing to break up the habit of kneeling in our congregations. Short, unctuous, fervent, pointed prayers in the pulpit is the first step to a reform in the interests of kneeling in our congregations.

Christian Advocate, November 29, 1890

Desire is said to be the will in action. It is a strong sensation excited in the mind by some good. Desire exalts the object and fixes the mind on it. Desire has choice and fixedness and flame in it. Prayer based on desire is explicit and specific—it knows its need and feels and sees the thing demanded.

Prayer is not the going through a performance; it is not an indefinite, widespread clamor. Desire while it kindles the soul, holds it to the object desired. Prayer ought to enter into the spiritual habits, but it ceases to be prayer when it is carried on by habit only. It is the depth and intensity of the spiritual desires that give intensity and depth to prayer. Desire gives fervor to prayer. The soul cannot be listless when some great desire fixes and inflames it. Desire gives importunity; the urgency of our desire holds us to the thing desired with an importunity that will not be denied, but stays and pleads and comes again, and will not go till its desires are met. Strong desires make strong prayers.

The secret of unanswered barren prayers is found in the weakness of our desires. The neglect of prayer is the fearful token of dead spiritual desires. The soul has turned away from God when desire after him no longer presses it to the closet. There can be no true praying without desire. There may be much seeming to pray without desire. We catalogue many things in our prayers; we cover a large area of ground; but do our desires make up the catalogue? Do our desires map out the region covered by our prayers? Desire is intense and narrow—it cannot spread itself over a wide field. It wants a few things, and it wants them badly—so badly that nothing but God's will can content it with any thing else.

"Blessed are they that hunger and thirst after righteousness, for they shall be filled." This is the basis of a prayer that fills us by its answer—this desire that has entered into the spiritual appetite and clamors to be satisfied.

Do not our prayers often lie in the sickly regions of a mere wish, or the feeble expression of a memorized concern or want? Sometimes our prayers are but stereotyped editions of set phrases and decent proportions whose freshness and life went out years ago.

It is the flame of a present and filling desire that mounts to God. It is the ardor created by desire that burns its way to the throne of mercy and gains its plea. It is the pertinacity of desire that gives triumph to the conflict in a great struggle of prayer. It is the burden of a weighty desire that sobers, and makes restless and reduces to quiet the soul in its mighty wrestlings. It is desire that arms prayer with a thousand pleas, and robes it with invincible courage and all-conquering force.

Christian Advocate, October 4, 1890

† † †

God has of His own motion placed Himself under the law of prayer, and has obligated Himself to answer the prayers of men. He has ordained prayer as a means whereby He will do things through men as they pray, which He would not otherwise do. Prayer is a specific divine appointment, an ordinance of heaven, whereby God purposes to carry out His gracious designs on earth and to execute and make efficient the plan of salvation.

When we say that prayer puts God to work, it is simply to say that man has it in his power by prayer to move God to work in His own way among men, in which way He would not work if prayer was not made. Thus while prayer moves God to work, at the same time God puts prayer to work. As God has ordained prayer, and as prayer has no existence separate from men, but involves men, then logically prayer is the one force which puts God to work in earth's affairs through men and their prayers.

Let these fundamental truths concerning God and prayer be kept in mind in all allusions to prayer, and in all our reading of the incidents of prayer in the Scriptures.

If prayer puts God to work on earth, then, by the same token, prayerlessness rules God out of the world's affairs, and prevents Him from working. And if prayer moves God to work in this world's affairs, then prayerlessness excludes God from everything concerning men, and leaves man on earth the mere creature of circumstances, at the mercy of blind fate or without help of any kind from God. It leaves man in this world with its tremendous responsibilities and its difficult problems, and with all of its sorrows, burdens and afflictions, without any God at all. In reality the denial of prayer is a denial of God Himself, for God and prayer are so inseparable that they can never be divorced.

Prayer affects three different spheres of existence—the divine, the angelic and the human. It puts God to work, it puts angels to work, and it puts man to work. It lays its hands upon God, angels and men. What a wonderful reach there is in prayer! It brings into play the forces of heaven and earth. God, angels and men are subjects of this wonderful law of prayer, and all these have to do with the possibilities and the results of prayer. God has so far placed Himself subject to prayer that by reason of His own appointment, He is induced to work among men in a way in which He does not work if men do not pray. Prayer lays hold upon God and influences Him to work. This is the meaning of prayer as it concerns God. This is the doctrine of prayer, or else there is nothing whatever in prayer.

Prayer puts God to work in all things prayed for. While man in his weakness and poverty waits, trusts and prays, God undertakes the work. "For from old men have not heard, nor perceived by the ear, neither hath the eye seen a God beside thee, which worketh for him that waiteth for thee."

Jesus Christ commits Himself to the force of prayer. "Whatsoever ye ask in my name," He says, "that will I do, that the Father may be glorified in the Son. If ye shall ask anything in my name, I will do it." And again: "If ye abide in me, and my words abide in you, ye shall ask what ye will and it shall be done unto you."

To no other energy is the promise of God committed as to that of prayer. Upon no other force are the purposes of God so dependent as this one of prayer. The Word of God dilates on the results and necessity of prayer. The work of God stays or advances as prayer puts forth its strength. Prophets and apostles have urged the utility, force and necessity of prayer. "I have set watchmen upon thy walls, O Jerusalem, which shall never hold their peace day nor night. Ye that make mention of the Lord, keep not silence, and give him no rest, till he establish, and till he make Jerusalem a praise in the earth."

Prayer, with its antecedents and attendants, is the one and only condition of the final triumph of the Gospel. It is the one and only condition which honors the Father and glorifies the Son. Little and poor praying has weakened Christ's power on earth, postponed the glorious results of His reign, and retired God from His sovereignty.

Prayer puts God's work in His hands, and keeps it there. It looks to Him constantly and depends on Him implicitly to further His own cause. Prayer is but faith resting in, acting with, and leaning on and obeying God. This is why God loves it so well, why He puts all power into its hands, and why He so highly esteems men of prayer.

Every movement for the advancement of the Gospel must be created by and inspired by prayer. In all these movements of God, prayer precedes and attends as an invariable and necessary condition.

In this relation, God makes prayer identical in force and power with Himself, and says to those on earth who pray: "You are on the earth to carry on My cause. I am in heaven, the Lord of all, the Maker of all, the Holy One of all. Now whatever you need for My cause, ask Me and I will do it. Shape the future by your prayers, and all that you need for present supplies, command Me. I made heaven and earth, and all things in them. Ask largely. Open thy mouth wide, and I will fill it. It is My work which you are doing. It concerns My cause. Be prompt and full in praying. Do not abate your asking, and I will not wince nor abate in My giving."

Everywhere in His Word God conditions His actions on prayer. Everywhere in His Word His actions and attitude are shaped by prayer. To quote all the Scriptural passages which prove the immediate, direct and personal relation of prayer to God, would be to transfer whole pages of the Scripture to this study. Man has personal relations with God. Prayer is the divinely appointed means by which man comes into direct connection with God. By His own ordinance God holds Himself bound to hear prayer. God bestows His great good on His children when they seek it along the avenue of prayer.

When Solomon closed his great prayer which he offered at the dedication of the temple, God appeared to him, approved him, and laid down the universal principles of His action. In 2 Chronicles 7:12–15 we read as follows:

> . . . the Lord appeared to Solomon by night and said unto him, I have heard thy prayer, and have chosen this place to myself, for a house of sacrifice.
>
> If I shut up heaven that there be no rain, or if I command the locusts to devour the land, or if I send pestilence among the people; if my people which are called by my name, shall humble themselves and pray, and seek my face, and turn from their wicked ways, then will I hear from heaven, and will forgive their sin, and will heal their land. Now my eyes shall be open, and my ears attentive to the prayer that is made in this place.

In His purposes concerning the Jews in the Babylonish captivity (Jer. 29:10–13) God asserts His unfailing principles:

> For thus saith the Lord, that after seventy years be accomplished, at Babylon, I will visit you, and perform my good word toward you, in causing you to return to this place. For I know the thoughts that I think toward you, saith the Lord, thoughts of peace, and not of evil, to give you an expected end. Then shall ye call upon me, and ye shall go and pray unto me, and I will hearken unto you. And ye shall seek me and find me, when ye shall search for me with all your heart.

In Bible terminology prayer means calling upon God for things we desire, asking things of God. Thus we read: "Call upon me and I will answer thee, and will show thee great and mighty things which thou knowest not" (Jer. 33:3). "Call upon me in the day of trouble, and I will deliver thee" (Ps. 50:15). "Then shalt thou call, and the Lord shall answer; thou shalt cry, and he shall say, Here I am" (Isa. 58:9).

Prayer is revealed as a direct application to God for some temporal or spiritual good. It is an appeal to God to intervene in life's affairs for the good of those for whom we pray. God is recognized as the source and fountain of all good, and prayer implies that all His good is held in His keeping for those who call upon Him in truth.

That prayer is an application to God, intercourse with God, and communion with God, comes out strongly and simply in the praying of Old Testament saints. Abraham's intercession for Sodom is a striking illustration of the nature of prayer, intercourse with God, and showing the intercessory side of prayer. The declared purpose of God to destroy Sodom confronted Abraham, and his soul within him was greatly moved because of his great interest in that fated city. His nephew and family resided there. That purpose of God must be changed. God's decree for the destruction of this evil city's inhabitants must be revoked.

It was no small undertaking which faced Abraham when he conceived the idea of beseeching God to spare Sodom. Abraham sets himself to change God's purpose and to save Sodom with the other cities of the plain. It was certainly a most difficult and delicate work for him to undertake to throw his influence with God in favor of those doomed cities so as to save them.

He bases his plea on the simple fact of the number of righteous men who could be found in Sodom, and appeals to the infinite rectitude of God not to destroy the righteous with the wicked. "That be far from thee to slay the righteous with the wicked. Shall not the Judge of all the earth do right?" With what deep self-abasement and reverence does Abraham enter upon his high and divine work! He stood before God in solemn awe, and meditation, and then drew near to God and spake. He advanced step by step in faith, in demand and urgency, and God granted every request which he made. It has been well said that "Abraham left off asking before God left off granting." It seems that Abraham had a kind of optimistic view of the piety of Sodom. He scarcely expected when he undertook this matter to have it end in failure. He was greatly in earnest, and had every encouragement to press his case. In his final request he surely thought that with Lot, his wife, his daughters, his sons, and his sons-in-law, he had his ten righteous persons for whose sake God would spare the city. But alas! The count failed when the final test came. There were not ten righteous people in that large population.

But this was true. If he did not save Sodom by his importunate praying, the purposes of God were stayed for a season, and possibly had not Abraham's goodness of heart overestimated the number of pious people in that devoted city, God might have saved it had he reduced his figures still further.

This is a representative case illustrative of Old Testament praying, and disclosing God's mode of working through prayer. It shows further how God is moved to work in answer to prayer in this world even when it comes to changing His purposes concerning a sinful community. This praying of Abraham was no mere performance, no dull, lifeless ceremony, but an earnest plea, a strong advocacy, to secure a desired end, to have an influence, one person with another person.

How full of meaning is this series of remarkable intercessions made by Abraham! Here we have arguments designed to convince God, and pleas to persuade God to change His purpose. We see deep humility, but holy boldness as well, perseverance, and advances made based on victory in each petition. Here we have enlarged asking encouraged by enlarged answers. God stays and answers as long as Abraham stays and asks. To Abraham God is existent, approachable, and all powerful, but at the same time He defers to men, acts favorably on their desires, and grants them favors asked for. Not to pray is a denial of God, a denial of His existence, a denial of His nature, and a denial of His purposes toward mankind.

God has specifically to do with prayer promises in their breadth, certainty and limitations. Jesus Christ presses us into the presence of God with these prayer promises, not only by the assurance that God will answer, but that no other being but God can answer. He presses us to God because only in this way can we move God to take a hand in earth's affairs, and induce Him to intervene in our behalf.

"All things whatsoever ye ask in prayer, believing, ye shall receive," says Jesus, and this all-comprehensive condition not only presses us to pray for all things, everything great and small, but it sets us on and shuts us up to God, for who but God can cover the illimitable of universal things, and can assure us certainly of receiving the very thing for which we may ask in all the thesaurus of earthly and heavenly good?

It is Jesus Christ, the Son of God, who makes demands on us to pray, and it is He who puts Himself and all He has so fully in the answer. He it is who puts Himself at our service and answers our demands when we pray.

And just as He puts Himself and the Father at our command in prayer, to come directly into our lives and to work for our good, so also does He engage to answer the demands of two or more believers who are agreed as touching any one thing. "If two of you shall agree on earth as touching anything, that they shall ask, it shall be done for them of my Father which is in heaven." None but God could put Himself in a covenant so binding as that, for God only could fulfill such a promise and could reach to its exacting and all controlling demands. God only can answer for the promises.

God needs prayer, and man needs prayer, too. It is indispensable to God's work in this world, and is essential to getting God to work in earth's affairs. So God binds men to pray by the most solemn obligations. God commands men to pray, and so not to pray is plain disobedience to an imperative command of Almighty God. Prayer is such a condition without which the graces, the salvation and the good of God are not bestowed on men. Prayer is a high privilege, a royal prerogative and manifold and eternal are the losses by failure to exercise it. Prayer is the great, universal force to advance God's cause; the reverence which hallows God's name; the ability to do God's will, and the establishment of God's kingdom in the hearts of the children of men. These, and their coincidents and agencies, are created and affected by prayer.

One of the constitutional enforcements of the Gospel is prayer. Without prayer, the Gospel can neither be preached effectively, promulgated faithfully, experienced in the heart, nor be practiced in the life. And for the very simple reason that by leaving prayer out of the catalogue of religious duties, we leave God out, and His work cannot progress without Him.

The movements that God purposed under Cyrus, king of Persia, prophesied about by Isaiah many years before Cyrus was born, are conditioned on prayer. God declares His purpose, power, independence and defiance of obstacles in the way of His carrying out those purposes. His omnipotent and absolutely infinite power is set to encourage prayer. He has been ordering all events, directing all conditions, and creating all things, that He might answer prayer, and then turns Himself over to His praying ones to be commanded. And then all the results and power He holds in His hands will be bestowed in lavish and unmeasured munificence to carry out prayers and to make prayer the mightiest energy in the world.

The passage in Isaiah 46 is too lengthy to be quoted in its entirety but it is well worth reading. It closes with such strong words as these, words about prayer, which are the climax of all which God has been saying concerning His purposes in connection with Cyrus:

> Thus saith the Lord, the Holy One of Israel, and his Maker: Ask me of things to come, concerning my sons, and concerning the work of my hands, command ye me. I have made the earth, and created man upon it; I, even my hands, have stretched out the heavens, and all their hosts have I commanded.

In the conclusion of the history of Job, we see how God intervenes in behalf of Job and calls upon his friends to present themselves before Job that he may pray for them. "My wrath is kindled against thee and against thy two friends," is God's statement, with the further words added, "My servant Job shall pray for you, for him will I accept," a striking illustration of God intervening to deliver Job's friends in answer to Job's prayer.

We have heretofore spoken of prayer affecting God, angels

and men. Christ wrote nothing while living. Memoranda, notes, sermon writing, sermon making, were alien to Him. Autobiography was not to His taste. The Revelation of John was His last utterance. In that book we have pictured the great importance, the priceless value, and the high position which prayer obtains in the movements, history, and unfolding progress of God's church in this world. We have this picture in Revelation 8:3, disclosing the interest the angels in heaven have in the prayers of the saints and in accomplishing the answers to those prayers:

> And another angel came and stood at the altar, having a golden censer, and there was given unto him much incense, that he should offer it with the prayers of all saints, upon the golden altar which was before the throne. And the smoke of the incense which came with the prayers of the saints, ascended up before God, out of the angel's hand. And the angel took the censer, and filled it with fire of the altar, and cast it into the earth, and there were voices, and thunderings and lightnings and an earthquake.

Translated into the prose of everyday life, these words show how the capital stock by which heaven carries on the business of salvation under Christ, is made up of the prayers of God's saints on earth, and discloses how these prayers in flaming power come back to earth and produce its mighty commotions, influences and revolutions.

Praying men are essential to Almighty God in all His plans and purposes. God's secrets, councils and cause have never been committed to prayerless men. Neglect of prayer has always brought loss of faith, loss of love, and loss of prayer. Failure to pray has been the baneful, inevitable cause of backsliding and estrangement from God. Prayerless men have stood in the way of God fulfilling His Word and doing His will on earth. They tie the divine hands and interfere with God in His gracious designs. As praying men are a help to God, so prayerless men are a hindrance to Him.

We press the scriptural view of the necessity of prayer, even at the cost of repetition. The subject is too important for repetition to weaken or tire, too vital to be trite or tame. We must feel it anew. The fires of prayer have burned low. Ashes and not flames are on its altars.

No insistence in the Scriptures is more pressing than prayer. No exhortation is oftener reiterated, none is more hearty, none is more solemn and stirring, than to pray. No principle is more strongly and broadly declared than that which urges us to prayer. There is no duty to which we are more strongly obliged than the obligation to pray. There is no command more imperative and insistent than that of praying. Art thou praying in everything without ceasing, in the closet, hidden from the eyes of men, and praying always and everywhere? That is the personal, pertinent and all-important question for every soul.

Many instances occur in God's Word showing that God intervenes in this world in answer to prayer. Nothing is clearer when the Bible is consulted than that Almighty God is brought directly into the things of this world by the praying of His people. Jonah flees from duty and takes ship for a distant port. But God follows him, and by a strange providence this disobedient prophet is cast out of the vessel, and the God who sent him to Nineveh prepares a fish to swallow him. In the fish's belly he cries out to the God against whom he had sinned, and God intervenes and causes the fish to vomit Jonah out on dry land. Even the fishes of the great deep are subject to the law of prayer.

Likewise the birds of the air are brought into subjection to this same law. Elijah had foretold to Ahab the coming of that prolonged drought, and food and even water became scarce. God sent him to the brook Cherith, and said unto him, "It shall be that thou shalt drink of the brook, and I have commanded the ravens to feed thee there. And the ravens brought bread and flesh in the morning, and bread and flesh in the evening." Can any one doubt that this man of God, who later on shut up and opened the rain clouds by prayer was not praying about this time, when so much was at stake? God interposed among the birds of the air this time and strangely moved them to take care of His servant so that he would not want food and water.

David in an evil hour, instead of listening to the advice of Joab, his prime minister, yielded to the suggestion of Satan, and counted the people, which displeased God. So God told him to choose one of three evils as a retribution for his folly and sin. Pestilence came among the people in violent form, and David betakes himself to prayer.

> And David said unto God, Is it not I that commanded the people to be numbered? Even I it is that hath sinned and done evil indeed. But as for these sheep, what have they done? Let thy hand, I pray thee, O Lord my God, be on me, and on my father's house; but not on thy people, that they should be plagued (1 Chron. 21:17).

And though God had been greatly grieved at David for numbering Israel, yet He could not resist this appeal of a penitent and prayerful spirit, and God was moved by prayer to put His hand on the springs of disease and stop the fearful plague. God was put to work by David's prayer.

Numbers of other cases could be named. These are sufficient. God seems to have taken great pains in His divine revelation to men to show how He interferes in earth's affairs in answer to the praying of His saints.

The question might arise just here in some over-critical minds as to the so-called "laws of nature," who are not strong believers in prayer, as if there was a conflict between what they call the "laws of nature" and the law of prayer. These people make nature a sort of imaginary god entirely separate of Almighty God. What is nature anyway? It is but the creation of God, the Maker of all things. And what are the "laws of nature" but the laws of God, through which He governs the material world. As the law of prayer is also the law of God, there cannot possibly be any conflict between the two sets of laws, but all must work in perfect harmony. Prayer does not violate any natural law. God may set aside one law for the higher working of another law, and this He may do when He answers prayer. Or Almighty God may answer prayer working through the course of natural law. But whether or not we understand it, God is over and above all nature, and can and will answer prayer in a wise, intelligent and just manner, even though man may not comprehend it. So that in no sense is there any discord or conflict between God's several laws when God is induced to interfere with human affairs in answer to prayer.

In this connection another word might be said. We used the form of words to which there can be no objection, that prayer does certain things, but this of course implies not that prayer as a human means accomplishes anything, but that prayer only accomplishes things instrumentally. Prayer is the instrument, God is the efficient and active agent. So that prayer in itself does not interfere in earth's affairs, but prayer in the hands of men moves God to intervene and do things, which He would not otherwise do if prayer was not used as the instrument.

It is as we say, "faith hath saved thee," by which is simply meant that God through the faith of the sinner saves him, faith being only the instrument used by the sinner which brings salvation to him.

Weapon of Prayer, Chap. 2

We are constantly on a stretch, if not on a strain, to devise new methods, new plans, new organizations to advance the church and secure enlargement and efficiency for the Gospel. This trend of the day has a tendency to lose sight of the man or sink the man in the plan or organization. God's plan is to make much of the man, far more of him than of anything else. Men are God's method. The church is looking for better methods; God is looking for better men. "There was a man sent from God whose name was John." The dispensation that heralded and prepared the way for Christ was bound up in that man John. "Unto us a child is born, unto us a son is given." The world's salvation comes out of that cradled Son. When Paul appeals to the personal character of the men who rooted the gospel in the world, he solves the mystery of their success. The glory and efficiency of the Gospel is staked on the men who proclaim it. When God declares that "the eyes of the Lord run to and fro throughout the whole earth, to show Himself strong in the behalf of them whose heart is perfect toward Him," He declares the necessity of men and His dependence on them as a channel through which to exert His power upon the world. This vital, urgent truth is one that this age of machinery is apt to forget. The forgetting of it is as baneful on the work of God as would be the striking of the sun from his sphere. Darkness, confusion, and death would ensue.

What the church needs today is not more machinery or better, not new organizations or more and novel methods, but men whom the Holy Ghost can use—men of prayer, men mighty in prayer. The Holy Ghost does not flow through methods, but through men. He does not come on machinery, but on men. He does not anoint plans, but men—men of prayer.

An eminent historian has said that the accidents of personal character have more to do with the revolutions of nations than either philosophic historians or democratic politicians will allow. This truth has its application in full to the gospel of Christ, the character and conduct of the followers of Christ—Christianize the world, transfigure nations and individuals. Of the preachers of the gospel it is eminently true.

The character as well as the fortunes of the gospel are committed to the preacher. He makes or mars the message from God to man. The preacher is the golden pipe through which the divine oil flows. The pipe must not only be golden, but open and flawless, that the oil may have a full, unhindered, unwasted flow.

The man makes the preacher. God must make the man. The messenger is, if possible, more than the message. The preacher is more than the sermon. The preacher makes the sermon. As the life-giving milk from the mother's bosom is but the mother's life, so all the preacher says is tinctured, impregnated by what the preacher is. The treasure is in earthen vessels, and the taste of the vessel impregnates and may discolor. The man, the whole man, lies behind the sermon. Preaching is not the performance of an hour. It is the outflow of a life. It takes twenty years to make a sermon, because it takes twenty years to make the man. The true sermon is a thing of life. The sermon grows because the man grows. The sermon is forceful because the man is forceful. The sermon is holy because the man is holy. The sermon is full of the divine unction because the man is full of the divine unction.

Paul termed it "my gospel"; not that he had degraded it by his personal eccentricities or diverted it by selfish appropriation, but the gospel was put into the heart and lifeblood of the man Paul, as a personal trust to be executed by his Pauline traits, to be set aflame and empowered by the fiery energy of his fiery soul. Paul's sermons—what were they? Where are they? Skeletons, scattered fragments, afloat on the sea of inspiration! But the man Paul, greater than his sermons, lives forever, in full form, feature, and stature, with his molding hand on the church. The preaching is but a voice. The voice in silence dies, the text is forgotten, the sermon fades from memory; the preacher lives.

The sermon cannot rise in its life-giving forces above the man. Dead men give out dead sermons, and dead sermons kill. Everything depends on the spiritual character of the preacher. Under the Jewish dispensation the high priest had inscribed in jewelled letters on a golden frontlet: "Holiness to the Lord." So every preacher in Christ's ministry must be molded into and mastered by this same holy motto. It is a crying shame for the Christian ministry to fall lower in holiness of character and holiness of aim than the Jewish priesthood. Jonathan Edwards said: "I went on with my eager pursuit after more holiness and conformity to Christ. The heaven I desired was a heaven of holiness." The gospel of Christ does not move by popular waves. It has no self-propagating power. It moves as the men who have charge of it move. The preacher must impersonate the gospel. Its divine, most distinctive features must be embodied in him. The constraining power of love must be in the preacher as a projecting, eccentric, an all-commanding, self-oblivious force. The energy of self-denial must be his being, his heart and blood and bones. He must go forth as a man among men, clothed with humility, abiding in meekness, wise as a serpent, harmless as a dove; the bonds of a servant with the spirit of a king, a king in high, royal, independent bearing, with the simplicity and sweetness of a child. The preacher must throw himself, with all the abandon of a perfect, self-emptying faith and a self-consuming zeal, into his work for the salvation of men. Hearty, heroic, compassionate, fearless martyrs must the men be who take hold of and shape a generation for God. If they be timid timeservers, place seekers, if they be men pleasers or men fearers, if their faith has a weak hold on God or His Word, if their denial be broken by any phase of self or the world, they cannot take hold of the church nor the world for God.

The preacher's sharpest and strongest preaching should be to himself. His most difficult, delicate, laborious, and thorough work must be with himself. The training of the twelve was the great, difficult, and enduring work of Christ. Preachers are not sermon makers, but men makers and saint makers, and he only is well-trained for this business who has made himself a man and a saint. It is not great talents or great learning or great preachers that God needs, but men great in holiness, great in faith, great in love, great in fidelity, great for God—men always preaching by holy sermons in the pulpit, by holy lives out of it. These can mold a generation for God.

After this order, the early Christians were formed. Men they were of solid mold, preachers after the heavenly type—heroic, stalwart, soldierly, saintly. Preaching with them meant self-denying, self-crucifying, serious, toilsome, martyr business. They applied themselves to it in a way that told on their generation, and formed in its womb a generation yet unborn for God. The preaching man is to be the praying man. Prayer is the preacher's mightiest weapon. An almighty force in itself, it gives life and force to all.

The real sermon is made in the closet. The man—God's man—is made in the closet. His life and his profoundest convictions were born in his secret communion with God. The burdened and tearful agony of his spirit, his weightiest and sweetest messages were got when alone with God. Prayer makes the man; prayer makes the preacher; prayer makes the pastor.

The pulpit of this day is weak in praying. The pride of learning is against the dependent humility of prayer. Prayer is with the pulpit too often only official—a performance for the routine of service. Prayer is not to the modern pulpit the mighty force it was in Paul's life or Paul's ministry. Every preacher who does not make prayer a mighty factor in his own life and ministry is weak as a factor in God's work and is powerless to advance God's cause in this world.

Power Through Prayer, Chap. 1

Preachers and Preaching

The Men Needed

This is a strong generation, and the men who take hold of it for God must be strong men—strong as God counts strength. Bishop Foster, of the northern Methodist Church, says: "With an army of over twelve thousand preachers the cry comes up in vain from all over the land for men to take hold of this generation." The bishop puts it well, but sadly, when he says the cry comes up in vain. Bishops cannot answer the cry, because they lack the material. This points the one commanding feature in the ministry, ability to take hold of a generation for God. If the cry were for men to please a generation, or for those who out of books could teach a generation theology, or if the call were for good sermonizers, taking pulpit declaimers, the cry might be easily satisfied. If the cry were for men who could reflect the times, and be impressed by its veering colors, the demand might be met. But when the call is for men who can handle and mold a generation for God, this requires a rare and costly material.

The men who do this work must have their credentials direct from God. Their faith in God's word must embrace in its grasp every verse from the first verse of the first chapter of Genesis to the last verse of Revelation. Backed by the consciously and constantly realized authority of God's commission and God's word, they must throw themselves into it with the abandon of a perfect faith. Hearty, heroic, compassionate, unselfish, strong, fearless, must these rulers of a generation be. The energy of a perfect self-denial must be as a fire in their bones. They must go forth as men among men, clothed with humility, abiding in meekness, but with the mien and dignity of princes empowered for their kingdom, (an) all-absorbing work. Seeking to please none but God, the conquerors of self and of the world, no time-servers, nor place-seekers, not afraid of men's faces, nor afraid of men's purses nor of men's power, hating ease, indulgence, enduring hardness as good soldiers.

"Our greatest present danger," the bishop adds, "is, that we may be crowding our ministerial ranks with young men imbued with the notion that the Church is to make a downy nest for them, and put up with imperfect service—young men with no intellectual fiber, no muscle for resolute work."

We repeat, with emphasis, this is our chief danger. As this prevails our glory is departed. Our Methodist system was made to guard against this fatal evil, but we are in danger of rushing blindly into it.

A ministry imbued with the idea that a church is to furnish them good places, with all possible amenities, has lost all the distinctive elements of the true ministry. They cannot be in any true sense the successors of the men who have formed and trained the generations for Christ.

Christian Advocate, December 13, 1890

The Leadership of Faith

God must have leaders in his church—men whose distinguished spiritual ability moves them to the front as an inspiration and example in the work of God. The distinguishing and elect element in these leaders is faith. Other elements may be material or immaterial; in other elements these leaders may be deficient, or in contrast, but in this one of faith they are a unit. It is faith that placed them on God's roll of position. Aspiring men destitute of faith may foist themselves into church leadership, but God has no hand in their elevation, for them he cast no vote, he had no voice in their election. The only true leaders are those whose faith in God has placed them at the head. These are the only men who can do God's bidding, be led by God's hand.

Faith is the imperial grace of Christ's system. A simple but very rare grace. Much of that which circulates as faith has but little if any of the elements of faith in it. If we subtract from this current article, education, sentiment, prejudice, enthusiasm, habit, we have but little left. Faith is the stuff out of which God makes his saints, martyrs, and apostles. Faith is a divine energy implanted in the heart by God. By it we have the foundation, the sight, and the vital force of the unseen and eternal. An energy it is that masters every thing for God; an eye that sees God in his nearness, majesty, and supremacy. Faith is not a subordinate principle, but supreme. It is not to be hid under a liberal education, not to play second-hand to a large brain, or much or little of anything else. Faith makes brain, educates God's leaders, gives them courage, conviction, bone, and muscle. It of itself makes God's leaders, and it must be the sovereign of all. Faith must be stronger than brain, must curb and direct brain. Faith must rise above education, talent, taste, genius, be more evident, more controlling than any of these.

None but men of commanding faith can project God's cause, grasp God's plans, lead God's hosts. Without faith leads intellect will fail, its wisest wisdom be but blunders, its keenest vision but blindness. God's leaders cultivate their faith above all things. Students they may be, but their studies are turned this way, they study God, and faith is the only school in which he can be studied. Gifted they may be, but all their gifts wait in lowly docility on the guidance of faith.

Faith is cultured by the Bible. God's leaders are too often ignorant of God's word. They may know it as the commentaries know it; they may know it as the lawyer knows his text-book; know it as the scholar knows his classics; to know it in the heart, to feed on it in the inner spirit, to water the roots and invigorate the life of faith by meditation on its essential truths. This is the way to pour the ocean streams of revealed truth into faith till it expands and grows to marvelous dimensions.

Fasting aids much in bringing faith to its throne. Faith will never be authoritative, supreme, where fasting has not fastened itself on the spiritual habits. Faith is founded or perfected by self-denial, and fasting is not only the symbol, but a cardinal grace in self-denial. It mortifies the flesh, lays it low, breaks the force of appetite and passion, and fits the soil to grow faith.

Faith is brought into leadership by secret prayer. Long, habitual, closeted interviews with God are the sunny seasons for the growth of faith; interviews in which God's searching eye and light discover all the hidden hinderances to faith; interviews in which God reveals himself so that faith is mightily strengthened. God's true leadership does more to strengthen its faith than to do any thing else. It seeks this one element of power, this secret of spiritual success, at the sacrifice of other things. It keeps its eye fixed not on place or plans, but on God. The leadership of faith has no alliance with ambition, they are eternal foes. Ambition may give leadership in the church, has done it, does do it, but faith has no part in this leadership. Faith is debauched by its touch. God is not in the leadership of ambition, but simony and sacrilege are.

The leadership of faith is the leadership of humility, and meekness is its bloom. Faith leads because it is lowlier than all. It is master of all because servant of all.

The leadership of faith is the leadership of convictions—convictions which reach into the unseen and eternal with such a real and absorbing hold as to lose sight of the seen and temporal. These convictions only grow and feed on the decay of the things that are seen and felt. The man who has a strong grasp on the seen and earthly has but a feeble hold on the unseen and heavenly. It is the province of faith to discover and bring near these unseen things, and fill itself with them, their grandeur and stability.

The leadership of faith is the leadership of the spiritual as distinguished from the material—the material, visible, secular church results, the getting the most money, the building the most churches is being put in the front. Made conspicuous by Conference tests and inquisition. This material leadership is doing great damage to the vital interests of spiritual life. It puts a low grade on ministerial character. By it spiritual estimates of the ministry are discounted, spiritual impulses hardened. Men of mighty faith we need in all the officers, commissioned or noncommissioned, in all the rank and file of God's army. The men of faith are the men of God's renown. The men of faith make God's history, work God's miracles, fight God's battles, gain God's victories.

Christian Advocate, October 18, 1890

Wesley's Way

The secret of the success of the men who have been greatly owned of God is not always an open secret. There is much confusion and blindness in searching after this secret. The world tries hard to hinder their success by opposing, defaming, and belittling. But when their success is secured, by changing its tactics, it does its most hurtful work. It then clothes them with fancied powers, great natural ability, it lauds them as heroes and statesmen, and puts the church on the sinful and foolish chase of worshiping them as heroes and extolling their worldly greatness. By this process the conscience and faith of the church are perverted, the flesh is exalted to boastfulness and pride, and God is robbed of his glory. The cause for which John Wesley suffered and labored is suffering from this condition of things. He was a man of God. The secret of Wesley's success is to be found in his consecration to God, not in his ability to lead, but in the greater ability—the ability to follow God. It was not Wesley's great plans, but Wesley's great faith that made him such an honored and useful instrument for God. It was not Wesley's great executive ability that mastered the situation, but his docility, fidelity, and meekness in executing God's plans. Wesley worked not to preach fine sermons; his conscience and his God would have disowned him had he done this. He worked to save the individual. By wholesale he preached to the thousands, by retail he handled the individual. If he had not worked with the individual he could not have worked with the mass. The crowd was much to him, but it did not cause him to overlook the individual. Like the sure gunner, his sight was not distracted by the number, nor his aim at the mass, he singled out the individual. His commission was not simply to man, but to the man, the first one he met, the next one he met. He sympathized with the race, prayed and sighed over its ruin, but his commission was to the individual. He preached from the church pulpit, but he erected a pulpit wherever he met a man. The preacher who preaches only from the pulpit does not preach at all. Professionalism cold as ice, as dead as a doornail, supremely selfish, can preach from the pulpit, but the preacher that hunts out and handles the individual, and presses the truth home on him personally is the preaching that tells and saves.

Wesley's zeal, skill, and power find an illustration in this phase of his work, a feature which we are so ready to forget when aggregating his elements of success. His commission embraced all times and all seasons, it made times and seasons, took advantage of all offered opportunities, and made other opportunities. We give some instances which illustrate his labor with the individual, and how he economized time and opportunity to do his work with the individual.

He had been often pressed not to speak to others only as his heart was free to it. He made the experiment for two days and records it:

"1. That I spoke to none at all for fourscore miles together; no, not even to him that traveled with me in the chaise, unless a few words at first setting out. 2. That I had no cross to bear or take up, and commonly in an hour or two fell fast asleep. 3. That I had much respect shown me wherever I came; every one behaving to me as to a civil, good-natured gentleman. O how pleasing is all this to flesh and blood!"

He held it his duty to speak to every one as he was thrown with them; they were in his commission.

On one occasion he had a great desire to speak to a young man, and rode with him three miles out of his way to do so, but he says: "I could fix nothing upon him. Just as we parted, walking over Caerlin bridge he stumbled and was likely to fall. I caught him and began to speak of God's care over us. Immediately the tears stood in his eyes, and he appeared to feel every word which was said, so I spoke and spared not. The same I did to a poor man who led my horse over the bridge; to our landlord and his wife; and to one who occasionally came in."

On another occasion his saddle slipping, his mare threw him. Some boys caught her and brought her to him; they were cursing and swearing. "I spoke plainly to them, and they promised to amend." As he set forward a man came after, joined by others, bringing his saddle-cloth. They swore likewise. "I turned," he says, "to one and another and spoke in love; they all took it well and thanked me." On this trip his horse lost a shoe. "This gave me," he says, "an opportunity of talking closely for near half-an hour, both to the smith and his servant."

This is the way John Wesley did the Lord's work. This was a flame of that zeal for God's house which consumed John

Wesley's Lord. This was the nature of that zeal that stirred Great Britain mightily for God. Not by John Wesley's might or power was this work done, but by John Wesley's zeal for God—a zeal which, as Robert Hall said, was the most remarkable trait about him—the quietest of all men, he stirred every thing around him.

Said the saintly Archbishop Leighton: "Were I again to be a parish minister I must follow sinners to their houses, and even to their ale-houses." The men who are possessed of this zeal for men they are the great ones with God, and the successful builders of his kingdom.

Christian Advocate, December 13, 1890

Mr. Wesley got much out of his meetings. He was their leader in prayer and praising God. If God's power rested on the people till they responded to it in mighty praises, Wesley was their leader in this. No mere professional preacher, no mere spectator was John Wesley of God's works. He filled others because God filled him full. He stirred others mightily because God stirred him mightily. He says: "I was much out of order, but forgot all my pain while we were praising God together."

Christian Advocate, January 14, 1892

Charles Simeon said of Henry Martyn's picture: "It seems always to be saying, be serious, be in earnest, don't trifle, don't trifle." It is said of Robert McCheyne that his manner was so holily impressive that persons were convicted by seeing his serious and devout attitude. We are neither the advocates nor apologists for austerity, sourness, nor long-facedness in the pulpit nor out of it; but we are not in danger that way now. We are drifting toward lightness of speech and frivolity of manner in dealing with the eternal verities of God. The condition of the people demands a serious setting forth of God's truth. Religion with the great mass of its professors is not a serious thing. Other interests are more engaging. The duties of this life press religion to the rear, dishonored. We need a serious ministry to call the people back to the serious claims of a serious religion. We need the sober, clear, sharp putting of Bible truths which will press them to the fore-front of our affairs and keep them there. We need a ministry brought face to face with the solemn facts with which Paul faced and charged Timothy—I charge thee before God and the Lord Jesus Christ, who shall judge the quick and dead, preach the word.

Sin, judgment, heaven, hell, time, eternity, are serious matters, and deserve and demand to be uttered and urged with great seriousness.

Some pulpits turn the whole matter into a joke, and have their stock of anecdotes and spicy sayings to provoke mirth and raise a laugh, when they ought to be breaking hearts with the deepest sorrow. This gospel of fun is not the gospel for sinners imperiled as we are. We doubt if it is the gospel that would be relished in heaven. We are sure it would not suit hell; hell is a serious place—too serious to suit the frivolity and foolery of many a pulpit.

The pulpit that seeks to entertain in a more elegant way than by joke, wit, or buffoonery, is also radically defective in the element of seriousness. As God's representative it is a failure. We need a pulpit baptized into all the seriousness of Christ's death, and all the perils induced by sin—sobered by the matchless value of immortal souls viewed from the agony of the cross and in the light of heaven and hell.

The Preaching Business

Whose business is it to preach? The business of the pulpit, says the pew. The business of both the pulpit and pew, says the Bible and common sense. The pulpit cannot reach the world of people, they will not attend its service nor heed its sermons. If there are no sermons but from the pulpit, religion will die or be disgraced.

The pulpit preaches to the crowd, the pew must preach to

the individual. The pulpit preaches on Sunday, the pew must repeat the sermon every day in the week. The pulpit may, like the general, arrange the campaign, but the individual members must execute his plans and fight his battles.

The pulpit may do its work well, but its voice has died and the words have too often faded from the heart ere he has opportunity to repeat the work; but these sermons are to be kept fresh on heart and conscience by the lives and voices of the pew at all points of contact, social, friendly, occasional, or accidental. Christ wrote no letters, he sends each disciple out as his letter of commendation, to reproduce in their lives the attractive power of his life and death as a continuous and powerful sermon.

This preaching from pulpit or pew must be personal and pressing; it must single out the individual and get him in a corner. It must take him by force and on purpose for Christ. The force may not be seen; it may be the gentlest, and yet the most pressing—irritating perhaps by its pertinacity. The purpose may be hid, the occasion accidental; but the arrow is not drawn at a venture. We must seek souls, we must make opportunities to save men. Business, recreation, friendship, society, may be the covert, but they should only be the covert, not the end—all subordinate to saving the individual.

The church needs a baptism of zeal for the salvation of the individual—individuals singled out as the object of salvation, upon whom our prayers, solicitude, efforts are to be centered.

To do this work of salvation well our own piety must be of a pure type; flaws in it will break the force of our efforts. Our religion must be strongly obtrusive, bright enough to herald itself, and strong enough to obtrude itself. If it has to be introduced or labeled to be known, it might as well be silent. An infant knows when the light is shining, though it does not smell or hear the match.

True preaching, whether by holy lives or from holy pulpits, will always offend some one. If no one is repulsed, no one will be drawn. The sermon that does not offend does not save. Let your lives be as pungent as salt, as bright, as sweet, as inviting as the light.

The truth is our religion ought to fill us so full that it will ooze out at every pore, and drop like myrrh or manna, and be felt at every point of contact. We ought to have so much of it that it would not only fill the great ocean channel, but press out and fill every bay, strait, and inlet, so that every place, every person, every duty, every thing would feel its presence and its force.

Christian Advocate, November 15, 1890

Preaching

Preaching is a simple thing. It would seem that in doing it one could scarcely miss doing it right and doing it well. But simple as preaching is, to do it well and secure its true ends, is no easy task. Much depends on the character of the man, on the condition of his heart and head, on the spirit, matter, and manner of the preaching, that its simplicity makes it complex and difficult.

The apostles found it necessary to separate themselves to it, and not allow the sacred duty of attending to the poor to divert them. To do it well they had to give themselves wholly to prayer and to the ministry of the word. The success of their preaching, their ability to do it well, centered in their ability to give themselves wholly to prayer and to the word of God.

There is much preaching that is much praised and much sought for that is not preaching. "Every place was crowded, the galleries filled, not a vacant chair in the vast room. I went an hour before the service, and found the people lining the pavement, waiting for the door to open. Not a syllable of gospel in the sermon, only a little flourish of it at the close." This is the statement of a sermon heard a few Sabbaths ago by one who knows what preaching is. This critic is not a censor in any sense of the word, always mild if not amiable in his judgment. We spent a Sabbath in a large village. There being no Methodist service we went elsewhere. In the morning we heard a dry, written discussion on some foreign, juiceless subject. At night we tried the Episcopal service. Our hungry soul was fed on a scented essay, as nourishing and as tasteless as a bouquet of flowers. The only food we got for our souls from these meetings was from the Episcopal service, and that was quite husky. We were saddened at the thought of palming off two services of that kind for the gospel, and sighed that Christ's sheep should have to graze and starve on such barren fields. No geographical progression, however far-reaching and rapid in its progression, will ever bring the millennium through such feeble and sickening efforts as these.

The *Christian at Work* touches up the way some popular sermons are made, and the vicious compound that sometimes passes current for the gold of the gospel:

> A sermon may be made up of scraps of philosophy, history, poetry, art criticisms, and literary allusions, so skillfully woven together and so admirably delivered with fitting tone and gesture as to be an intellectual and esthetic feast, and yet be absolutely devoid of spiritual power and beauty. Such discourses may exercise a temporary charm, but they can never transform the soul nor exalt it into vital and joyful communion with its Maker and Redeemer; indeed they are properly speaking, not sermons at all, only wretched perversions of the time and the place where real sermons ought to be presented.

A man called of God, with common sense, and eye single to God's glory, who is much with God in prayer and with his Bible in his hand and in his heart, cannot miss the thing. He will be honest, direct, and simple; self in every form will be crucified, Christ and souls only sought. His sermons may not pass the criticism of worldly taste, nor fit the homiletical straitjacket, nor gather the dust of the theological library, but they will perform the divine mission of bringing many sons to glory. Gospel preaching is a simple, easy thing for a gospel preacher, with a gospel heart, to do. He must be a man of prayer, and a man of one book, the Bible must be in him in a way that discounts his connection with all other books. The Bible, not theology, not books about the Bible, not commentaries, must be his study. The Bible must be in the very blood and bone of his being. As the eating of the roll was Ezekiel's preparation to speak to Israel, as the eating of the little book by John was essential to his prophesying, so the Bible ought to be devoured by the preacher till it forms the nutriment of his soul, and makes the richest blood and strongest spiritual nerve. Not till the word of God is incarnate in the preacher is he equipped for preaching.

† † †

A preacher that will draw is the modern demand. The New Testament knows much of a holy preacher, of a faithful preacher, and of the elements of saintly character; but it knows nothing of a preacher that will draw. The New Testament knows something of a Church that will draw men to it by a spiritual gravitation; draw them by the holiness of their lives, by the attractive forces of godliness. A preacher that draws is generally a compound of sensation, genius, with a double portion of self mixed with the least moiety—of Christ. He proposes to do by lively, taking, original ways what the church ought to do by its inherent Christliness. The drawing preacher is an illusive and vicious substitute for the solidity and piety of the church. A drawing preacher is the bait that a worldly church throws out to catch the world, and to cover the appalling fact that it has no power to draw men to Christ.

Christian Advocate, January 7, 1892

† † †

It is not reason, said the apostles, that we should leave the word of God and serve tables. The feeding of God's poor was a very sacred office, but it distracted the apostles, engaged their time and attention, and prevented them from giving their whole force, time, and strength to prayer and the ministry of the word. Leave all lower things to chosen stewards, and let the preachers put in all their time praying and studying God's word and delivering it, and things will move on a higher plane, and more strongly. This is apostolic. Many a preacher is so filled with sacred religious secularities that the gospel coming out of him has no projective force.

The power of the pulpit is found in its essential unworldliness. That in its utterances, in manner, measure, or grade there shall be no semblance of the world. That in the preacher himself there are to be no points of worldly contact or stain, literally crucified to the world and the world to him. Unworldly as Christ, not a *nexus* of the breadth of a hair binding him to the world. That a great gulf fixed rolls between him and the world, a gulf bridged by no longings, no regrets, no desires on his part.

Christian Advocate, October 4, 1890

Revolutionizing Preachers, Part I

God can work wonders if he can get a suitable man. Men can work wonders if they can get God to help them. The full endowment of the spirit that turned the world upside down would be eminently useful in these latter days. Men who can stir things mightily for God, whose spiritual revolutions change the whole aspect of things, is the universal need of the church.

The church has never been without these men; they adorn its history; they are the standing miracles of the divinity of the church; their example and history are an unfailing inspiration and blessing. An increase in their number and power should be our prayer.

That which has been done in spiritual matters can be done again, and be better done. This was Christ's view. He said: "Verily, verily, I say unto you, He that believeth on me, the works that I do shall he do also; and greater works than these shall he do; because I go unto my Father." The past has not exhausted the possibilities nor the demands for doing great things in the church. The church that is dependent on its history for its miracles of power and grace is a fallen church. We illustrate our meaning, and make the point and force of this article by an example. The story has been often told, it will bear the strain of many more tellings.

Louis Harms was born in Hanover in 1809. He was powerfully convicted of sin. "I have never in my life," said he, "known what fear was; but when I came to the knowledge of my sins I quaked before the wrath of God so that my limbs trembled." He was mightily converted to God by reading the Bible. Rationalism, a dead orthodoxy, and worldliness held the multitudes around Hermansburg, his native town. His father, a Lutheran minister, dying, he became his successor. He began with all the energy of his soul to work for Christ and develop a church of a pure and strong type. The fruit was soon evident—a quickening on every hand, the attendance on church increased, reverence for the Bible grew, conversation on sacred things revived, infidelity, worldliness, and dead orthodoxy vanished like a cloud. A conscious and present Christ, the Comforter, in the full energy of his mission, proclaimed the revival of apostolic piety and power. All the neighborhood of his parish became at once regular attendants at church, the Sabbath was restored to its sanctity and hallowed with strict devotion, family altars erected in all the homes, and when the noon bell sounded every head was bowed in prayer. The whole aspect of the country was changed in a short time.

Such a spiritual revolution cannot be confined. It is irrepressible. The world is its objective point. Africa and India were not too remote to be affected by this revolution in an obscure town in Germany. The pastor's thoughts and heart were turned to Africa. He spoke to his people in private and public. As the pastor prayed and preached and worked the people caught the fire, it could not be otherwise, the missionary movement took shape. He selected a dozen young peasants, and gave them a training of four years. He had no means. Without asking a single man he prayed to God for money, or, to use his own expression, "knocked on the dear Lord in prayer." The money began to come in, the first contribution, a silver penny, from a child, sixpence from a poor laborer, six shillings from a widow. Such are the humble beginnings of faith. One man gave his farm and himself. They built a ship and sent out 8 missionaries. . . . The training school was kept full, usually numbering about 50. In 1856 a second company, chiefly farmers and maids, was found ready to go out; in 1857 still another company, numbering 46, of whom 12 were missionaries, the rest colonists. On one occasion more than 100 stood ready to go at one time. At the end of the first decade of this mission, 1864, they had founded 24 stations and started 2 more, and baptized 190 converts.

How well this work was founded in God is evident from the fact that at the death of Mr. Harms, in 1866, the work was not arrested, but prospered; the workman died, but the work went on.

In 1886 the income of the Society was $48,500, its missionaries and native helpers numbered 219, of whom 40 were ordained Europeans, 50 laymen, and 42 women, likewise Europeans. The native communicants numbered 4,680, and baptized persons, 12,120. The gain of the year was 260 communicants.

In addition to the South African work they were doing mission work in India, Australia, and New Zealand. Instead of being exhausted by this work the home work was increased with enlarged activities and greater efficiency. Many charitable institutions sprung into life—an asylum, and a publishing house from which issued the whole range of missionary and gospel literature.

The secret of his power is the open secret of every man who does mighty things for God. He was a man of mighty faith and mighty prayer. He moved spiritual things because he moved God mightily. His personal, conscious, and close union with God consumed and quickened every thing by its intensity. He was charged with being crazy, a charge to which every one who does any thing for God in a way to harm hell or the world, is exposed. He lived and died a martyr to his work—the only ones whose work and blood are the seeds of the church. He worked for God with a force which nothing could arrest or for a moment divert in its irresistible and impetuous flood.

The king of Hanover, knowing that Harms was in the city, did him the honor to send a high official and a state carriage to invite him to the palace. "Give my regards," he said, "to the king; I would obey his order if duty allowed, but I must go home and attend to my parish." The official was indignant; but the king said, "Harms is the man for me." So God had said, "Harms is the man for me."

This revolutionizing work must be done by every preacher, or else nothing is done worth the name. The feebleness and obscurity of the agents are not hinderances, but conditions of usefulness for God. Not the men who worry and work to make themselves great, but the men who feel and know their littleness, and whom God makes great are the great workers for God.

God is in great need of men by whom he can revolutionize missions, circuits, stations, districts.

"Give me," said John Wesley, "one hundred preachers who fear nothing but sin, and desire nothing but God, and I care not a straw whether they be clergymen or laymen, such alone will shake the gates of hell, and set up the kingdom of God on earth."

Such a man was Louis Harms; such a man in spirit and power, in their measure and sphere, will every one be who has the faith, prayer, and energy and communion with God that he had. Nothing keeps us from revolutionizing things for God but our self-bigness and our faith-littleness.

Christian Advocate, July 26, 1890

† † †

Revolutionizing Preachers, Part II

We put it as our most sober judgment that the great need of the church in this and all ages is men of such commanding faith, of such unsullied holiness, of such marked spiritual vigor and consuming zeal that their ministry will be of such a radical and aggressive form as to work spiritual revolutions which will form eras in individual and church life.

We do not mean men who get up sensational stirs by novel devices, nor those who attract by a pleasing entertainment; but men who can stir things, and work revolutions by the preaching of God's word, and by the power of the Holy Ghost, revolutions which change the whole current of things.

Natural ability and educational advantages do not figure as factors in this matter; but a capacity for faith, the ability to pray, the power of a thorough consecration, the ability of self-littleness, an absolute losing of one's self in God's glory and an ever present and insatiable yearning and seeking after all the fullness of God. Men who can set the church ablaze for God, not in a noisy, showy way, but with an intense and quiet heat that melts and moves every thing for God.

We instance John Fletcher as a type and pattern. Madeley, the place of his work, was given over to wickedness of the lowest kind. Holy things were decried, the forms of religion held up to contempt, the restraints of decency disregarded. It was a crowded, debauched, heathenish population, without seemliness or promise. A dismaying prospect to any save a strong faith. Without hope of recovery save by the gospel of the Son of God in its genuine and divine form. Into this seething mass of corruption the ministry of Fletcher was injected. It was like caustic or salt on a sore, there were kickings and adversaries and opposition and insults of all kinds from the worldly clergy as well as from the wicked rabble. His words were wrested, his actions misrepresented, his name cast out as evil. But his ministry came with resurrection power, the valley of death was shaken as by the archangel's voice and the trump of God. Fletcher gave them the words of God, and it reproved their sins, convicted their consciences, exposed their guilt and their doom. Dauntless, self-sacrificing, on fire with holy zeal, he affected them despite their opposition, he influenced them despite their hate. His scantily attended church was soon overflowing. The whole aspect changed, a mighty work was wrought, the community transformed. Madeley became the rendezvous for religious persons, a privileged and honored place, a sort of Christian Jerusalem. The influence still remains. A late distinguished Methodist writer says: "Madeley will long be a kind of Mecca to the Methodists." Three Established and seven Methodist churches formed out of his work attest the present and enduring results of his labors.

What were the elements by which this revolution was secured? He preached the word of God in its entirety with great fidelity. He sought persistently, daily, hourly, and all the time the increased energy and conscious power of God's Spirit, enabling him and enabling the word.

He was untiring and urgent in securing personal holiness. An example he was of the Methodist doctrine of perfect love, and of that ceaseless groaning after it which always characterizes those who are its partakers. He was a saintly character, his holiness was not of the tame, conservative, insipid type; but pungent, aggressive, fresh, radiant as the morning, hostile as a bannered host against sin. With touches gentler than a woman's to the brokenhearted, Fletcher went out after his people, he followed them to their haunts, preached in their dens, broke into their assemblies of lust and wickedness with a vehement and holy indignation. He solved the question of reaching the masses, the question that has given so much theoretical trouble to professional preachers. The man who reaches his church for God will reach the masses. A quickened church and a holy ministry is the secret of reaching the masses. Fletcher was stirred mightily for God, and he moved toward God with impetuous and fiery burnings. No man can stir things mightily for God who is not himself stirred mightily for and toward God.

Simple, frugal, self-denying, and unworldly in his piety, he labored with the single eye, and his heart in heaven. His zeal knew no abatement, tireless and consuming, his whole being was aflame for God and his glory; nothing selfish, low, or earthly, adulterated this pure flame.

He was mighty in prayer; the wall of his room still bears the stains of his breath where he poured out his soul to God day and night. His faith and desires for God were mightily helped by fasting. He had a mighty faith, a wrestling spirit, believed in God mightily, and, as its results, worked for men mightily. God was with him, as he will be with every man who seeks him as Fletcher sought him, honor every man who honors him as Fletcher did. Fletcher lived singly, simply, and only for God, and these are the only men by whom God will work mighty works. Had Fletcher thought of salary, had an eye or half an eye to self, mixed his motives with desires for place or position, then he had never wrought his work for God, then Madeley would never have felt the pressure, force, and revolution of his ministry. Then Fletcher never would have had a place in the calendar of saints. He said when offered another place: "Too much money and too little work." With this crucified earthliness he began, continued, and wrought out his work. Such men God delights to honor.

Christian Advocate, August 2, 1890

† † †

Revolutionizing Preachers, Part III

God is in a great strait for men of the right sort. "The eyes of the Lord run to and fro throughout the whole earth, to show himself strong in the behalf of them whose heart is perfect toward him." So spake God's prophet; so might every prophet of God speak down to this hour. God is dependent on men to get into this world, with saving efficacy. His revelations now are incarnate. God is not so careful about numbers as about quality. Numbers cannot atone for the lack of quality, but quality may atone for the lack of numbers. It is not simply volunteers that God is looking for. Many persons are eager to go. Bishop Thoburn had one hundred volunteers for India, but the searching of his devout and practiced eye sifted them down to three. God wants elect men—men out of whom self and the world have gone by a severe crucifixion, by a bankruptcy which has so totally ruined self and the world that there is neither hope nor desire of recovery; men who by this insolvency and crucifixion have turned toward God perfect hearts.

God found one of the men he was looking for in David Brainerd, whose name and work have gone into history. No sublimer story has been recorded in earthly annals than that of David Brainerd; no miracle attests with diviner force the truth of Christianity than the life and work of such a man. Alone in the savage wilds of America, struggling day and night with a mortal disease, unschooled in the care of souls, having access to the Indians for a large portion of time only through the bungling medium of a pagan interpreter, with the word of God in his heart and in his hand, his soul fired with the divine flame, a place and time to pour out his soul to God in prayer, he fully established the worship of God and secured all its gracious results. The Indians were changed with a great change from the lowest besotments of an ignorant and debased heathenism to pure, devout, intelligent Christians, all vice reformed, the external duties of Christianity at once embraced and acted on, family prayer set up, the Sabbath instituted and religiously observed; the internal graces of religion exhibited with growing sweetness and strength.

The solution of these results is found in David Brainerd himself, not in the conditions or accidents or God's peculiar election, but in the man Brainerd. He was God's man, for God, first, and last, and all the time. God could flow unhindered through him. The omnipotence of grace was neither arrested nor straitened by the conditions of his heart; the whole channel was broadened and cleaned out for God's fullest and most powerful passage, so that God with all his mighty forces could come down on the hopeless, savage wilderness, and transform it into his blooming and fruitful garden; for nothing is too hard for God to do if he can get the right kind of a man to do it with.

Brainerd lived the life of holiness and prayer. His diary is full and monotonous with the record of his seasons of fasting, meditation, and retirement. The time he spent in private prayer amounted to many hours daily. "When I return home," he said, "and give myself to meditation, prayer, and fasting, my soul longs for mortification, self-denial, humility, and divorcement from all the things of the world." "I have nothing to do," he said, "with earth but only to labor in it honestly for God. I do not desire to live one minute for any thing which earth can afford."

Men of this spirit and power are the crowning glory of the gospel, its crying need, its exacting demand. Methodism has stressed this need, her successes have been won by men of this spirit. While not ignoring the incidentals, Methodism has demanded that this one feature of holiness should be central and commanding in her ministry. Her demands on this line are epitomized in the statement of an eminently saintly Scottish preacher; "It is not great talents God blesses so much as great likeness to Jesus. A holy minister is an awful weapon in the hand of God." One of Wesley's Conferences gives this unfailing remedy to revive decayed churches: "Let every preacher read carefully the life of David Brainerd. Let us be followers of him as he was of Christ in absolute self-devotion, in total deadness to the world, and in fervent love to God and man. Let us but secure this point, and the world and the devil must fall under our feet."

These three men—Harms, Fletcher, and Brainerd—who transformed the whole face of things for God, by the power of a faith that deadened them to the world and self and made them alive to God, with a purpose too ardent, too insatiable, too triumphant and forceful to allow division or remission. They are the true representatives of a God-ordained and a God-anointed ministry.

These three men differ in almost every thing; the conditions around them are different, but in the one and only element of the preacher's success they are a unit. In deadness to the world, in devotedness to God, in absorption in his glory and the salvation of men, in faith, humility, self-denial, they are one.

We say of them all as Wesley said of one of them in his journal: "I preached and afterward made a collection for the Indian schools in America. A large sum of money is now collected; but will money convert heathens? Find preachers of David Brainerd's spirit, and nothing can stand before them; but without this what will gold or silver do? No more than lead or iron."

Christian Advocate, August 23, 1890

Resurrection of the Body

The whole system of Jesus Christ is based on the immortality of the man. It is not the philosophical idea or guesses of the immortality of the soul, but the immortality of the man. The whole man, in his dual or triune nature, is to live forever. The spirit or higher department defies death; the body is to come out of the ruins and prison house of death and be raised to life. Man immortal; the whole man, soul, body, spirit, immortal—this is the keystone and keynote of the redemption by Christ. The deathless nature of the soul has been taught in the philosophies of earth, pagan and Christian, but the resurrection of the body is distinctively a Christian doctrine. It belongs to the revelation of God's Word. It is found in the Bible, and nowhere else. Nature may have echoes, analogies, figures; but nowhere is the doctrine fully asserted, fully assured, but in the Scriptures which contain the revealed will of God.

This doctrine of the resurrection of the body is not a mere inference from Bible statement. It is the statement itself, the key of its arch, the corner stone of its foundation. It is not a rich afterthought of the gospel, but coordinate "Jesus and the resurrection" are the gospel.

Faith can make no appeal to reason or the fitness of things; its appeal is to the Word of God, and whatever is therein revealed faith accepts as true. Faith accepts the Bible as the word and will of God and rests upon its truth without question and without other evidence.

Faith accepts the Word of God as indubitable evidence of any fact, and rejoices in the fact as true because God asserts it in his Word. Many of the facts revealed to us in the Bible receive the credence of our reason as fit and proper things. Others extend beyond the range of reason, and it has neither vision nor analogy to measure them.

The resurrection of the human body, its coming back into life from the ravages, decay, and oblivion of the grave, is one of these supernatural facts. It has been the anxious and tearful question of the ages: "Can the dead live? Is there strength anywhere to vanquish death? Is there any hope of victory over the grave?" Reason has neither answer to the question nor hope for the questioner. Analogy starts some faint light, but this goes out amid the increasing night of the tomb.

There are but two questions to quicken and satisfy faith in the resurrection of the body. These questions are of promise and ability: Has God promised to raise the body from the dead? Is he able to perform his promise in this respect? The body is a distinct, a very important part of the man. It is the part seen, known, handled, described as the man, the organ, the outlet, through which the man comes into contact, sympathy, and action with the world around. A part, an all-important, indispensable part, of the man, the body belongs to the man, is an original, organic part of the man, evident and conspicuous— will this body rise from the dead where it has been laid amid tears and heart-breaking farewells? Its death is a fact distinct and clearly outlined. "Will it live again?" is the passionate question of love and longing.

The heathen world sighed out their upbraidings, emptiness, and despair. The flowers, said they, die by the chill of winter, but spring's warm breath brings them to life again. The day declines into darkness and night, but rises again into the full day; suns set, but come again full-orbed out of the eclipse of their setting; moons wane, but wax into fullness and brightness again; but their loved ones leave them, eclipsed and lost in the darkness of death, but no spring, no morn, no rising ever brings them again.

Christianity hushes these sighs, fills this emptiness, lifts this despair. She lights the darkness of the grave with the morning star of hope, and sheds the luster of the resurrection day upon the night of the tomb. Faith asks of unbelief, of doubt and despair: "Why should it be thought a thing incredible with you that God should raise the dead? Is anything too hard for God?" She declares: "All that sleep in their graves shall hear the voice of the Son of God and shall come forth."

Faith puts the brightness of an immortal hope amid our graveyard griefs; writes on every tombstone, "I am the resurrection and the life"; calls aloud to every mourner, "Thy dead shall live." Christianity is not agnosticism, but faith, assurance, knowledge; not negative, but positive. "I believe in the resurrection of the body," is a fundamental and enduring item of her creed.

Christianity is not rationalism, but faith in God's revelation. A conspicuous, all-important item in that revelation is the resurrection of the body.

The attitude of Jesus Christ to the doctrine of the resurrection of the dead is one of familiarity and matter of course. In the sixth chapter of John with what an emphatic, authoritative manner he deals with it as a generally acknowledged, great basic fact! "For I came down from heaven, not to do mine own will, but the will of him that sent me. And this is the Father's will which hath sent me, that of all which he hath given me I should lose nothing, but should raise it up again at the last day."

This resurrection he puts as the declared purpose and will of God, that he should raise them up at the last day. This was imperative if he accomplishes God's design. The capsheaf of God's purposes for Jesus Christ was that he should raise the dead. Again he returns to this great thought, purpose, and fact: "And this is the will of him that sent me, that every one which seeth the Son, and believeth on him, may have everlasting life: and I will raise him up at the last day."

Again he iterates the fact, and declares that he is committed to it. The Father commits it to him. The resurrection power is lodged in Jesus. "No man can come to me, except the Father which hath sent me draw him: and I will raise him up at the last day." Again Jesus gives utterance to the important statement: "Whoso eateth my flesh, and drinketh my blood, hath eternal life; and I will raise him up at the last day."

Death and him that had the power of death—that is, the devil—against these, the author of evil and his works, Jesus Christ set himself. He declared himself to be the resurrection and the life, that death in every form, in every way, and at every place, must yield to him. We stress and iterate the fact that he is life. "If a man keep my saying, he shall never see death." "Whosoever liveth and believeth in me shall never die." "He that believeth in me, though he were dead, yet shall he live." "I am the first and the last, and the Living One; and I was dead, and behold, I am alive for evermore, and I have the keys of death and of Hades." "I am come that they might have life, and have it more abundantly." Life against death is he. Jesus Christ, the source of all deathless energy, by absolute and eternal fitness, by a matter of course, and by character he is the foe, the destruction of death. He is coequal, coeternal with the Father, and pours the Father's full tide of life on the world. "For the Father loveth the Son, and showeth him all things that himself doeth: and he will show him greater works than these, that ye may marvel. For as the Father raiseth up the dead, and quickeneth them; even so the Son quickeneth whom he will. For the Father judgeth no man, but hath committed all judgment unto the Son: Verily, verily, I say unto you, He that heareth my word, and believeth on him that sent me, hath everlasting life, and shall not come into condemnation; but is passed from death unto life. Verily, verily, I say unto you, The hour is coming, and now is, when the dead shall hear the voice of the Son of God: and they that hear shall live. For as the Father hath life in himself; so hath he given to the Son to have life in himself; And hath given him authority to execute judgment also, because he is the Son of man."

"Marvel not at this: for the hour is coming, in the which all that are in the tombs shall hear his voice, and shall come forth: they that have done good, unto the resurrection of life; and they that have done ill, unto the resurrection of judgment." He had made strong declarations of life, eternal life, and of a spiritual resurrection; seeing their wonderment, he goes on to declare a greater marvel still—the resurrection of the body from the grave as the inevitable sequence of the life in his Father and in himself. All shall come forth—death shall yield its hold, and the grave deliver its prisoners long held. All shall come forth—not a body left—not an atom of the grave's dust but shall have the touch and taste of the resurrection life. Jesus Christ tells his disciples that when he comes in the glory of his Father with the holy angels he will reward every man according to his works. To secure this end, the resurrection is a necessity.

The transfiguration of Jesus is one of the typical facts of the resurrection of the body; not only of the glorious change, but of the renewed life of the body and of the general judgment day. The presence of Moses and Elijah there are the trophies as they appear in glory of the resurrection power of Christ. It is a distinct prophecy and foreshadowing of the coming of the body out of the power and ravages of death. Moses and Elijah appear at this hour as the first fruits of the resurrection glory. It is worthy of remark that it is here as well as in the continuous ministry of Christ that the body, this body of our humiliation, has its sign and pledge of its future glory.

"I will raise him up at the last day." These iterated words deserve great and grave consideration—there is to be a day, a great day, a tremendous day; the last day, the closing of this world's history. Time shall be no more. Eternity, changeless eternity, will begin its new history for man. Paul calls it "the day of wrath and revelation of the righteous judgment of God"; the day when "the dead, small and great, shall stand before God." The raised dead—raised from their sleep in proud city cemetery or the silent forsakenness of the unmarked loneliness of the country sleeper; from the ocean depths, shrouded and entombed for ages in its restless, defiant, fathomless caves; from the dismal abodes of the Hades whose waves and fires were but the voices which told of deeper waves and fiercer fires to come. This is the day when Christ is committed to the raising of his dead ones, when his and man's last enemy, death, shall be destroyed.

"Last day!" Day of God's glory and power! Day of terror and alarm to the unbelieving and impenitent—their eternal doom! Day of renown and victory to Jesus Christ, of infinite comfort to all his saints. Infinite comfort! Infinite in measure and infinite in length. This last day is one of God's appointed days—God's decreed days.

The future of man will be divinely glorious and divinely illustrious. He is to share the place of Jesus, where Jesus and his followers are to be. This is the specific teaching of Jesus. "I go to prepare a *place* for you," said Jesus; "and if I go and prepare a *place* for you, I come again, and will receive you unto myself; *that where I am, there ye may be also.*" In his sacerdotal prayer Jesus said: "Father, that which thou hast given me, I will that, where I am, they also may be with me; that they may behold my glory, which thou hast given me." The statement in the Apocalypse is very exalted, very strong, and very clear: "He that overcometh, I will give to him to sit down with me in my throne, as I also overcame, and sat down with my Father in his throne."

Jesus must have the place of greatest dignity, of highest honor in the universe. God has awarded this to him without question or limitation—a name above every name, a place above every place. Jesus calls it paradise, a place of ineffable beauty, God-adorned and exuberant in its divine embellishments—untold beauty to fascinate the eye and ravish and intoxicate the heart. The divine word is that Jesus will shepherd all the blessed flock of that thrice-blessed land. With them Jesus will be, and for them Jesus will be. The honor, dignity, power, and glory bestowed on him will be theirs. They are joint heirs with him of all God's most generous inheritance. Rich indeed, surpassing rich, shall be the saints in that large, exhaustless, immortal store.

"I am fully persuaded of this as of a most necessary and infallible truth: that as it is appointed unto all men once to die, so it is determined that all men shall rise from death, that the souls separated from our bodies are in the hands of God and live, that the bodies dissolved into dust or scattered into ashes shall be recollected in themselves and reunited to their souls, that the same flesh which lived before shall be revived, that the same numerical bodies which did fall shall rise, that this resuscitation shall be universal, no man excepted, no flesh left in the grave, that all the just shall be raised to a resurrection of life, and all the unjust to a resurrection of damnation; that this shall be performed at the last day when the trump shall sound, and this I believe the resurrection of the body."

With what acclamations will saints, rising from the dead, applaud the Redeemer! How will the heaven of heavens resound his praises forever! "Thanks be to God" will be the burden of their song; and angels will join in the chorus and declare their consent with a loud AMEN! HALLELUJAH!

The Resurrection, Chaps. **3, 6, 23**

Revival

Revivals That Stay

Revivals are among the charter rights of the church. They are the evidences of its divinity, the tokens of God's presence, the witness of his power. The frequency and power of these extraordinary seasons of grace are the tests and preservers of the vital force in the church. The church which is not visited by these seasons is as sterile in all spiritual products as a desert, and is not and cannot meet the designs of God's church. Such churches may have all the show and parade of life, but it is only a painted life.

The revival element belongs to the individual, as well as to the church, life. The preacher whose experience is not marked by these inflows of great grace may question with anxious scrutiny whether he is in grace. The preacher whose ministry does not over and over again find its climax of success and power in these gracious visitations of God may well doubt the genuineness of his call, or be disquieted as to its continuance.

Revivals are not simply the reclamation of a backslidden church. They do secure this end, but they do not find their highest end in this important result. They are to invigorate and mature by one mighty act the feeble saints; they also pass on to sublimer regions of faith and experience the advanced ones of God's elect. They are the fresh baptisms—the more powerful consecration of a waiting, willing, working church to a profounder willingness, and a mightier ability for a mightier work. These revivals are the pitched battles and the decisive victories for God, when the slain of the Lord is many, and his triumph glorious.

There are counterfeit revivals well executed, well calculated to deceive the most wary. These are deceptive and superficial, with many pleasant, entertaining, delusive features, entirely lacking in the offensive features which distinguish the genuine ones. The pain of penitence, the shame of guilt, the sorrow and humiliation of sin, the fear of hell—these marks of the genuine are lacking in the counterfeit. The test of a genuine revival is found in its staying qualities. The counterfeit is but a winter spurt, as evanescent and fitful as the morning cloud or early dew—both soon gone—and the sun but the hotter for the mockery of the cloud and because of the fleeting dew. These surface revivals do more harm than good, like a surface thaw in midwinter which only increases the hardness and roughness of tomorrow's freeze. The genuine revival goes to the bottom of things; the sword is not swaddled in cotton, nor festooned with flowers, but pierces to the dividing asunder of soul and spirit and of the joints and marrow.

A genuine revival marks an era in the life of the church. It plants the germs of the great spiritual principles which grow and mature through all the changing seasons that follow. Revival seasons are favoring seasons, when the tides of salvation are at their flood, when all the waves and winds move heavenward . . . days of emancipation and return and rapture. The church needs revivals; it cannot live, it cannot do its work without them. Revivals which will lift it above the sands of worldliness that shallow the current and impede the sailing. Revivals which will radicate the great spiritual principles, which are worn threadbare in many a church. It is true that in the most thorough work some will fall away, but when the work is genuine and far-reaching, as it ought to be, the waste will scarcely be felt in the presence of the good that remains.

The first element, in a revival whose effects will stay, is that the revival spring from within the church, the native outgrowth of the spiritual condition of the church. The so-called revivals do not spring from the repentance, faith, and prayers of the church, but are induced by foreign and outside forces. Many of the religious movements of the day have no foundation in the travailing throes of the church. By outside pressure, the presence and reputation of an evangelist, of imported singers and imported songs, an interest is awakened, a passing impression made, but these are quite different from the concern aroused by the presence of God and the mighty power of his almighty Spirit. In the manufactured revival there is an interest which does not deepen into conviction, which is not subdued into awe, which cannot be molded into prayer, nor agitated by fears. There is the utter absence of the spirit of prayer; neither has the spirit of repentance any place; lightness and frivolity reign; tears are strange and unwelcome visitors. The church-members, instead of being on their knees in intercession, or mingling their wrestling cries with the wrestling penitents, or joining in rapturous praise with their rapturous deliverance, are simply spectators of a pleasing entertainment, in which they have but a momentary interest, the results of which, viewed from a spiritual stand-point, are far below zero. A revival means a burdened church and a burdened pastor and burdened penitents.

The revival whose results are gracious and abiding must spring from the spiritual contact of pastor and church with God. A season of fasting and prayer of deep humiliation and confession are the conditions from which a genuine and powerful work springs.

The nature of the preaching is of the first importance. Its character will grade the converts and measure the depth of the work. The word of God in its purity and strength must be given. The law of God in its spiritual demands must arouse the conscience, and pierce and lay bare the heart. If there ever is a time for sentimental anecdotes, for the exercise of wit, if the preacher is ever justified in pausing to soften the sympathies or inflame the fancy, it is not at this period.

The object must not be to increase the impulses, or move on the surface, or work on tender emotions, but to convict the conscience, search out the sinner and expose his sins, to alarm the guilty soul, and intensify the faith and effort of the believer. The word of God is the imperishable and vitalizing seed. The Spirit of God is the quickening energy that is to be let loose. The word of God is the sword of the Spirit. The sword must be unsheathed, and cut with both edges.

The spirit of prayer must be the one evident and prevailing spirit. The spirit of prayer is but the spirit of faith, the spirit of reverence, the spirit of supplies, ... [incomplete] ... and increased. This spirit holds in its keeping the success of the word and power of the Holy Ghost; as the spirit of prayer fail these fail. If the spirit of prayer is absent or is quenched, God is not in the assembly. He comes and stays only in the cloud of glory formed by the incense of a church whose flame of prayer is ascending to him. All genuine revivals are simply God coming with great grace to his Church. The revival that springs from heart contact of the church with God, which is directed and intensified by the pure preaching of the pure word of God, and in which, and through which, prayer, mighty prayer, prevails, will be a revival that will stay in its coming.

Christian Advocate, December 6, 1890

We have advanced a good step when we can see and feel our need of a revival of religion. We fear many have not advanced to this first step. It is well, too, if this sense of the need of a revival presses on us from a clear view of our perils. That we are in peril from the many forms and many floods of worldliness that are flowing in on us is not to be debated. No time must be wasted with the man who is too blind to see this. Other perils confront us, but perils or no perils, perils ordinary or perils extraordinary, we need a revival. The church cannot prosper in the most peaceful times nor meet her feeblest foes without revivals. She will be becalmed in the happiest hours like "a painted ship on a painted ocean." Without them she will backslide though ever so well situated spiritually. The Methodist Church must have revivals or die spiritually. She must have revivals or she will save no souls. Her sacraments cannot save. She has no priestly hands to impose priestly absolution. The Methodist Church must have the genuine article or nothing. She has no fictions to impose, no secondhand wares to deal out. Her revivals have educated her into the highest form of spiritual life and made her adept in the soul-saving trade. To lose the revival is for her right hand to lose its cunning.

But to have the revival is most serious business. It does not come for the saying. Most serious business it is for us in our present state. If any one desires to ascertain what a heavy job he has on hand let him try to secure a revival in the average Methodist Church. Let him discard all methods which tend to create a sensation or get up a stir by dint of generalship, machinery, or manipulation. Let him reduce the whole movement to a spiritual basis and labor to secure a revival in the church, as the product of the relation of the church to God. If the one who undertakes such a discrediting task does not find himself like a sparrow alone upon the housetop he must be accounted as one of the most favored of men.

The revival means serious work with the church. It means a church intent on a great interest. It means more than an interested church, for the church may be interested in seeing the preacher gather them in. The stewards will always be interested in seeing men of financial ability coming in. The church doors will always be open to those who have influence and who come to join us. The true revival means a great deal more than concern for additions to the church roll, much more than increase of social or financial ability. It means a church in tears, a church in confession, a church in travail of soul. It means a church weighed down with interest and agony as Christ was weighed down. It means a church in sorrow for sin as he was in sorrow. A church in prayer. . . .

It must go down to the church life, and transform, elevate, and mightily quicken it. It must go down, and with sharp incisiveness divorce the church from its sins and from the world.

A revival means a heartbroken pastor—means a heartbroken membership. A revival means a church on its knees confessing its sins—the sins of the individual and of the church—confessing the sins of the times and of the community, the sins of the sinners and the sins of the saints as well.

That the revival may begin in the church the church must enter into closer relations with God. The travailing spirit must be in it. The intense desire for God's glory must move it. The church must sit down with the sinner in dust and ashes, must in its penitence represent the sinner and seek God with a broken heart, and while crying to God for mercy to the sinner must unite itself in interest and sin, and cry: "Have mercy on *us*." The church too often assumes the role of a spectator, interested, it is true, but still a spectator. The preacher and church too often turn the whole matter over to an evangelist or visiting brother, and if he, perchance, has in him the force of God, some good may be accomplished. If he be a professional revivalist an interest will be manufactured, a well-executed counterfeit of a genuine revival will be passed off on them, and neither preacher nor church will have discernment enough to discover its baseness, and when by sad experience they find out the bad fruits they will make a wholesale discredit of all revival efforts.

The great preparation for the revival ought to be in the hearts of the leading officials. These chief ones should be first in this good and great work, but they are too often content to see that the assessments are well up, and if an extra effort must be made to save souls the poorer members and humbler ones must see to the business. The leading ones have no time and no taste for the exactions of this work. It is time that we were seeing to this work. Other churches have accepted the revival feature as the aggressive force of the church; as distinctive of spiritual operations, as the feature that links us to Pentecost. To let the revival flame grow feeble on our altars while others are kindling it to a brighter glow and an intenser flame is to surrender our glory to them and to fall to the rear in ignoble ease and spiritual senility. It will not do to say that we have changed the phase of our work; that we are solidifying, edifying, polishing. The church that lacks the spiritual force for a thorough revival lacks the edifying, solidifying elements. Nothing edifies, matures, unites like a revival. The preacher whose ministry does not culminate in a revival does not culminate in anything else essentially spiritual. The ministry that does not deal in the wholesale revival work of soul saving is a failure in the retail business of soul saving.

It has been said that the history of revivals is the history of religion, and no one can study their history without being impressed with their mighty influence upon the destiny of the race. To look back over the progress of the divine kingdom upon earth is to review revival periods which have come like refreshing showers upon dry and thirsty ground, making the desert to blossom as the rose, and bringing new eras of spiritual life and activity just when the church had fallen under the influence of the apathy of the times, and needed to be aroused to a new sense of her duty and responsibility. "From one point of view, and that not the least important," writes Principal Lindsay, in "The Church and the Ministry in the Early Centuries," "the history of the Church flows on from one time of revival to another, and whether we take the awakenings in the old Catholic, the medieval, or the modern Church, these have always been the work of men specially gifted with the power of seeing and declaring the secrets of the deepest Christian life, and the effect of their work has always been proportionate to the spiritual receptivity of the generation they have spoken to."

As God, from the beginning, has wrought prominently through revivals, there can be no denial of the fact that revivals are a part of the Divine plan. The kingdom of our Lord has been advanced in large measure by special seasons of gracious and rapid accomplishment of the work of conversion, and it may be inferred, therefore, that the means through which God has worked in other times will be employed in our time to produce similar results. "The quiet conversion of one sinner after another, under the ordinary ministry of the Gospel," says one writer on the subject, "must always be regarded with feelings of satisfaction and gratitude by the ministers and disciples of Christ; but a periodical manifestation of the simultaneous conversion of thousands is also to be desired, because of its adaptation to afford a visible and impressive demonstration that God has made that same Jesus, Who was rejected and crucified, both Lord and Christ; and that, in virtue of His Divine Mediatorship, He has assumed the royal sceptre of universal supremacy, and 'must reign till all His enemies be made His footstool.' It is, therefore, reasonable to expect that, from time to time, He will repeat that which on the day of Pentecost formed the conclusive and crowning evidence of His Messiahship and Sovereignty; and, by so doing, startle the slumbering souls of careless worldlings, gain the attentive ear of the unconverted, and, in a remarkable way, break in upon those brilliant dreams of earthly glory, grandeur, wealth, power and happiness, which the rebellious and God-forgetting multitude so fondly cherish. Such an outpouring of the Holy Spirit forms at once a demonstrative proof of the completeness and acceptance of His once offering of Himself as a sacrifice for sin, and a prophetic 'earnest' of the certainty that He 'shall appear the second time without sin unto salvation,' to judge the world in righteousness."

And that revivals are to be expected, proceeding, as they do, from the right use of the appropriate means, is a fact which needs not a little emphasis in these days, when the material is exalted at the expense of the spiritual, and when ethical standards are supposed to be supreme. That a revival is not a miracle was powerfully taught by Charles G. Finney. There might, he said, be a miracle among its antecedent causes, or there might not. The Apostles employed miracles simply as a means by which they arrested attention to their message, and established its divine authority. "But the miracle was not the revival. The miracle was one thing; the revival that followed it was quite another thing. The revivals in the Apostles' days were connected with miracles, but they were not miracles." All revivals are dependent upon God, but in revivals, as in other things, He invites and requires the assistance of man, and the full result is obtained when there is co-operation between the Divine and the human. In other words, to employ a familiar phrase, God alone can save the world, but God cannot save the world alone. God and man unite for the task, the response of the divine being invariably in proportion to the desire and the effort of the human.

This cooperation, then, being necessary, what is the duty which we, as coworkers with God, require to undertake? First of all, and most important of all—the point which we desire particularly to emphasise—we must give ourselves to prayer. "Revivals," as Dr. J. Wilbur Chapman reminds us, "are born in prayer. When Wesley prayed England was revived; when Knox prayed, Scotland was refreshed; when the Sunday School teachers of Tannybrook prayed, 11,000 young people were added to the Church in a year. Whole nights of prayer have always been succeeded by whole days of soul-winning."

When D. L. Moody's church in Chicago lay in ashes, he went over to England, in 1872, not to preach, but to listen to others preach while his new church was being built. One Sunday morning he was prevailed upon to preach in a London pulpit. But somehow the spiritual atmosphere was lacking. He confessed afterwards that he never had such a hard time preaching in his life. Everything was perfectly dead, and, as he vainly tried to preach, he said to himself, "What a fool I was to consent to preach! I came here to listen, and here I am preaching." Then the awful thought came to him that he had to preach again at night, and only the fact that he had given the promise to do so kept him faithful to the engagement. But when Mr. Moody entered the pulpit at night, and faced the crowded congregation, he was conscious of a new atmosphere. "The powers of an unseen world seemed to have fallen upon the audience." As he drew towards the close of his sermon he became emboldened to give out an invitation and as he concluded he said, "If there is a man or woman here who will tonight accept Jesus Christ, please stand up." At once about 500 people rose to their feet. Thinking that there must be some mistake, he asked the people to be seated, and then, in order that there might be no possible misunderstanding, he repeated the invitation, couching it in even more definite and difficult terms. Again the same number rose. Still thinking that something must be wrong, Mr. Moody, for the second time, asked the standing men and women to be seated, and then he invited all who really meant to accept Christ to pass into the vestry. Fully 500 people did as requested, and that was the beginning of a revival in that church and neighborhood, which brought Mr. Moody back from Dublin, a few days later, that he might assist the wonderful work of God.

The sequel, however, must be given, or our purpose in relating the incident will be defeated. When Mr. Moody preached at the morning service there was a woman in the congregation who had an invalid sister. On her return home she told the invalid that the preacher had been a Mr. Moody from Chicago, and on hearing this she tuned pale. "What," she said, "Mr. Moody from Chicago! I read about him some time ago in an American paper, and I have been praying God to send him to London, and to our church. If I had known he was going to preach this morning I would have eaten no breakfast. I would have spent the whole time in prayer. Now, sister, go out of the room, lock the door, send me no dinner; no matter who comes, don't let them see me. I am going to spend the whole afternoon and evening in prayer." And so while Mr. Moody stood in the pulpit that had been like an ice-chamber in the morning, the bedridden saint was holding him up before God, and God, who ever delights to answer prayer, poured out His Spirit in mighty power.

The God of revivals who answered the prayer of His child for Mr. Moody, is willing to hear and to answer the faithful, believing prayers of his people today. Wherever God's conditions are met there the revival is sure to fall. Professor Thos. Nicholson, of Cornell College relates an experience on his first circuit that impresses anew the old lesson of the place of prayer in the work of God.

There had not been a revival on that circuit in years, and things were not spiritually hopeful. During more than four weeks the pastor had preached faithfully, visited from house to house, in stores, shops, and out-of-the-way places, and had done everything he could. The fifth Monday night saw *many of the official members at lodges*, but only a corporal's guard at the church.

From that meeting the pastor went home, cast down, but not in despair. He resolved to spend that night in prayer. "Locking the door, he took Bible and hymn book and began to inquire more diligently of the Lord, though the meetings had been the subject of hours of earnest prayer. Only God knows the anxiety and the faithful, prayerful study of that night. Near the dawn a great peace and a full assurance came that God would surely bless the plan which had been decided upon, and a text was chosen which he felt sure was of the Lord. Dropping upon the bed, the pastor slept about two hours, then rose, hastily breakfasted, and went nine miles to the far side of the circuit to visit some sick people. All day the assurance increased.

"Toward night a pouring rain set in, the roads were heavy and we reached home, wet, supperless, and a little late, only to find no fire in the church, the lights unlit, and no signs of service. The janitor had concluded that the rain would prevent the service. We changed the order, rang the bell, and prepared for war. Three young men formed the congregation, but in that 'full assurance' the pastor delivered the message which had been prayed out on the preceding night, as earnestly and as fully as if the house had been crowded, then made a personal appeal to each young man in turn. Two yielded, and testified before the meeting closed.

"The tired pastor went to a sweet rest, and next morning, rising a little later than usual, learned that one of the young men was going from store to store throughout the town telling of his wonderful deliverance, and exhorting the people to salvation. Night after night conversions occurred, until in two weeks we heard 144 people testify in forty-five minutes. All three points of that circuit saw a blaze of revival that winter, and family after family came into the church, until the membership was more than trebled.

"Out of that meeting one convert is a successful pastor in the Michigan Conference, another is the wife of one of the choicest of our pastors, and a third was in the ministry for a number of years, and then went to another denomination, where he is faithful unto this day. Probably none of the members ever knew of the pastor's night of prayer, but he verily believes that God somehow does for the man who thus prays, what He does not do for the man who does not pray, and he is certain that 'more things are wrought by prayer than this world dreams of.'"

All the true revivals have been born in prayer. When God's people become so concerned about the state of religion that they lie on their faces day and night in earnest supplication, the blessing will be sure to fall.

It is the same all down the ages. Every revival of which we have any record has been bathed in prayer. Take, for example, the wonderful revival in Shotts (Scotland) in 1630. The fact that several of the then persecuted ministers would take a part in solemn convocation having become generally known, a vast concourse of godly persons assembled on this occasion from all quarters of the country, and *several days were spent in social prayer*, preparatory to the service. In the evening, instead of retiring to rest, the multitude divided themselves into little bands, and *spent the whole night in supplication and praise*. The Monday was consecrated to thanksgiving, a practice not then common, and proved the great day of the feast. After much entreaty, John Livingston, chaplain to the Countess of Wigtown, a young man and not ordained, agreed to preach. He *had spent the night in prayer* and conference—but as the hour of assembling approached his heart quailed at the thought of addressing so many aged and experienced saints, and he actually fled from the duty he had undertaken. But just as the kirk of Shotts was vanishing from his view, those words, "Was I ever a barren wilderness or a land of darkness?" were borne in upon his mind with such force as compelled him to return to the work. He took for his text Ezekiel 36:25, 26, and discoursed with great power for about two hours. *Five hundred conversions* were believed to have occurred under that one sermon, thus prefaced by prayer. "It was the sowing of a seed through Clydesdale, so that many of the most eminent Christians of that country could date their conversion, or some remarkable confirmation of their case, from that day."

Of Richard Baxter it has been said that "he stained his study walls with praying breath; and after becoming thus anointed with the unction of the Holy Ghost he sent a river of living water over Kidderminster." Whitefield once thus prayed, "O Lord, give me souls or take my soul." After much closet pleading, "he once went to the Devil's fair and took more than a thousand souls out of the paw of the lion in a single day."

Mr. Finney says: "I once knew a minister who had a revival fourteen winters in succession. I did not know how to account for it till I saw one of his members get up in a prayer meeting and make a confession. 'Brethren,' he said, 'I have been long in the habit of praying every Saturday night till after midnight for the descent of the Holy Ghost among us. And now, brethren (and he began to weep), I confess that I have neglected it for two or three weeks.' The secret was out. That minister had a praying church."

And so we might go on multiplying illustration upon illustration to show the place of prayer in revival and to demonstrate that every mighty movement of the Spirit of God has had its source in the prayer chamber. The lesson of it all is this, that as workers together with God we must regard ourselves as in not a little measure responsible for the conditions which prevail around us today. Are we concerned about the coldness of the church? Do we grieve over the lack of conversions? Does our soul go out to God in midnight cries for the outpouring of His Spirit?

If not, part of the blame lies at our door. If we do our part, God will do His. Around us is a world lost in sin, above us is a God willing and able to save; it is ours to build the bridge that links heaven and earth, and prayer is the mighty instrument that does the work.

And so the old cry comes to us with insistent voice, "Pray, brethren, pray."

Purpose in Prayer, Chap. 12

Satan

We have no genesis of the devil in the Bible as a direct statement. The Bible is not his full history. It gives no intimation of his birth and no description of his creation. The Bible is only concerned with the devil as he has part in the great crises of man's history, and only gives us occasional glimpses of him in his work of ruin and death as explanatory, or as putting his acts in striking contrast and opposition to the works and aims of Christ. There are not lacking in these intimations and inferences, sidelights which indicate an original purity, a high relation to God, and a heavenly character and conduct. It is not a fanciful conjecture that he was and is the head of the angels who kept not their first estate. Peter in his first epistle gives the angel crises and fall as one of the signal events which illustrate God's justice, its certainty and fearfulness. He says, "God spared not the angels that sinned, but cast them down to hell, and delivered them into chains of darkness to be reserved unto judgment." Jude speaks after the same order of God's inflexible wrath when he tells us that "the angels which kept not their first estate, but left their own habitation, he hath reserved in everlasting chains under darkness unto the judgment of the great day."

The Revelation of John adds its testimony with addition to this fact: "And there was war in heaven; Michael and his angels fought against the dragon; and the dragon fought and his angels, and prevailed not; neither was their place found any more in heaven. And the great dragon was cast out, that old serpent, called the devil, and Satan, which deceiveth the whole world; he was cast out into the earth, and his angels were cast out with him."

To the Word of God we must go, assured that we will find the traces of the devil's steps and the unfolding of his conduct whose bad schemes have eclipsed so much of earth's brightness and blasted so much of its promise and hope.

If we have the childlike spirit of docility and trust, if we will "lay aside all filthiness and superfluity of naughtiness, and receive with meekness the engrafted word," we will find satisfaction and illumination, not satisfaction as to curiosity, nor illumination in the niceties or subtleties of philosophy, but satisfaction and illumination in all things which pertain to the highest and weightiest truth for the thoughtful, trustful and prayerful mind.

In the Bible we have the facts and history of man's redemption. Incidentally or essentially, other worlds and other beings are brought prominently on the stage of redemption purposes and plans. These revealed facts whether incidental or essential, whether casual or regular, are to our faith what the facts of nature are to the student of nature. They must shape theories and settle opinions. They must not be set aside, for weighty and final they must be. Reason must not ignore nor reject them, but must lay them deep and solid as the foundation of all investigation, the basis of every hypothesis. These Bible facts demand our faith, though we may not be able to reach out beyond into the unknown regions where harmony reigns.

The Word of God brings clearly to light the unseen world, its persons, places, facts and history, not, we say, in minute detail, but full enough to provoke thought and reflection, and to create and inspire faith.

The Bible nowhere enters into an argument to prove the person and being of God. It assumes His being and reveals His person and character. Without preface or introduction, the Bible brings God before us in all His majesty and omnipotence. God is at the world's beginning, and He it was who created the beginning of all things. "In the beginning God created the heavens and the earth." How sublime and awe-inspiring our first glimpse of God! God is revealed not by argument but by work. We learn what He is from what He does.

In like manner is the revelation of the devil. He is before us in full person without introduction or ceremony as the evil one, a graduate in the work of guile and evil. The curtain is drawn and the chief actor is in full dress. A world is at stake, man is to be seduced, Eden is to be blasted. No light is shed upon his past history, no knowledge of the school where he learned his dire trade. He was before earthly life. Eden does not date his birth, and is not the first chapter of his history, nor is it the first trial of his hellish art. We have no access to the archives of the past. Eden bounds our horizon, and the devil is there. Henceforth his history is to run parallel with our race. Man is to be the object of his schemes, his ruin, and his ambition. Earth is to be the favorite scene of his exploits. He is at the cradle of man, and has much to do in shaping his character and determining his destiny.

The Bible is a revelation, not a philosophy nor a poem, not a science. It reveals things and persons as they are, living and acting outside the range of earthly vision or natural discovery.

Bible revelations are not against reason but above reason, for the uses of faith, man's highest faculty. The powers of reason are not able to discover these Bible facts, and yet they are for reason's use, its light, strength and higher elevation, but more essentially to form, to nourish and to perfect faith.

The Bible reveals the devil as a person, not a mere figure, not an influence simply, not a personification only, but a real person. In the eighth chapter of John, Christ is arraigning the cruelty and murderous malignity, the falsehood, deceit and hypocrisy of the Jews. Jesus says, "Ye are of your father the devil, and the lusts of your father ye will do." He was a murderer from the beginning and abode not in the truth, because there is no truth in him.

Many myths may have gathered around the person of the devil by the accretion of ages, much of poetry, sentiment and tradition, and even our fears may have caricatured his person, exaggerated his character, and colored his conduct. But there is truth in regard to him, naked and simple truth. There is much truth that needs to be learned about the devil, and no age needs the plain, unvarnished truth about the devil more than this age. We need the light of that truth as a warning, as an incentive to vigilance, and an inspiration to effort. We need the knowledge of the enemy, his character, presence and power to arouse men to action, for this is vital to victory.

It is wholly at variance with any Christian idea of the perfection of truthfulness in Christ, who was truth itself, to suppose Him to have used such plain and solemn words repeatedly before His disciples and the Jews in encouragement and furtherance of a lying superstition.

A denial of the reality of demonical possessions on the part of any one who believes the Gospel narrative to be true . . . may justly be regarded as simply and plainly inconceivable.

When the devil fell, others fell with him. This is the lesson of God's Word.

Of the number of these fallen spirits we have no census. In Ephesians, quoting from the Revised Version, in the summary of these unseen foes we have "spiritual hosts," an uncounted, uncountable number.

How innumerable they are, we cannot tell. The demoniac of Gadara was named "legion because many devils were entered into him." A legion if exact was somewhat less than six thousand. Their number must be great, enabling them to spare so many to swarm into and possess one man, or even seven in one woman, as Mary Magdalene.

The statement in Revelation that the great red dragon with "his tail did draw the third part of the stars of heaven and did cast them to the earth," may be a reference to the fall of the angels and their number.

The Bible is clear in many references and some direct statements that the devil has a host of angelic followers who are ready, eager in their efforts to hurt man and defeat God's kingdom on earth.

The devil is a person of marked emphatic character. Character gives dignity, place and value to the person, or character degrades the person. Character is that which is inner, cut in and graven. Character abides, forms action and shapes life. Character is a fountain. It is the head and stream of conduct; character often versus reputation. Character is what we are. Reputation is what folks think we are. The *real* and the *think so* are often two worlds. It would be well every way if reputation were based on character, if the real and the reputed were one. A bad reputation may be coupled with a good character. Then the times are sadly out of joint or the environments, and the folks are more sadly out of joint than the times. A good reputation may be but the veneering of a bad character. The devil has this characteristic with him. Reputation is based on character. They are one. His reputation is bad, because his character is worse.

The devil is *a created being*. He is therefore not self-existent nor eternal, but limited and finite. There was a time when he was not, when he began to be. His creation was after the order of the angels. The angels were not the offspring of the family relation. Cradlehood and all the tender ties, training, sweetness and growth are unknown to them. The pains and joys of childbirth are not theirs. Each angel is created, not born, created directly, personally, by God. The devil was created good, doubtless very good. His purity, as well as exaltation, were sources of congratulation, wonderment and praise in heaven.

The devil is *a positive character*. He wears disguises, but his ends are single and lie in only one direction, double-faced but never double-minded, never undecided, never vague nor feeble in his purposes or ends. No irresolution, nor hesitant depression nor aimless action spring from him. The devil has character if not horns, for character is often harder and sharper than horns. Character is felt. We feel the devil. He orders things, controls things. He is a great manager. He manages bad men, often good men and bad angels. Indirect, sinister, low and worldly, is the devil as a manager.

Is Christ a person? He puts the devil in opposition and contrast to Himself as a great mighty malignant person the sower of all evil—as Christ is the sower of all good. "The field is the world; the good seed are the children of the kingdom; but the tares are the children of the wicked one; the enemy that sowed them is the devil; the harvest is the end of the world; and the reapers are the angels."

Is Christ impersonal? Are the children of the kingdom impersonal? Are the children of the wicked one impersonal? Are not Christ and the children of the kingdom personal and persons? Are not the children of the wicked one and the devil personal and persons also?

In the Bible the personality of the devil is made emphatic. He is not only the source of evil to others, but the embodiment of evil in a person. The Revised Version makes this emphatic. The petition in the Lord's Prayer, "Deliver us from evil," becomes personal, "Deliver us from *the evil one*." So we find Christ praying not only that His disciples should be delivered from evil, all evil, impersonal and general, but "that thou shouldst keep them from the evil one." The statement by John that "the whole world lieth in wickedness," becomes personal, for in the Revised Version, all wickedness concentrates in a person. "The whole world lieth in the evil one." Here, too, the devil is called the "wicked one." Personality is attributed to him. Fatherhood is attributed to him, the father of all evil, the enemy of Jesus, malignant, active, crafty, cautious, cowardly.

The devil and his angels are of a higher order than the fallen sons of Adam, by rank, order, and intelligence. The devil is called in the Bible a prince, a world ruler, "prince of this world." He is designated as "the devil and his angels." He and they are held accountable, are condemned for their sins and for revolt in leaving their "first estate," the sphere for which they were created, and in which they were originally placed by God. This fact of their fall, and all the other statements, direct and incidental, emphasize them as persons, living, acting, free, accountable. That they had a chief prince in all their movements, prime in wisdom, prime in skill and in leadership, is clear from all Scriptural statements concerning the devil and his angels.

In 2 Corinthians 11:13, Paul says: "For such are false apostles, deceitful workers, transforming themselves into the apostles of Christ. And no marvel; for Satan himself is transformed into an angel of light. Therefore it is no great thing if his ministers also be transformed as the ministers of righteousness, whose end shall be according to their works." "Satan himself" is an emphatic declaration of personality. He has ministers. An influence does not have ministers. Paul is writing of persons, wily, fraudulent and alluring, and he introduces the great person, the pattern and inspirer of all their fraud, hypocrisy and error, his apostles, false as he, the arch-impostor.

Jude has a statement which brings into view many persons: "Likewise also these filthy dreamers defile the flesh, despise dominion, and speak evil of dignities. Yet Michael, the archangel, when contending with the devil, he disputed about the body of Moses, durst not bring against him a railing accusation, but said, The Lord rebuke thee."

The "filthy dreamers" were persons. Moses was a great person. Michael an archangel was a person. The devil, what was he, if not a person? Living in the Mosaic dispensation, the devil was contending with the highest dignity under that dispensation of angels. Did the mighty archangel have to appeal for help against a mere influence, a shadowy, dreamy personification? This statement in Jude declares the devil to be a high dignity, whose person and presence are not to be treated with indignity or by frivolity or raillery.

The statement in Peter is after the same order and to the same end. The devil is a person of great dignity. "The Lord knoweth how to deliver the godly out of temptation, and to reserve the unjust unto the day of judgment to be punished. But chiefly them that walk after the flesh in the lust of uncleanness, and despise government. Presumptuous are they, self-willed, they are not afraid to speak evil of dignities. Whereas angels, which are greater in power and might, bring not railing accusation against them before the Lord. But these, as natural brute beasts made to be taken and destroyed, speak evil of the things that they understand not, and shall utterly perish in their own corruption."

Note how James puts the mightiest persons in contrast and opposition: "Submit yourselves therefore to God. Resist the devil and he will flee from you. Draw nigh to God and he will draw nigh to you." Why such a combination and contrast? Is God not a person? How can we then reduce him who is so in God's way to a mere influence? The passage teaches a personal devil as surely as a personal God.

Why are God and the devil in like manner conjoined in Peter's urgent exhortation? "Humble yourselves, therefore, under the mighty hand of God, that he may exalt you in due time; casting all your care upon him, for he careth for you. Be sober, be vigilant; because your adversary, the devil, as a roaring lion, walketh about, seeking whom he may devour." Why casting all care on Him? Why be sober and vigilant? "Your adversary" can be no less than a person against whom the Christian has to be armed with God. "Your adversary!" Hate and ruin are in his opposition. Can he be less than a person? The devil, "walking about like a roaring lion," strong, full of passions, and deadly hate! Can anything less than a person of infernal passion and infernal power answer this divine portraiture? To Peter the existence and person of this powerful adversary had a sad demonstration in his own experience. The words were still on his conscience and heart and memory. "Simon, Satan hath desired to have you that he may sift you as wheat."

In the directions in the Sermon on the Mount about swearing, affirmations and conversation, Jesus says, "Let your communication be Yea, yea; Nay, nay: for whatsoever is more than these is of the evil one."

Under the powerful operations of the cross and the Spirit, as well as the restraining influences of the Gospel, evil would soon be driven from the earth, branded and banned, were it not for the mighty personality and executive ability of the devil.

We find many references, hints and reminders of the power and person of the devil, coming out in the ministry of Christ. The name "devil" invests him with an infamous personality, and clothes him with all the deceit, craft and cruelty attaching to that name. By the name "Satan," Christ puts him as the adversary of God and man. By designating him as "the prince of this world," Christ recognizes his royal power and ruling authority for evil in this world. The devil's agency in the ills that affect the body is not merely hinted at, but comes out as being taken for granted.

How strenuous and ever continuing the conflict between the devil and Jesus, is learned by the Lord's prayer, that perfect and universal prayer which Jesus puts in the heart and lips of His people in all ages, for as we have seen, according to the Revised Version, that petition of conflict, peril, warning, and safety is, "Deliver us from the Evil One." Evil is comparatively harmless, feeble and inert without the presence of its mighty inspirer. Deliverance from the devil is deliverance from the many evils of which he is the source and inspiration.

In the sixth chapter of Ephesians, the Christian soldier-hood, its character, armor, conduct and courage are challenged, and he is urged, because of the devil's power, and because the Christian's warfare is mainly against him, to this effect: "Put on the whole armour of God, that ye may be able to stand against the wiles of the devil. For we wrestle not against flesh and blood, but against principalities, against powers, against the rulers of the darkness of this world, against spiritual wickedness in high places."

The Christian's comfort as administered by Paul in the sixteenth chapter of Romans is not only the impartation of, "The grace of the Lord Jesus Christ be with you," but also, "And the God of peace shall bruise Satan under your feet shortly."

Peter's vital exhortation has a double imperative in it, not only the "casting all our care on God," but a loud and urgent call to watch and pray. "Be sober, be vigilant; because your adversary the devil, as a roaring lion, walketh about, seeking whom he may devour." Peter recognized in the deadly crime of Ananias and Sapphira the hand of Satan, and remonstrates thus: "Ananias, why hath Satan filled thine heart to lie to the Holy Ghost, and to keep back part of the price of the land?"

The warning and exhortation which Christ sends to the church at Smyrna to prepare and nerve to endurance involves the person and power of the devil. "Fear none of those things which thou shalt suffer; behold, the devil shall cast some of you into prison, that ye may be tried; and ye shall have tribulation ten days. Be thou faithful unto death, and I will give thee a crown of life." The explanation of the parable of the tares puts the malignity, person, and power of the devil in contrast with Christ. "The field is the world; the good seed are the children of the kingdom; but the tares are the children of the wicked one. The enemy that sowed them is the devil; the harvest is the end of the world; and the reapers are the angels."

The defense of Christ against the pharisaic charge of violating the Sabbath puts the devil conspicuous in his work of evil: "And ought not this woman, being a daughter of Abraham, whom Satan hath bound, lo, these eighteen years, be loosed from this bond on the Sabbath day?"

The statement about Judas, "And supper being ended, the devil having now put into the heart of Judas Iscariot, Simon's son, to betray him;" is a statement not of an influence nor a personification, but of a person outside of Judas, making suggestions to him, and urging him on to his act of hypocrisy, and the suggestion is strictly in keeping with the character of the devil. "And after the sop Satan entered into him. Then said Jesus unto him, That thou doest, do quickly." How much an advance in fulness and power of action and influence is this act compared with his work in paradise! There he used a serpent as his instrument. Here a man, a chosen, trusted apostle. "A messenger of Satan," says Paul, "to buffet me." The exalted revelation and experience of the person and power of Christ are closely followed by the revelation and experience of the person and power of the devil.

The fearful doom of the wicked at the judgment is thus set forth by Christ: "Then shall he say also unto them on the left hand, Depart from me, ye cursed, into everlasting fire, prepared for the devil and his angels." The final doom of Satan is revealed in these words, "And the devil that deceived them was cast into the lake of fire and brimstone, where the beast and the false prophets are, and shall be tormented day and night for ever and ever."

These extracts are not only arguments to prove the existence or personality of the devil, but are logical conclusive references to a person whose being is taken for granted, universally accepted and thoroughly believed by them all.

A singular case would that mind be in its attitude to God's Word, who should profess to accept that Word and not believe in the existence of the devil. This would be a great breach both in the logic and faith of such a mind, as if the play *Macbeth* were accepted in utter failure to recognize the person or existence of Lady Macbeth, whose character forms the entire plan and color of the whole.

The encounters with those who were possessed of devils illustrates Christ's constant recognition of them as personal beings. He recognizes their distinct individuality. He talks to them and commands them as persons. They know Christ, confess His divinity, bow to His authority, obey, however unwillingly, His commands. He makes the clear distinction between the *human personality* possessed by the devil, and *the personality of the devil* who holds possession. The two are to his eye *two persons*.

That the exercising of these did give a severe blow to Satan's kingdom is declared by Christ's exclamation at the return and report of the seventy. "That even the devils are subject unto us through thy name." He exclaimed, "I beheld Satan as lightning fall from heaven," and then amid their ecstasy and His joy He renewed their commission. "Behold, I give unto you power to tread on serpents and scorpions, and over all the power of the enemy, and nothing shall by any means hurt you. Notwithstanding, in this rejoice not, that the spirits are subject unto you; but rather rejoice because your names are written in heaven." "Over all the power of the enemy." The devil is the enemy of Christ, of man. Power over all the devil's power.

To Christ, the devil was one of the most real persons. He recognized his person, felt and acknowledged his power, abhorred his character, and warred against his person and kingdom.

To the Holy Spirit, the substitute representative and successor of Jesus Christ, was committed this work of breaking the deadly power of the world by breaking the power of its prince. There was the necessary and continuous reminder that the devil occupied the royal position of the world's prince, already adjudged and condemned, and upon whom the sentence and penalty were to be executed. "Nevertheless, I tell you the truth: It is expedient for you that I go away; for if I go not away, the Comforter will not come unto you; but if I depart, I will send him unto you. And when he is come, he will reprove the world of sin, and of righteousness, and of judgment; of sin because they believe not on me; of righteousness, because I go to my Father, and ye see me no more; of judgment, because the prince of this world is judged."

"The prince of *this world*" he is, though the awful doom awaiting unbelief, sin and unrighteousness are his.

In these declarations of Jesus Christ, we have the clear revelation of what the devil is in his relation to the world as a prince and ruler. We understand why the world is so alien to God, to God's Son, to His cause, and how attachment to the world is at once estrangement and bitter enmity to God, because in the world's beauty and charms there is the enmity of the devil to God. The world is the beauteous harlot with her snares of death and hell.

The devil is recognized by Jesus Christ to be the prince of

this world, not lawfully, but in its rebellion against God, not to be submitted to, but to be renounced as a lawless one, dethroned as a usurper and conquered as a rebel. To secure these ends, to dethrone and conquer the devil, the mission of the Son of God is charged. We see how readily Jesus Christ acknowledges the position and power of the devil. It is of the devil He speaks, and conjoins him with the world. The stroke of the Son of God falls on both: "Now is the judgment of this world; now shall the prince of this world be cast out. And I, if I be lifted up, will draw all men to me." The world is condemned by the power of the cross. The sweet attractive potencies of the cross dissolve the fatal fascinations of the world. The power of that same cross casts out from his world ruling throne the prince of this world. Christ affirms the devil's high position, but signs and seals his destiny and doom. "God anointed Jesus of Nazareth with the Holy Ghost and with power; who went about doing good, and healing all that were oppressed of the devil, for God was with him."

Again does the Son of God recognize the position which the devil holds as crowned prince by the world's franchises. How his presence quiets the Son of God. Man's words are not to be victors in this conflict. God's words in the temptation broke the power of his assault and defeated his fell intents, but left him still a sovereign with his kingly crown. The Son of God is awed into silence at the devil's approach. The cross, its agony and shame, its deep humiliation, bitter agony and untold shame, its defeat and despair, all these it would take to lift the crown from Satan's brow and bring his throne down to dust and ashes. The adorable Son of God "saw the travail of His soul in that hour and was satisfied." He saw also what it would cost Him, and what it would cost every son of heaven, to discrown that prince, and He lapsed into a solemn silence, the prestige of His victory. "Hereafter I will not talk much with you, for the prince of this world cometh, and hath nothing in me."

If there be any virtue in not being an infidel, the devil may claim this virtue. If it be any praise to be always busy, the devil may claim that praise, for he is always busy, and very busy. But his character does not spring from his faith. His faith makes him tremble, his character makes him a devil.

The devil is a very busy character. He does a big business, a very mean business, but he does it well, that is, as well as a mean business can be done. He has large experience, big brains, a black heart, great force, and tireless industry, and is of great influence and great character. All his immense resources and powers are laid out for evil. Only evil inspires his activities and energies. He never moves to relieve or bless, a stranger alike to benevolent doing and kindly feeling.

Satan's history antedates the history of man—the only beings, he and his angels, who know by sad experience, Heaven, Earth and Hell. These three words are familiar to him. He has walked the streets of Heaven side by side with its purest and best. He has felt the thrill of its purest joys. He knows the bitterest anguish of hell, and has felt its keenest flames.

He does a big business on earth. He is a prince and a leader. Men and devils are his agents, and the elements are often by him debauched from their benignant purposes, and are made to destroy. He is busy tempting men to evil. He has large experience in this business and is an adept at it. By him sin loses its sinfulness, the world is clothed with double charms, self is given a double force, faith is turned into fanaticism and love into hate.

A spiritual character can work through agencies or directly on the spirit. He infuses thoughts, makes suggestions and does it so deftly that we do not know their paternity. He tempted Eve to take the forbidden fruit. He put it into David's mind to number Israel, thereby provoking the wrath of God. He influenced Ananias and Sapphira to lie to God. Peter's yielding to presumption was at his instance. Judas' betrayal was from the same baneful source. The temptation of Christ was a typical and master piece of his business in seeking to seduce our Lord from God, showing his power to array agencies and pleas, and to back these by all forms of sanctity and persuasiveness. He is blasphemous, arrogant and presumptuous. He slanders God to men and infuses into men hard thoughts of God. He intensifies their enmity and inflames their prejudice against Him. He leads them to deny His existence and to traduce His character, thereby destroying the foundations of faith and all true worship. He does all he can by insinuation and charges to blacken saintly character and lower God's estimate of the good. He is the vilest of calumniators, the most malignant and artful of slanderers. Goodness is the point of his constant attack. He says nothing good about the good, nothing bad about the bad. He is always at church before the preacher is in the pulpit or a member in the pew, to hinder the sower, to impoverish the soil, or to blast the seed, that is, when courage and faith are in the pulpit, and zeal and prayer in the pew. But if dead orthodoxy or live heterodoxy are in the pulpit, he then puts in his time elsewhere at some point of danger.

Christ expressly declared that some sickness, at least, was the direct infliction of Satan.

The devil goes about to do evil and oppress men, at every point the antagonist of Him who went about to do good and heal all that were oppressed of the devil. In some way he had power over death and worked a fearful work of bondage and fear and death. Through death, Christ works to destroy him that had the power of death, that is the devil. He puts a thorn in Paul's flesh and makes a special effort and requisition for Peter. He directs the whirlwind, kindles the fire and orders the disease which overwhelm and devastate Job and his property. He arms the thieving Chaldeans and Sabeans against him and gets into his wife, and directs the divers agencies of his empire to ruin this one saint. He will wreck an empire at any time to secure a soul. He sows the tares in the wheat, the bad among the good, bad thoughts among the good thoughts. All kinds of evil seed are sown by him in the harvest fields of earth. He is always trying to make the good bad and the bad worse. He fills the minds of a Judas and inflames and hurries him on to his infamous purpose. He fills Peter with an arrogant pride which tries to thwart the divine plans and to inject human views into the purpose of Christ instead of God's purpose.

The devil goes about as fierce, as resolute, and as strong as a lion, intent only to destroy, restrained by no sentiments which soften and move human or divine hearts. He has no pity and no sympathy. He is great, but only great in evil. A great intellect, he is driven and inspired by a malignant and cruel heart.

At the threshold of Christ's ministry there we meet with His temptations by the devil,—one of those conflicts on which one of the mightiest issues turn. The history of the case presents the devil as a spiritual person, the head and embodiment of all evil, making a fierce, most wily, and protracted assault on the Son of God. We are not informed as to what shape he assumed to veil the treachery and wickedness of his attack. The temptation is noted as one of the preliminary and pivot facts of Christ's ministry, and can no more be resolved into the visionary than can His baptism, the descent of the Spirit, His wilderness trip, or His fasting. It was no influence tempting Christ. The whole transaction forbids that. "He was led of the Spirit into the wilderness to be tempted of the devil." The devil came to Him and the devil left Him, and then "the angels came and ministered to him."

In this temptation the methods, hypocrisy and craft of the devil are seen. How materially and benevolently he comes to the weak, exhausted Son of God! How innocent is the suggestion that Jesus use His power to relieve His hunger! What could be more allowable than that? To use His spiritual power for temporal ends! How often is it done? What a world of evil to religion when it is used to subserve the natural. Man living for bread alone. The temporal the first. The secular and worldly prime. Religion not simply to serve money or business, but religion secondary or subservient to business. The heavenly used for the earthly, the spiritual for the natural, more intent on daily food than on daily grace, eyeing the seen more than the unseen. That is the devil's main business—to materialize, earthlyize religion, to get man to live for bread alone, to make earth bigger than heaven. Time is more engaging than eternity. What a fearful conflict is being carried on in that quiet wilderness between the fainting Son of God and Satan, between the earthly and the heavenly, between God's religion and the devil's religion!

The conflict surges around three points. The fleshly, the presumptuous, and the worldly. But this little circle holds all the shapes and forms of temptation, all the crafty devices, all the hidden depths, all the glittering seductions which Satan has devised to swerve men from the lofty allegiance which faith demands. The devil's assault on Christ is in striking contrast with his temptation to beguile Eve, and in more striking contrast with his fearful ordeal through which he tried Job's integrity. No suspicion cast on God's goodness as with Eve, no terrific, curdling sorrow as in Job's case. All is friendly, sympathetic and inviting.

The second temptation includes in it, not merely the fanatical presumption of overheated zeal and brainless devotion, but all the methods of sensational and abnormal piety by all those short cut processes by which the severe and tedious principles of a genuine faith are set aside, and spurious, superficial and flesh-pleasing substitutes are brought in to make a more attractive and popular guise of faith. It seeks to take man-devised methods, easy, fragrant of sentiment, rank and material, in the stead of God's lowly way of godly sorrow, strict self-denial, and prayerful surrender.

Then the last, the world, its kingdoms and its glory, these as the reward of his devotion to Satan, worship the devil, that is, the world's god. How the devil massed all his forces! Religion was invoked. The world and the flesh all conspired, under Satan's power, to tempt the Son of God. With what reluctance the pure soul of the Son of God went unto this close conflict with Satan is seen in Mark's statement: "And immediately the Spirit driveth him into the wilderness." No wrestling can warp this statement into a mere influence. It is history, fact—plain, simple, historical fact. Reread the record as to the devil. How clearly, without a doubt or figure of speech, does it stamp the whole transaction with personality. "Then was Jesus led up of the Spirit into the wilderness to be tempted of the devil. And he was there in the wilderness forty days tempted of Satan; and was with the wild beasts; and the angels ministered unto him. Then the devil leaveth him, and, behold, angels came and ministered unto him." These are not figures of speech, but the narrative of a transaction and of persons engaged in the transaction. The wilderness and the fasting are literal. The beings are all literal, the wild beasts, the angels, Jesus and the devil.

The conflict of Jesus with Satan is not incidental, nor

accidental, nor casual, but essential and vital. Satan held man and man's world in thrall. They had fallen into his hands and were held by him in bondage and ruled by him with desperate power.

The record has been made, "And when the devil had ended all the temptation, he departed from him for a season."

The season has ended and he is back again as though he had brought seven other spirits more wicked than himself. Gethsemane is the sum of the devil's most maddened and desperate methods. The guises are off. He appears there as he is. It is a rare thing to get a clear, true light on the devil. He assumes so many roles, acts so many parts, wears so many guises. Here we have him in life size and in perfect features. The air is heavier by his breath, the night is darker by his shadow, the ground is colder, and his chill is on it. Judas is more false still, and Peter more cowardly and dastardly, because Satan is there. On the threshold of Gethsemane he exclaims, "My soul is exceeding sorrowful unto death," and he began to be sore amazed and very heavy. Why? Because "this is your hour and the power of darkness." Why? Because "now is the judgment of this world: now shall the prince of this world be cast out." Silence is there, dread and horror, and a great darkness and a fearful conflict. Why? "For the prince of this world cometh and hath nothing in me."

How different the devil's method now with Christ than in the wilderness. Then there was mildness, an assumed sympathy, the spirit of an inquirer, one desirous to relieve. The most pleasant and attractive and satisfying ministries to flesh did Satan then offer, something of the gentleness of the lamb, the interest and sympathy of a friend. But now how changed! The lamb is transformed into the lion, a roaring lion, maddened and desperate. Jesus could not be seduced by the flesh, nor self, nor the world in the wilderness. He must be overwhelmed with dread and horror, and be driven. His steadfastness must be overcome by weakness and fear. So comes he to many a saint in the fierceness and power of the lion when the gentle inducements fail.

The devil is too wise, too large in mental grasp, too lordly in ambition, to confine his aims to the individual. He seeks to direct the policy and sway the scepter of nations. In his largest freedom, and in his delirium of passion and success, "he goes out to deceive the nations which are in the four quarters of the earth." He is an adept in deception, an expert in all guileful arts. An archangel in execution, he often succeeds in seducing the nations most loyal to Christ, leading them into plans and principles which pervert and render baneful all Christly principles. The church itself, the bride of Christ, when seduced from her purity, degenerates into a worldly ecclesiasticism.

The "gates of hell shall not prevail" against the church. This promise of our Lord stands against every Satanic device and assault: But this immutable word as to the glorious outcome does not protect the church from the devil's stratagems which may, and often do, pervert the aims of the church and postpone the day of its final triumph.

The devil is a hydra-headed monster, but he is hydra-headed in plans and wisdom as well as in monstrosities. His master and supreme effort is to get control of the church, not to destroy its organization, but to abate and pervert its divine ends. This he does in the most insidious way, seemingly innocent, no startling change, nothing to shock nor to alarm. Sometimes the revolutionizing and destructive change is introduced under the disguise of a greater zeal for Christ's glory. Introduced by some one high in church honor, often it occurs that the advocate of these measures is totally ignorant of the fact that the tendency is subversive.

One of the schemes of Satan to debase and pervert is to establish a wrong estimate of church strength. If he can raise false measurements of church power; if he can press the material to the front; if he can tabulate these forces so as to make them imposing and aggregating in commands, influence, and demand, he has secured his end.

In the Mosaic economy, the subversion of the ends of the church and the substitution of material forces was guarded against. Their kings were warned against the accumulation, parade, and reliance on material forces.

It was in the violation of this law that David sinned when he yielded to the temptation of Satan to number the people.

It was to this end some suggest that the devil contended with Michael, the archangel, about the body (or system) of Moses, referred to in Peter and Jude and narrated by Zechariah, third chapter. At which time there was given that redoubtable, rallying text which asserts the eternal separation of spiritual forces from and their antagonism to the material. *"Not by might nor by power, but by my Spirit*, saith the Lord."

To this, the third temptation of our Lord was directed. In measure, such temptation by which the devil tried Jesus was intended to subvert the ends of His kingdom by substituting material elements of strength for the spiritual.

This is one of the devil's most insidious and successful methods to deceive, divert and deprave. He marshals and parades the most engaging material results, lauds the power of civilizing forces and makes its glories and power pass in review till church leaders are dazzled, and ensnared, and the church becomes thoroughly worldly while boasting of her spirituality. No deceiver is so artful in the diabolical trade of deception as Satan. As an angel of light he leads a soul to death. To mistake the elements of church strength is to mistake the character of the church, and also to change its character [and] all its efforts and aims. The strength of the church lies in its piety. All else is incidental, and is not of the strength of things. But in worldly, popular language of this day, a church is called strong when its membership is large, when it has social position, financial resources; when ability, learning, and eloquence fill the pulpit, and when the pews are filled by fashion, intelligence, money and influence. An estimate of this kind is worldly to the fullest extent.

The church that thus defines its strength is on the highway to apostasy. The strength of the church does not consist of any or all of these things. The faith, holiness and zeal of the church are the elements of its power. Church strength does not consist in its numbers and its money, but in the holiness of its members. Church strength is not found in these worldly attachments or endowments, but in the endowment of the Holy Ghost on its members. No more fatal or deadly symptom can be seen in a church than this transference of its strength from spiritual to material forces, from the Holy Ghost to the world. The power of God in the church is the measure of its strength and is the estimate which God puts on it, and not the estimate the world puts on it. Here is the measure of its ability to meet the ends of its being.

On the contrary, show us a church, poor, illiterate, obscure and unknown, but composed of praying people. They may be men of neither power nor wealth nor influence. They may be families that do not know one week where they are to get their bread for the next. But with them is "the hiding of God's power," and their influence will be felt for eternity, and their light shines, and they are watched, and wherever they go, there is a fountain of light, and Christ in them is glorified and His kingdom advanced. They are His chosen vessels of salvation and His luminaries to reflect His light.

There are signs everywhere unmistakable and of dire import that Protestantism has been blinded and caught by Satan's dazzling glare.

We are being seriously affected by the material progress of the age. We have heard so much of it, and gazed on it so long, that spiritual estimates are tame to us. Spiritual views have no form nor comeliness to us. Everything must take on the rich colorings, luxuriant growth and magnificent appearance of the material, or else it is beggarly. This is the most perilous condition the church has to meet, when the meek and lowly fruits of piety are to be discounted by the showy and worldly graces with which material success crowds the church. We must not yield to the flood. We must not for a moment, not the hundredth part of an inch, give place to the world. Piety must be stressed in every way and at every point. The church must be made to see and feel this delusion and snare, this transference of her strength from God to the world, this rejection of the Holy Ghost by the endowment of "might and power," and this yielding to Satan. The church more and more is inclined not only to disregard, but to despise, the elements of spiritual strength and set them aside, for the more impressive worldly ones.

We have been and are schooling ourselves into regarding as elements of church prosperity only those items which make showings in a statistical column, and which impress an age given up to the materialization of secular facts and figures; and as the most vital spiritual conditions and gains cannot be reduced to figures, they are left out of the column and its aggregates, and after a while they will neither be noted nor estimated. If we do not call a halt and change our methods, the whole estimate of the strength of a church will be supremely worldly. However imposing our material results may be, however magnificent and prosperous the secular arm of the church appears, we must go deeper than these for its strength. We must proclaim it, and iterate and reiterate it with increased emphasis, that the strength of the church does not lie in these things.

These may be but the gilded delusions which we mistake for the true riches, and while we are vainly saying, "We are rich and increased in goods," God has written of us that we are "wretched, and miserable, and poor, and blind, and naked." They will be, if we are not sleeplessly vigilant, but the costly spices and splendid decoration which embalm and entomb our spirituality. True strength lies in the vital godliness of the people. The aggregate of the personal holiness of the members of each church is the only true measure of strength. Any other test offends God, dishonors Christ, grieves the Holy Spirit, and degrades religion.

A church can often make the fairest and best showing of material strength when death in its deadliest form is feeding on its vitals. There can scarcely be a more damaging delusion than to judge of the conditions of the church by its material exhibits or churchly activity. Spiritual barrenness and rottenness in the church are generally hidden by a fair exterior and an obtrusive parade of leaves and an exotic growth. A spiritual church converts souls from sin soundly, clearly and fully, and puts them on the stretch for perfect holiness, and those who are straining to get it, to keep it, and to add to it.

This spirituality is not a byplay, not to be kept in a corner of the church, not its dress for holiday or parade days, but it is its chief and only business. If God's church is not doing this work of converting sinners to holiness and perfecting saints in holiness, wherever and whenever this work is not blazing and conspicuous, wherever and whenever this work becomes secondary, or other interests are held to be its equivalent, then the church has become worldly. Wherever and whenever the material interests are emphasized till they come into prominence, then the world comes to the throne and sways the scepter of Satan. There is no readier and surer way to make the church worldly than to put its material prosperity to the front, and no surer, readier way to put Satan in charge. It is an easy matter for the assessments to become of first moment by emphasizing them till a sentiment is created that these are paramount. When collecting money, building churches, and statistical columns are to stand as evidences of real church prosperity, then the world has a strong lodgment, and Satan has gained his end.

Another scheme of Satan is to eliminate from the church all the lowly self-denying ordinances which are offensive to unsanctified tastes and unregenerate hearts, and reduce the church to a mere human institution, popular, natural, fleshly and pleasing.

Satan has no scheme more fearfully destructive and which can more thoroughly thwart God's high and holy purposes, than to transform God's church and make it a human institution according to man's views. God's right arm is thereby paralyzed, the body of Christ has become the body of Satan, light turned into darkness and life into death.

Men who sit in apostolic seats often through a marvelous blindness, sometimes through a false attachment to what they deem truth, and for what they consider the honor of Christ, are found trying to eliminate from the system of Christ those painful, offensive, unpopular, and self-denying features to which it owes all its saving efficacy, and beauty and power, and which stamp it as divine.

We have a painful illustration most instructive and warning in Peter, recorded thus:

> From that time forth began Jesus to shew unto his disciples, how that he must go unto Jerusalem, and suffer many things of the elders and chief priests and scribes, and

be killed, and be raised again the third day. Then Peter took him, and began to rebuke him, saying, Be it far from thee, Lord; this shall not be unto thee. But he turned, and said unto Peter, Get thee behind me, Satan: thou art an offense unto me; for thou savourest not the things that be of God, but those that be of men. Then said Jesus unto his disciples, If any man will come after me, let him deny himself, and take up his cross, and follow me. For whosoever will save his life shall lose it; and whosoever will lose his life for my sake shall find it. For what is a man profited, if he shall gain the whole world, and lose his own soul? or what shall a man give in exchange for his soul? For the Son of Man shall come in the glory of his Father with his angels; and then he shall reward every man according to his works.

Here is a lesson most suggestive, a lesson for all times, a warning for each man, for all men, for church men, for saintly men and for apostolic men. An apostle has become the mouthpiece of Satan! Alarming, horrible, unnatural and revolting picture! An apostle, zealous for his Master's glory, advocating with fire and force a scheme which would forever destroy that glory! An apostle, the apostle Peter, Satan's vicegerent! The apostle who had but just made that inspired confession, "Thou art the Christ, the Son of the living God," which placed him in highest honor and commendation with Christ and the church! Before the words of that divine and marvelous confession had died from his lips, this same apostle is the inflamed and self-willed advocate of views and plans which will render his confession a nullity, and raze the impregnable and eternal foundations of the church.

Peter, a chief apostle, fathering and advocating schemes which would discrown Christ of His messiahship, and bring heaven's favorite plan to a most disastrous and shameful end! How came this? What baneful impulse impels Peter? Satan has entered him and for the time being, has mastered his purposes, and so Christ reproves Peter, but in the reproof strikes a crushing blow at Satan. "Get thee behind me, Satan," a reminder and duplicate of the wilderness temptation. "Thou art an offense (a stumbling block) to me." The devil's trigger to catch Christ in the devil's trap—"Thou savourest not the things which be of

God, but those that be of men." The devil is not in sight. Man appears and his views are pressed to the front. The things which men savor in church plan and church life are against God's plan. The high and holy principles of self-denial, of unworldliness of life, and of self-surrender to Christ, are all against men's view of religion, a losing thing with them. The devil does not seek to destroy the church only indirectly. Men's views would eliminate all these unpopular principles of the cross, self-denial, life surrender and world surrender. But when this is done, the devil runs the church. Then it becomes popular, cheery, flesh-pleasing, modern and progressive. But it is the devil's church, founded on principles pleasing in every way to flesh and blood. No Christ is in it, no crucifixion of self, no crucifixion of the world, no second coming of Christ, no eternal judgment, no everlasting hell, no eternal heaven. Nothing is in it that savors of God, but all that savors of men. Man makes the devil's church by turning Christ's church over to men leaders. The world is sought and gained in the devil's church, but the man, the soul, heaven, are all lost, lost to all eternity.

The very heart of this disgraceful apostasy, this dethroning Christ and enthroning the devil, is to remove the Holy Spirit from His leadership in the church and put in unspiritual men as leaders to plan for and direct the church. The strong hands of men of great ability and men with the powers of leadership have often displaced God's leadership. The ambition for leadership and the enthronement of man-leadership, is the doom and seal of apostasy. There is no leadership in God's church but the leadership of the Holy Spirit. The man who has the most of God's Spirit is God's chosen leader, ambitious and zealous for the Spirit's sovereignty, ambitious to be the least, the slave of all.

There are two ways of directing the church, God's way and the devil's way. God's way and man's way of running the church are entirely at poles. Man's wise plans, happy expedients and easy solutions, are Satan's devices. The cross is retired, the world comes in, self-denial is eliminated, all seems bright, cheerful and prosperous, but Satan's hand is on the ark, men's schemes prevail, the church fails under these taking, pet devices of men, and the bankruptcy is so complete that the court of heaven will not even appoint a receiver for the collapsed and beggarly corporation.

All God's plans have the mark of the cross on them, and all His plans have death to self in them. All God's plans have crucifixion to the world in them. But men's plans ignore the offense of the cross or despise it. Men's plans have no profound, stern or self-immolating denial in them. Their gain is of the world. How much of these destructive elements, esteemed by men, does the devil bring into the church, until all the high, unworldly and holy aims, and heavenly objects of the church are retired and forgotten?

One of these taking, man-savoring, Satanic devices is to pervert the aims of the church after this manner of statement and effort, that the main object of the church today is not so much to save individuals out of society, as to save society, not to save souls so much as to save the bodies of men, not to save men out of a community so much as to save men and manhood in the community. The world, not the individual, is the subject of redemption.

This popular, seductive and deadly fallacy entirely subverts the very foundation of Christ's church. Its materializing trend is so strong that it will sweep away every vestige of the spiritual and eternal if we do not watch, work and speak with sleepless vigilance, tireless energy, and fearless boldness. The attitude and open declaration of much of the religious teaching we now hear is in the same strain and spirit which characterized Unitarian, Jewish, or rationalistic utterances half a century ago.

To save society is a kind of religious fad to which much enterprising, lauded church work is committed. Advanced thinkers and discoverers have elaborated the same idea. They seem not to realize their true condition, which is one of going back, and not going forward. This backward step entombs religion in the grave where Judaism has been buried all these centuries. It may well accord with the idle dreams of the worldly rabbis to think of regenerating the world and ignoring the individual.

The phrase "to save the world," has a pompous sounding; and right taking to flesh and blood is it for the church to apply itself to bettering the temporal surroundings of the individual, and improve his sanitary conditions; to lessen the bad smells that greet his nose, to diminish the bacteria in his water, and to put granite in the pavement for him to walk on instead of wood or brick. All this sounds finely, and agrees well with a material age, and becomes practical in operation, and evident and imposing in results. But does this agree with the sublime dignity and essential aim of the church? Do we need any church to secure these ends? Councilmen of common talent, an efficient street commissioner, and the ordinary vigilance of the average policeman, will secure these results in their best way. It needs no church, no Bible, no Christ, no personal holiness, to secure these ends, and this is the point to which all this vaunted advance tends. If the ends of the church are directed to those results which can be as well or better secured by other agencies, the church will soon be regarded as a nuisance, a thing to be abated by the most summary process.

The purposes of the church of God rise in sublime grandeur above these childish dreams and effete philosophies. Its purpose is to regenerate and sanctify the individual, to make him holy and prepare him by a course of purifying and training for the high pursuits of an eternal life. The church is like the seine cast into the sea. The purpose is not to change the sea so much as to catch the fishes out of the sea. Let the sea roll on in its essential nature, but the net catches its fishes. No bigger fools would ever be found than fishermen who were spending all their force trying by some chemical process to change the essential elements of the sea, vainly hoping thereby to improve the stock of the fish that they had not and never could catch. By this method, personal holiness, the great desideratum for church operation and ends, would be impossible, and heaven would be stricken from creed and life and hope.

To save the world and ignore the individual, is not only utopian, but every way damaging. It is the process, fair and laudable in name, to save the world, but in results it is to lose the church, or, which amounts to the same, making the church worldly, and thereby unfitting her for her holy and sublime mission. Christ said that gaining the world and saving the man are antagonistic ends. Christ teaches Peter that his satanic device would gain the world to and for the church, but would lose the soul. Everything would seem thrifty to the cause when in reality all was death.

The church is distinctly, preeminently and absolutely a spiritual institution, that is, an institution created, vitalized, possessed and directed by the Spirit of God. Her machinery, rites, forms, services and officers have no comeliness, no pertinency, no power, save as they are depositions and channels of the Holy Spirit. It is His indwelling and inspiration which make its divine being and secure its divine end. If the devil can by any methods shut the Holy Spirit out from the church, he has effectually barred the church from being God's church on earth. He accomplishes this by retiring from the church the agencies or agents which the Holy Spirit uses, and displaces them by the natural, which are rarely if ever the media of His energy. Christ announced the universal and invariable law when He said, "That which is born of the flesh, is flesh; that which is born of the Spirit, is spirit." The church may have a holy preacher, a man of great prayerfulness, of great grace, filled with the Spirit. But if Satan can by any method retire him, and put a man of no prayerfulness, plausible, eloquent and popular, the church may seem to have gained, but it has gained by the substitution of natural for spiritual forces, a gain which has all unconsciously revolutionized the church. Officer a church with holy men, not highly cultured, but well-versed in the deep things of God, and strong in devotion to Christ and His cause, not wealthy, nor of high social position. Now change these officers and put in men who are every way decent in morality, but not given or noted for prayer and piety, men of high social position and fine financiers, and the church scarcely marks the change save marked improvement in finances. But an invisible and mighty change has taken place in the church, which is radical. It has changed from a spiritual church to a worldly one. The change from noonday to midnight is not more extreme than that.

At this point Satan is doing his deadliest and most damning work, the more deadly and damning because unnoticed, unseen, producing no shock and exciting no alarm.

It is not by positive, conspicuous evil that Satan perverts the church, but by quiet displacement and by unnoticed substitution. The higher is being retired, the spiritual gives place to the social, and the divine is eliminated, because it is made secondary.

The perversion and subversion of the church is secured by Satan when the spiritual forces are retired or made subordinate to the natural, and social entertainment, and not edification becomes the end. This process involves not only the aims and ends of entertainment, but it is intended to soften and modify the distinctly spiritual aim, and to widen from what is deemed the rigid exclusiveness of spiritual narrowness. But in the end it eliminates all that is distinctly spiritual, and that which is in any sense deeply religious will not survive the death of the spiritual. Edification as the end of God's church is wholly lost sight of, and entertainment, that which is pleasing and pleasant, comes to the front. The social forces not only retire the spiritual forces, but effectually destroy them.

A modern church with its kitchen and parlor, with its club and lyceum, and with its ministries to the flesh and to the world, is both suggestive and alarming. How suggestive in the contrast it presents between the agencies which the primitive church originated and fostered, as the conserver of its principles and the expression of its life, and those which the modern and progressive church presents as its allies or substitutes. The original institutions were wholly spiritual, calculated to strengthen and cultivate all the elements which combine to make a deep and clear experience of God. They were training schools for the spiritual life, subservient to its culture as the chief end. They never lingered in the regions of the moral, the aesthetic and the mental. They fostered no taste nor inclination which was not spiritual, and did not minister to the soul's advance in divine things.

They took it for granted that all who came to them, really desired to flee from the wrath to come, and were sincerely groaning after full redemption, and that their obligation to furnish to these the best aids were of the most sacred and exacting kind. It never occurred to them that the lyceum or sociable were channels through which God's grace would flow and could be laid under tribute for spiritual uses. These social and fleshly forces are regarded in many quarters as the perfection of spiritual things. These agencies are arrayed as the mature fruit of spiritual piety, flavored and perfected by its culture and progress, and ordained henceforth as the handmaids of the prayer and testimony meeting. We object most seriously to the union. What have they in common? "How indeed can two walk together unless they be agreed?"

What elements of piety are conserved by the lyceum or sociable? What phases of spiritual life do they promote? By what feature of the lyceum is faith invigorated? Where do you find in it any elements which are distinctly pious, or are aids to piety? How does the sociable produce a more prayerful, a holier life? What secret springs has it to bring the soul nearer to God? Wherein does it form or strengthen the ties of a Christly fellowship? Is it not frivolous and worldly? Is it not sensuous and fleshly? Does it not cater to and suit the tastes of the carnal, the light and worldly? What unity of purpose and spirit is there between the lyceum and witnessing for Christ? The one is intensely spiritual. The other has in it no jot or tittle of spiritual uses.

We might as well add to the list of heavenly helpers, the skating rink, calisthenics and the gymnasium. If the young people desire to join a lyceum, enjoy a sociable or establish a bank, let them do so, but do not deceive them and degrade piety by calling these things holy institutions and feeders of spiritual life.

Disguise it as we may; reason about it as we will; apologize for it as we do; vainly philosophize of growth and change and culture, the truth is, we have lost that intense type of personal experience, that deep conviction of eternal things which are such evident features of all great spiritual movements. Many preachers and people have fallen so low in their experience that they do not relish these distinct and strongly spiritual agencies; and are devising schemes and institutions to gratify their nonspiritual tastes with schemes which are midway between Christ and the world; which, while not essentially wrong, do not possess one grain of spiritual power, and can never be the channels of heavenly communications.

It is said we cannot get the people to attend the distinctly spiritual means of grace. What is the trouble? Are the institutions worn out and no longer of value to the humble, pious soul? Who will dare affirm this? The tastes of the people are low and perverted. Shall we then change the agencies to suit the unsanctified appetites? No; let us tone up the appetite for spiritual things, and correct and elevate the tastes of our people. Let the revolution begin with the preacher. Let him wrestle with God until his ordination vow becomes vitalized, so that all can feel the pressure of his aim, the ardor of his zeal, his singleness of purpose, and the holiness and elevation of his life, and until the people catch the fire and purpose of his heart, and all press on to the regions of perfect love, panting for all the fulness of God. Under this united, mighty, divine impulse the social and the lyceum will be forgotten and become stale, and all saintly assemblies will be attractive and delightsome.

The church cannot confederate with non-spiritual agencies. By this she breaks the tension of her faith and discards the Holy Ghost. She cannot be the purveyor to unsanctified desires. Neither is it her province to fall down to the beggarly task of entertaining the people. This is her saddest mistake, when her solemn assemblies are surrendered to the concert and lecture, her praise turned into worldly music, her classrooms into parlors, her sociables more popular than her prayer meetings, the house of God made a house of feasting, and social cheer is sought after rather than a house of prayer. The unity of the Spirit and the holy brotherhood are displaced and destroyed to make room for social affinities and worldly attractions. Her high and royal duty, that by which she maintains her spotless fidelity to her Lord, is to stress holiness and afford all means for its advancement and perfection. This done, spiritual character and affinities will order all the rest.

There is no more fundamental statement than that the world is to be renounced by every true disciple of Christ, and that to love the world and the things of the world puts us in open and standing enmity to God. By virtue of the relationship of love or friendship to the world, we are the enemies of God. There needs no other sin, no other crime by virtue of our attachment to the world. By that alone, we are the enemies of God.

Christ Jesus lays it down as an obvious truth that between the world and His disciples there would be hatred. The two discipleships to Himself and to the world were inimical and impossible. The call, the touch and choice of Christ when accepted and obeyed, becomes at once the secret and the source of the world's hatred.

Jesus declares the native and inevitable enmity of the world to His followers: "The world hath hated them because they are not of the world even as I am not of the world." Again, in the sacerdotal prayer, He declares this distinct and eternal separation and conflict: "They are not of the world, even as I am not of the world." By virtue of their relation to Christ they are separated from and are in conflict with the world.

The two persons, Jesus and Adam, their natures, affinities and opposition, are declared in the clearest language: "The first man is of the earth, earthy; the second man is the Lord from heaven. As is the earthy, such are they also that are earthy; and as is the heavenly, such are they also that are heavenly. And as we have borne the image of the earthly, we shall also bear the image of the heavenly." How strong is the opposition to the world declared and demanded. The love of the world is hostile to and destructive of the love of God. The two cannot coexist.

> Ye adulteresses, know ye not that the friendship of the world is enmity with God? Whosoever therefore would be the friend of the world maketh himself an enemy of God (James 4:4, R.V.).

Nothing is more explicit than this, nothing is more commanding, authoritative and more exacting. "Love not the world." Nothing is more offensive to God, nothing is more criminal, more abominable, violative of the most sacred relationship of the soul with God. "Adulteresses"—purity gone and shame and illicit intercourse exist. Friendship for the world is heaven's greatest crime and God's greatest enemy.

The world is one of the enemies which must be fought and conquered on the way to heaven. "For this is the love of God, that we keep his commandments; and his commandments are not grievous. For whatsoever is born of God overcometh the world, and this is the victory that overcometh the world, even our faith. Who is he that overcometh the world, but he that believeth that Jesus is the Son of God?"

The Gospel is represented as a training school in which to deny worldly desires is one part of its curriculum. "For the grace of God that bringeth salvation hath appeared to all men, teaching us, that denying ungodliness and worldly lusts, we should live soberly, righteously and godly, in this present world; looking for that blessed hope, and the glorious appearing of the great God and our Saviour Jesus Christ; who gave himself for us, that he might redeem us from all iniquity, and purify unto himself a peculiar people, zealous of good works." There is something somewhere in the world which makes it a deadly foe to the salvation of Christ and which poisons us against heaven.

What is "this world," which so effectually alienates us from heaven and puts us by virtue of our relation to it and in flagrant enmity to God, and friendship to which violates our wedding vow to God, whose love is enmity to God, whose friendship is criminal to the most abominable and utmost degree? What is it? "The world, the lust of the flesh, the lust of the eye, the pride of life." What are they? The world includes the whole mass of men alienated from God, and therefore hostile to the cause of Christ. It involves worldly affairs, the aggregate of things earthly, the whole circle of earthly goods, endowments, riches, advantages, pleasures, and pursuits, which although hollow, frail and fleeting, stir desire, seduce from God, and are obstacles to the cause of Christ. The divorced or torn relation between heaven and earth, between God and His creatures, finds its expression in the term, "the world."

Our English word, "desire," expresses the meaning of the word *lust*, including the whole world of active lusts and desires, to which the seat of desire and the natural appetites impels.

Alford's Commentary says:

The world was constituted at first in Adam, well pleasing to God and obedient to Him. It was man's world, and in man it was summed up, and in man it fell into the darkness of selfish pursuits and by which man has become materialized in spirit and dragged down so as to be worldly and sensual. The world is man's world in his fall from God. The "lust of the flesh," human nature averse to God; "lust of the eyes," that sense which takes note of outward things and is inflamed by them. The "pride of life," the manner of life of worldly men among one another whereby pride is to display and pomp is cherished.

Bengel says:

"The lust of the flesh" means those things on which the sense of enjoyment, taste and touch, feed. "Lust of the eyes" means those things by which the senses of investigation, the eye and sight, hearing and smelling, are occupied. "Pride of life" means when any one assumes too much to himself in words or actions. Even those who do not love arrogance of life may possibly pursue the "lust of the eyes," and they who have overpowered this yet frequently retain the lust of the flesh, for this prevails in the greatest degree and to the widest extent among the poor, the middle classes and the powerful, even among those who appear to exercise self-denial.

John Wesley says:

The desire of the flesh means the pleasures of the outward senses, whether of taste, smell or touch. The "desire of the eye," the pleasures of the imagination (to which the eye chiefly is subservient), of that internal sense whereby we relish what is grand, new or beautiful. The "pride of life" means all that pomp in clothing, houses, furniture, equipage and manner of living which generally procure honor from the bulk of mankind, and so gratify pride and vanity. It therefore directly includes the desire of praise and remotely covetousness. All these desires are not from God, but from the prince of this world.

This world arrays itself and all its forces against heaven. Worldliness is the epidemic foe to heaven. To live for this world is to lose heaven by counter attraction. The Son of God declares of His disciples, and reiterates the declaration to His Father as one of prime importance: "Thou gavest them me out of the world. They are not of the world, even as I am not of the world." It remains true to this hour that all the true disciples of Jesus are not of the world, but are chosen out of the world, have left the world, have renounced the world, and are crucified to the world.

Fundamental and eternal are these truths, of which heaven has an illustration in every follower of Jesus.

What gives the world its fatal charms? What makes its witchery so deadly? Sometimes its beauty is all withered, its brightness all night, its hope all despair, its joy the bitterest anguish, and all its prospects decay and desert, but still it holds and binds. We are loath to leave it. Whence is its deadly sorcery and its fatal snares? Whence is its malignant hate? Whence is its hostility to God and its alienation from heaven? This world is the devil's world. In that fatal hour when man fell from his allegiance and devotion to God, he carried the world with him in his rebellion against God. Man was the world's lord, and it fell with its lord. This is the solution of its full influence, its malignant rivalry, and its intense opposition to heaven. The devil has his kingdom here. It is his princedom. He clothes it with all beauty and seductive power as the rival of heaven. Heaven's trinity of foes are the world, the flesh, and the devil. The world is first, the most powerful and engaging. They all center in and are strong for evil because the devil inspires and inflames them. The flesh wars with the spirit simply because the devil inflames its desires. The world gets its deadly and fascinating snares from the devil. The world is not simply the ally, but is the instrument and the agent of Satan. It represents him with the most servile and complete loyalty.

The text from John already quoted, "Love not the world, neither the things that are in the world," needs, for its full understanding, to have the preface which reads: "I write unto you, young men, because ye have overcome the wicked one. I write unto you, little children, because ye have known the

Father. I have written unto you, fathers, because ye have known him that is from the beginning. I have written unto you, young men, because ye are strong, and the Word of God abideth in you, and ye have overcome the wicked one."

To "overcome the wicked one," the world, its love and its things must be abjured. There stands at the threshold of many a church door these words, which in spirit belong to the sacred honor of every soul's true espousal to Christ: "Dost thou renounce the devil and all his works, the vain pomp and glory of the world, with all covetous desires of the same, and the carnal desires of the flesh, so that thou wilt not follow or be led by them?" "I renounce them all," was the answer solemnly said in the serious hour, and the preacher and the people and our own hearts, if true, said, "Amen." And Amen let it be now and forever.

This world must be renounced and this is to renounce Satan. This is the deadliest blow at his rule. The friendship of the world is violative of our marriage vows to heaven.

We will not understand James in his severe denunciations of the world, where he makes its friendship so criminal and declares that to be the friend of the world is of itself to be the enemy of God, except we note how he is declaring that the world's friendship is the devil's religion, earthly, sensual, devilish; and that we can get back to God only by renouncing the friendship of the world and by cleansing our hearts and hands of its soiling touch. We draw nigh to God by resisting the devil. We resist the devil by renouncing the world.

The Apostle James sums up the distinct characteristics of the devil's world-counterfeit religion. Passion, appetite and pleasure reign and make war. How much of this passion, pleasure and world religion has there been in church annals? Too often its history is a history of passion, strife, ambition and blood. Its ecumenical councils are the battlefield of passion in its unbridled, most malignant form. "Earthly, sensual, devilish," is the divine stigma put on it, and obloquy is put on much of that which marks and mars ecclesiastical history. What volumes of this worldly religion, unwritten volumes, a world full of volumes, belong to the lives of many old reputed saints and to many modern church members and church goers. They are friends of the world, its advocates and lovers. They do not pray and only say prayers in order not to miss praying. There is no drawing nigh to God and no fighting against the devil and driving him from the field of action. Their religion and its performances and worship descendeth not from above, but is "earthly, natural, devilish." "Submit to God" and "resist the devil," is the keynote of an unworldly religion. A personal God and a personal devil are among the primary articles of creed and experience in true religion. Surrender to God, draw nigh to Him, live close to Him, fight against the devil, and get rid of him by denouncing and abjuring the world.

The divine warning against the course of the world, against the fashion of the world and against the spirit of the world, finds its solution in the fact that the devil is directing the world's course, the devil is creating the world's spirit, and the devil is cutting the pattern of the world's fashion. The touch of the world pollutes because Satan's fingers are in its touch. Its desires are deadly and heaven-quenching because Satan kindles its desires. The world and its things are contraband in the Christian warfare because Satan is the ruler of the world and the administrator of its affairs.

In Ephesians, Satan and his legions are called the "world-rulers." We quote from the Revised Version: "Put on the whole armour of God, that ye may be able to stand against the wiles of the devil. For our wrestling is not against flesh and blood, but against the principalities, against the powers, against the world rulers of this darkness, against the spiritual hosts of wickedness in heavenly places." The "world rulers" are principalities and powers under the direction of the devil. How they rule this world by ruling the things which rule this world! How Satan seizes and directs all the mighty forces of this world! War he seizes, and instead of it being the patriot's struggle for freedom and for the defense of home and native land, it becomes the pliant tool of despotism, crushes liberty and right, enslaves freedom, and carries on a campaign of lust, rapine, cruelty, desolation and death.

Money is another of the world's ruling forces which might be used to Edenize earth and to lay up a good foundation against the time to come. It ought to be used to ease the burdens of the poor, to banish beggary, and to brighten the homes of widowhood and orphanage. A mighty world-ruling power is money. The devil rules it and instead of flowing at the command of pitying love, it is diverted by Satan to all selfish and unholy purposes. Inflaming into covetousness and hardening into callousness, men become noted, illustrious and esteemed, as they are money-getters and money-keepers.

Education, a mighty world-ruling force, Satan chains this to his car, and it becomes the source of pride and ungodly power, and its mighty engineering is turned into "higher criticism," and under the guise of Christian learning, it becomes the most powerful ally to Satan, unsettling faith in God's Word in multitudes of hearts, and opening a wide door of skepticism in the temple of God.

In Ephesians the devil is called the "prince of the power of the air." The very atmosphere of this world ministers to his cause and is under his baneful rule. How much of storm and cyclones, terror and ruin is he responsible for we may not know. "And you hath he quickened who were dead in trespasses and sins; wherein in time past ye walked according to the course of this world, according to the prince of the power of the air, the spirit that now worketh in the children of disobedience. Among whom also we all had our conversation in times past in the lusts of our flesh, fulfilling the desires of the flesh and of the mind; and were by nature the children of wrath, even as others." "Among whom we all had our conversation," says Paul of himself and the saints. They formerly lived in Satan's kingdom, and he ruled them by the lusts of the flesh, "fulfilled the desires of the flesh and the mind." We see in this how Satan rules through the world. He is the god of this world, and by the world he excites its desires, both low and high, low in the desires of the flesh, and high in the desires of the mind. Whether the world fills the passions or appetites, or draws out and chains the mind in its high worldly pursuits and refined tastes, it is all of

Satan, because of the world. The "lust of the flesh, the lust of the eyes and pride of life," these are of the world, and Satan is the exciter of them, "and lust when it is finished bringeth forth death."

"We know that whosoever is begotten of God sinneth not, but he that was begotten of God keepeth him and the evil one toucheth him not. We know that we are of God and the whole world lieth in the evil one" (Revised Version). The world "lieth," means that it is in the power of the devil, is held in subjection by him, and is fixed and established. The devil is pictured not only as trying to kindle into a flame the desires which may remain in a good man's heart after conversion, but also as folding in his arms the whole world and making it subject to his power and submissive to his absolute control.

When the world comes in at many a door, it comes in in many a form, but at whatever door and in whatever form it comes, it is always as the devil's servant. It comes in to do his work as his most obsequious and faithful slave. When the world comes in, dressed in its most seductive and beautiful garb, the devil has fashioned its clothing and ordered its coming. The world is the devil's heaven. Its rest, crown and good are here. When the world comes in, God's heaven goes out. It fades from the eye and heart. The struggle for it ends, and God's heaven, with its fadeless and eternal glories, is lost.

In these declarations of the Bible about the world and the devil, we see why the world opposes heaven. We learn the enmity of the two. Heaven is Christ's place, the place where He is, and to which He would win men. The world is Satan's place. His power is here. To fix our hearts on the world, is to be loyal to him. To fix our hearts on heaven, is to be loyal to Christ.

Here we have the solution of the cruel hatred of the world to Jesus and why it has persecuted so bitterly and to death His followers. We see why it is that the Spirit lusteth against the flesh and the flesh against the Spirit, and likewise we see why these are not only contrary to one another, but at war with one another. The devil is in the flesh and rules it. Christ is in the Spirit. This world leads from Christ. It is the invincible foe of Christ.

This great truth is illustrated and enforced by the fact that

Christ's work is to get possession of the world and make its attractive power further His purposes. But He establishes a kingdom of heaven which is not of this world. A new power has come in, a new kingdom established and a new world made. It will take the fires of the judgment and the new creative power to make a new heaven and a new earth before the stains and ruin of the devil's debasing and death-dealing hands can be removed, and this alien and hell-debauched, yet beautiful, world fitted for God's holy purposes.

The Christian, by the urgent demand made upon him to forswear allegiance to the world, is, by his very relation to Jesus Christ, lifted out of the world's deadly embraces, and its polluting witcheries are broken. In this subserviency of the world to the devil, we have the solution of the world's intense hatred to Jesus Christ, and we see why it has armed itself with all its forces under the power of the devil to destroy the cause of Christ. The world's opposition and enmity have been always against true religion, but often its smiles are more fatal than its hate.

In all we have seen, instead of minifying the power of the devil, Jesus exalts him to the pinnacle of power as a prince, with this world as his princedom.

In the prominent features of Christ's life the devil appears as the one being and the one evil agent which Christ has in mind, to whose rule He is opposed. We have seen how soon the devil followed in the wake of our Lord's baptism at the Jordan, after the anointing of the Holy Ghost, and His public entrance on His ministry. When He first commissioned His disciples, among other great miracles they were to "cast out devils." When the seventy returned to report their work to Christ, they said, with evident surprise and gratulation, "Even the devils are subject to us through thy name." He replied: "I beheld Satan as lightning fall from heaven." When He is opening their hearts to receive the great comfort of that great promise of the Holy Spirit, He declares that one of the trinity of great ends to be executed by the Holy Spirit was "to convict the world of judgment, because the prince of this world is judged."

In one of His troubled and impassioned outbreaks, as the shadows and pain of His great agony are coming on Him, He cries, "Now is my soul troubled." The darkness is relieved by a gleam of light in which He sees the ruins of Satan's kingdom and the devil spoiled, dethroned, cast out by the almightiness of His cross, "Now is the judgment of this world; now shall the prince of this world be cast out. And I, if I be lifted up from the earth, will draw all men unto me."

But as the darkness grows deeper, and the anguish more bitter, He sees the approaching form of him whose hour and power of darkness it is. Hushed into silence in the presence of this relentless and cruel foe, the Son of God says to His sorrowing and awe-struck disciples: "Hereafter I will not talk much with you; for the prince of this world cometh, and hath nothing in me."

The devil's sad and mighty influence is farther set forth on the circle of chosen disciples. Peter staggers under the blow of the devil; his narrow, shameful escape of Peter is thus referred to by Christ: "Simon, Simon, behold, Satan hath desired to have you, that he might sift you as wheat: but I have prayed for thee, that thy faith fail not: and, when thou art converted, strengthen thy brethren."

Jesus Christ acknowledges the great power and authority which the devil has in the present deranged and usurped order of things. He declares, "Now is the judgment of this world, now shall the prince of this world be judged."

How defiant Satan is, and how he opposes Christ stubbornly with reckless and too often successful courage is plainly revealed. Into the chosen circle of the twelve he entered, into the one who had been trusted as their treasurer, the receiver, the depositor and the disburser of their money and their charity.

How close he comes, and how large his successes! One of the sacred twelve he has seduced, possessed and moved to carry out in the most hypocritical, false way his infamous designs. How near he came adding Peter to the black roll of his immortal ones, immortal in infamy, is very evident. That the devil had much every way to do with Peter's dastardly course, his lying and blasphemy, is evident from the words of Christ, "And the Lord said unto Simon, Simon, behold Satan hath desired to have you that he may sift you as wheat. But I have prayed for thee, that thy faith fail not; and when thou art converted, strengthen thy brethren. And he said unto him, Lord, I am ready to go with thee, both into prison, and to death. And he said, I tell thee, Peter, the cock shall not crow this day, before that thou shalt thrice deny that thou knowest me."

In the parable of the sower, Christ sets forth the unseen but powerful influence which the devil exerts to neutralize the word of God. In the record of this parable by Matthew, the devil is termed the "wicked one," a statement of personality and of the concentration and comprehension of preeminent wickedness. He catches away the word sown with vigilant and diabolical hate. "Then cometh the devil and taketh the word." He is the destroyer of the seeds of good. So powerful is he that the word of God, incorruptible and eternal, is prevented from securing its benign and saving efforts by his vigilance and influence over the mind.

In the story of Job and his sore trials, we see the Sabeans and Chaldeans are ready to respond to his suggestion to make their predatory raids on Job's herds. Satan's power is not limited to outside influence, but is direct and powerful, getting into the inside, and making suggestions of evil, almost godlike sometimes, and again so inflaming our passions or principles that we cannot see the wrong till too late, as in the case of Satan's suggestion to David to number Israel. His power is so great that even good men, the best, who are able to resist his temptations, yet for a time are under his power. The Christians at Smyrna were so under his power that while he could not alienate their affections or disturb their loyalty, he could put them in prison. Paul felt all his life the rankling poison of a wound inflicted by Satan's power.

Peter was in his hands and tossed about, and was brought nigh to the fatal verge by his power. Job was for a while put in his power, and was driven and torn and desolated like a cruel and reckless tempest, wherein everything was wrecked and lost but his patience. How great was Satan's power to destroy fortune and family and friends and reputation! The Son of God was in his mysterious and all desolating power, led to the mountains and led to the temple by the fearful spell of Satan. Angels retired and heaven hushed its music and was draped in silence and trembled in awe while Satan's dread power was allowed to spend its dark force on heaven's Anointed One. The power of disease was in the devil's hands. He smote Job. Christ said of the woman with the spirit of infirmity: "Ought not this woman, being a daughter of Abraham, whom Satan hath bound, lo! these eighteen years, be loosed from this bond on the Sabbath day?" Doubtless much of sickness is due to the power of the devil. To this there is reference in the statements of Christ's work. "When the even was come, they brought unto him many that were possessed with devils; and he cast out the spirits with his word, and healed all that were sick. That it might be fulfilled which was spoken by Isaiah, the prophet, saying, Himself took our infirmities, and bare our sicknesses." "How God anointed Jesus of Nazareth with the Holy Ghost and with power; who went about doing good, and healing all that were oppressed of the devil; for God was with him."

Satan's power did not extend to death in Job's case, but it did in that of his children. The Smyrna Christians he could hold in prison but ten days, but thousands of others he held unto death. His own cruel, deadly hands weaved for them the martyr's crown of gold and glory.

The power of the devil over the body is further seen and illustrated by numbers of cases in the New Testament, of demoniacal possessions. The devil had possession by some of his imps of the bodies of persons. Some of the cases were fearfully tormented in body and almost wrecked in mind, others had functions of the body suspended, some were made dumb by him, and others made deaf and blind. These cases were many in number and of great variety. The great power and malignity of Satan is seen in that among the most distressing cases were those who were not noted for great sins, but the young and comparative innocent ones were the victims of his dread power. The whole person came under the power of this alien spirit. The power of Satan, his nearness and personality, had a constant and destructive manifestation in these cases.

Of these demoniacal possessions it has been well said that

the Gospel narratives are distinctly pledged to the historic truth of these occurrences. Either they are true or the Gospels are false.

Nor can it be said they represent the opinions of the times. They relate to us words spoken by the Lord Jesus in which the personality and presence of the devil are distinctly stated. Now either our Lord spoke these words or He did not. If He did not, then we must at once set aside the concurrent testimony of the evangelists to a plain matter of fact. In other words, we establish a principle which will overthrow equally every fact related in the Gospels.

The power of Satan is far greater than that of God's highest and saintliest earthly ones. In the third chapter of Zechariah we have the picture of his power with God's high official representatives. Joshua, the high priest, is there, the angel of the Lord is there, and standing at Joshua's right to resist all his righteous acts is Satan. Joshua and the angel, realizing their insufficiency when contending with Satan, they send a cry to heaven, "The Lord rebuke thee, O Satan."

Jude gives us this item. "Michael the archangel, when contending with the devil he disputed about the body of Moses, durst not bring him a railing accusation, but saith, The Lord rebuke thee."

Whatever this obscure text may mean in regard to this contest between Michael and the devil, while it teaches us spirit and tongue control, it does, without obscurity or doubt, clearly show that an archangel's strength is not sufficient to contend single-handed and alone with the devil.

Daniel gives a side glance into the power and conflicts which exist in the unseen and spiritual world which lies so near our own, which has so much to do with us where our spiritual battles are fought, and victories won. Daniel had been praying three weeks before the angel and the answer came. "Then said he unto me, Fear not, Daniel, for from the first day that thou didst set thine heart to understand and to chasten thyself before thy

God thy words were heard and I am come for thy words. But the prince of the kingdom of Persia withstood me one and twenty days; but lo, Michael, one of the chief princes, came to help me." We see how he plans. If he cannot keep people from praying nor absolutely prevent the answer to prayer, he can cause delay in the answer to prayer that he may discourage and break down faith and discount urgent, importunate praying.

He has power to cast into prison. To the little pious church at Smyrna, Jesus Christ writes in commendation, warning and consolation: "Fear none of those things which thou shalt suffer; behold, the devil shall cast some of you into prison, that ye may be tried; and ye shall have tribulation ten days. Be thou faithful unto death, and I will give thee a crown of life."

There are special seats or headquarters of his power, places where the devil makes his home and rules with an absolute sway. To this Christ refers in His letter to the church of Pergamos: "I know thy works, and where thou dwellest, even where Satan's seat is; and thou holdest fast my name, and hast not denied my faith, even in those days wherein Antipas was my faithful martyr, who was slain among you, where Satan dwelleth."

Some said they were Jews, but were the "synagogue of Satan." Are there churches which are called Christian, but are churches of Satan?

In Christ's letters to the seven churches in Asia, we see how the ascended and enthroned Son of God presents the same view of the devil. The "depths" of Satan are referred to in the address to Thyatira. In this revelation of Christ to John, the devil is still declared to be "the great dragon, the old serpent, the devil, and Satan." He is declared to have great "wrath."

The devil's power is greatly and strangely enhanced by his system of worship, which, while it degrades, it fascinates and holds. The system of pagan worship and devotion is very powerful. It holds its devotees by iron chains. It is not a work of chance, neither does it spring from native religious instincts. It is a system of rare power and of rare skill, constructed by a graduate in the craft of seduction and delusion. Satan's hand and head are in it, all planning, ordering, and inspiring it. It is this fact which gives its strength and influence.

Of Jeroboam, who perverted the religious instinct and

debased worship for sinister, worldly, and selfish purposes, it is said he ordained him priests for the devils. The psalmist declared they sacrificed unto devils. The New Testament declares that "the things which the Gentiles sacrifice, they sacrifice to devils, and not to God; and I would not that ye should have fellowship with devils. Ye cannot drink the cup of the Lord and the cup of devils; ye cannot be partakers of the Lord's table and of the table of devils." Again we have it declared, "Now the Spirit speaketh expressly, that in the latter times some shall depart from the faith, giving heed to seducing spirits, and doctrines of devils."

The intensity and power of the devil's worship is illustrated and enforced in the last book of the New Testament, showing how his worship would increase in intensity and would militate against the worship of the Lamb. We have all along rival altars and rival worship. The devil is the author, inspirer, and protector of the one, and Christ is the author, inspirer and protector of the true and pure worship. There are wonders in each, miracles and martyrs in the false and devilish, as well as in the true and heavenly.

Revelation summarizes the situation: "And they had a king over them, which is the angel of the bottomless pit, whose name in the Hebrew tongue is Abaddon, but in the Greek tongue hath his name Apollyon. One woe is past; and, behold, there come two woes more hereafter."

These are not lawless woes, nor are their authors lawless bands, disorderly and reckless mobs. They are organized. The strictest obedience to the devil prevails. "devil with devil damned firm concord holds." They are "principalities and powers," not only of high and first order in creation, not only of great personal power and dignity, but ordered and sub-ordered, coordinate and subordinate. There is the most perfect government, military in its drill and discipline, absolute and orderly in its arrangement, under one supreme, dictatorial, powerful head, with rank and file and officers complete. "For our wrestling is not against flesh and blood but against principalities, against the powers, against the world, rulers of this darkness, against the spiritual hosts of wickedness in the heavenly places." These high and wicked spirits are everywhere. They fill the air, are everywhere intent on evil, following the direction of their leader carrying out his plans with hearty accord, ready obedience and implicit confidence. How loathsome their nature! How marvelous and miracle-working their power! How high and kingly their influence! How martial their purposes! All this is vividly and strongly set forth in the sixteenth chapter of Revelation: "And I saw three unclean spirits like frogs come out of the mouth of the dragon, and out of the mouth of the beast, and out of the mouth of the false prophet. For they are the spirits of devils, working miracles, which go forth unto the kings of the earth and of the whole world, to gather them to the battle of that great day of God Almighty."

The power of Satan finds its great increase and expression in the efforts and instrumentality of the unregenerate, who are by Bible teaching under his power, subjects of his kingdom of darkness. More than that, so intimate is their connection with Satan, so close the unity, purpose and relationship, that they belong to his family. His paternity gives birth and character to them, his fatherhood binds them in a strong embrace.

The power of the devil—how defiant, bold, sacrilegious, presumptuous! How near the sacred person of Christ he came! See how he invaded the sacred circle of His chosen apostles. Judas falls from his high position—tempted, possessed by Satan and filled with remorse and infamy, committing suicide, and hell is his forever. Peter acts as the spokesman of the devil, becomes the advocate of a noncross-bearing, nonself-denying, worldly religion. He is so affected by the devil's power that he curses and swears and lies, and finds himself all besmirched, bemired and befouled, from which he is only saved by the prayers and look of Christ. John and James fell a prey to the devil as they wanted fire to come down from heaven and burn up the Samaritans. Christ sharply shows that they had not His Spirit, but the other spirit, the spirit of the destroyer which actuated them. Paul had his apostolic plans interfered with and hindered by the devil. To the Thessalonians, he writes: "Wherefore we would have come unto you, even I, Paul, once and again; but Satan hindered us." And he bore to his grave the marks of the power of this inveterate foe to apostolic fidelity.

The power of Satan is not supreme. It is limited. It was so in Job's case. Satan could go only so far to afflict. Since the Son of God came into the world, the devil's power has been curtailed. The cross gave a shock to Satan and his power. Death, his realm has been abolished, and "life and immortality brought to light through the gospel." His kingdom received its death stroke on Calvary. The almighty forces of the Gospel are laying hold of the mighty forces of Satan.

The careless and halfhearted Christian knows nothing of the devil or his devices, but the souls astir for God and the good, on a stretch for heaven, they are the ones who demand his attention, provoke his ire and call forth his machinations.

Says that marvelous man of faith and power, Pastor Blumhart: "He who is ignorant of the wiles and artifices of the enemy, only beats the air, and the devil is not afraid of him." Blumhart himself is an illustration. "In interesting myself in behalf of one possessed," he says, "I became involved in such a fearful conflict with the powers of darkness as is not possible for me to describe."

Christians may live and die all unaware of the devil's being and hate, and he may be as indifferent to their religion because they are unharmful of his kingdom. But wherever one of the Blumhart type lives, there is a big commotion and fear in Satan's realm.

Satan works by imitation. To make something as near like the true as possible, and thereby break the force and value of the genuine. This is one of his favorite methods. As Jannes and Jambres withstood Moses by their false tricks, so is he carrying on by lying wonders his work. As his apostles are transformed into angels of light, so his wonders are looked on as first class miracles. They do indeed discount true miracles.

What of the revelations of his person? God and Christ have been revealed to men in bodily shape, by figure, by representation. Matchless, majestic, beatific theophanies have holy men seen of God. Has the devil power to clothe himself in form and object to the eye? Can he incarnate himself? He seems to have clothed himself in some visible shape at the temptation of Christ.

The form is not recorded. Perhaps in that of a man, doubtless a pious man, gathering in the assembly of the righteous, or as a pious hermit in the seclusion and retirement of the desert. In the days of Christ he revealed himself by taking absolute possession and sway over the person, and used other personalities through which to manifest his being and power. His manifestations are disguises, insidious and deceptive. Sometimes as "an angel of light," with the bloom, beauty, and spices of paradise on him. His person unearthly in splendor, his voice gentle, musical, winning, with no lines or traces of the fall.

The devil affects the body, and through the body affects loyalty to Christ. Job was tried by his sickness. So the devil tries us by sickness. In the days of Christ, he carried on a large business by affecting the body, not simply by ordinary diseases, but by what is termed, "possessed with a devil." In those cases his work was by breaking down the body in some of its chief functions.

His method is to assume that shape which will suit his purposes at the time. Doubtless there was something in the shape or character of the serpent which gave him the readier access to Eve. Garbed as an angel of light his appearance commends him fully to the pure and unsuspecting. As a thorn he desires to give only pain to those who, like Paul, cannot be seduced nor swerved from the fixed course of fidelity. The Christians at Smyrna he puts in prison that by that process he may fetter their bodies whose souls he could not fetter. With matchless cunning and unspeakable fidelity he plies his trade to seduce and damn.

He has access to the minds of men from which he ought forever to be barred. But he has so much of diabolical trickery that he clothes the meanest act with the fairest guise, and conceals a world of infamy with beautiful rainbow colorings. He hoodwinked good David and provoked him to number Israel in opposition to God's will, and brought swift and fearful judgment on the nation.

He readily snatches away from the mind the truth that is superficially received. He also blinds the minds of them which believe not and obstructs the light of saving truth. His process of taking the word out of the heart to prevent faith, and of blinding the mind to the beauties and light of salvation, is a very common one with him. . . .

In the parable of the sower, we are taught the devil's ability to work on the mind, and take away the good impression there made. "And those by the wayside are they that have heard; then cometh the devil, and taketh away the word from their heart, that they may not believe and be saved." We are also taught how the devil influences the mind to do the most dastardly things, in the case of Judas, chosen as an apostle, into high and holy fellowship, a royal vocation, a select company. Satan had much to do in influencing Judas to the great crime that brought him to despair and suicide, and to immortal infamy in this world and hell in the next. . . .

To the Son of God in the wilderness, he comes not as he did to Job in lowering and seething storms of distress, but in the form of apparent sympathy and friendliness. It may have been in the guise of a saintly hermit in the wilderness. "If thou be the Son of God"—you want this matter of your sonship to God settled, and so do I. You are very hungry and faint. "Command that these stones be made bread." An innocent and a proper way to settle at once a great question and to appease a great hunger.

Then he comes to Christ with the sanctity of the holiest place, and affords Him an opportunity to attest before the wondering and awestruck worshippers His Messiahship, a shorter and a better road this to gain credence to His mission than the slow and thankless process of daily teaching and daily ministering, and marching to the cross with the dark shadows of its shame and heaviness ever darkening His way.

Satan's desperate venture was to seduce Him by the world's array of grandeur, power and glory. Satan plunged Job from serene and cloudless, heavenly height down to a midnight, starless and stormy. To the Son of God he would be a present friend to save Him from pain, poverty, hunger, shame, toil and death.

The devil is rarely seen in his movements and methods. He has rare tact in getting others to do his work and execute his plans.

His methods are to blind, to put a veil on the evil results and all the sad consequences of sin. He so blinds that the evil cannot be seen. So with the keen-eyed David, brave, true and clear-eyed for God, yet Satan blinded him completely to the treachery, infamy and murder in Uriah's case. So sinners are held by him in unbelief. He puts out their eyes to all the light and glory of the Shining Sun of Righteousness. "In whom the god of this world hath blinded the minds of them which believe not, lest the light of the glorious gospel of Christ, who is the image of God, should shine unto them."

The power of the devil extends to the mind. He can influence the mind, insinuate thoughts, suggest purposes, excite the imagination, inflame the passions, stir the appetites, kindle the fleshy fires, awaken old habits, and fan old dead flames or light new ones. The artless purity of Eve he beguiled. He entered into the half traitorous Judas and possessed him fully, and made his half-formed treason full and his treachery immortal in its infancy. He was in the private council of Ananias and Sapphira, a party of their fraud, and suggested their lying plan to deceive the apostles. His access to the mind is evident in that he snatches away the divine seed implanted by holy lips in the soil of the heart as taught in the parable of the sower. . . .

The devil uses this world as a veil to shut out the truth of God, the light of His glorious Gospel, and to close the eyes of faith to all the discoveries in the unseen and eternal.

The antagonism between the children of the world possessed by Satan, and the children of God possessed by God, is set forth by John. "Ye are of God, little children, and have overcome them; because greater is he that is in you, than he that is in the world. They are of the world; therefore speak they of the world, and the world heareth them. We are of God; he that knoweth God heareth us; he that is not of God heareth not us. Hereby know we the spirit of truth and the spirit of error."

Who is in us? God. Who is in the children of the world? The devil. Our faith, our hope and our final triumph are in the truth of the Word of God. "Greater is he that is in us than he that is in the world."

Satan perverts the things which are truly works of God and misemploys miracles to obscure God's glory.

The devil often tries to break the soul down and reduce it to despair. He tells us to discourage us that we shall never succeed. The way is too hard and narrow and the burden too heavy.

He takes advantage of weak and distracted nerves, and suggests fears. Grace is hid from the sight, shortcomings are magnified and infirmities are classed as gross sins. Sometimes the fear of death is used by Satan to quench the fire of faith, and the grave becomes something awful. He darkens the future. Heaven and God will be out of sight, hidden by a thick veil of tomorrow's cares, trials and needs. The imaginary disasters, failures and evils of tomorrow are powerful weapons in Satan's hand. He suggests that the Lord is a hard master, and that His promises will fail. He works on the remaining corruption in the heart, and raises a great storm in the soul. . . .

He tempts to evil tempers, to hasty words, to impatience and to carnal reasoning, which is his powerful ally in our minds. Back to Christ. More of His Spirit-renewed and thorough self-dedication, and in darting prayers upward by an uplifted eye and heart—thus will we be able to resist and conquer the great adversary of our souls.

The devil may tempt us to think too meanly of ourselves as Moses did, and too highly of ourselves as Peter did. In one sense, we cannot think too meanly of ourselves, but in another we can. He persuades us that we are so poor and weak we can do nothing, and so we are weakened in faith and broken in effort. But his master method is to fill us with self, self-importance and self-ability, and then not only is faith weakened, but destroyed. Our efforts and doings may increase in number and vain show, but the seal of self and Satan are on them all.

John Wesley notes: "I preached at eight on that delicate device of Satan to destroy the whole religion of the heart. The telling Christians not to regard frames or feelings, but to live by naked faith, is in plain terms, not to regard either love, joy, peace or any other fruit of the Spirit; not to regard whether they feel them or the reverse; whether their souls be in a heavenly or hellish frame. Satan's method with some is to make them rely too much on frames and feelings. With others he deals the reverse and urges them to discard all frames and feelings."

Many anxious errors sprang up with the rank growth in Wesley's day, and he pruned and trimmed with a master's hand. Naked faith is often nothing but a sapless, arid, fruitless, unconscious thing, and brings an arid, fruitless, unconscious salvation with it, if it brings salvation at all.

Whatever may be his method, how numberless his devices, the words of his conqueror to us are these: "Behold, I give unto you power to tread on serpents and scorpions, and over all the power of the enemy; and nothing shall by any means hurt you." Of this text, Miss Havergal writes: "Why, this is grand—*power over all the power* of the enemy. Just where he is strongest there they shall prevail. Not over the very center of his power, not over his power here and there, nor now and then, but over *all* his power. And Jesus said, Is not that enough to go into battle with?"

The devil's brain is prolific in plans. He has many ways of doing many things. Perhaps he has many ways of doing each thing. With him nothing is stereotyped. He never runs in ruts. Fruitful, diverse and ever fresh, is his way of doing things. Indirect, disingenuous, insidious and graceful are his plans. He acts by artifice and always by guile.

His plans by Bible statement are "wiles." The original word means to follow up or investigate by method and settled plan. It is not a bad word but one of order, arrangement and methods, conceived and executed. But when the word gets into the devil's hand it is defined by his dictionary. It receives a strong tincture, a deep coloring of cunning and trickery.

Sometimes Satan comes disrobed of his heavenly garments, a thorn, sharp and pointed and painful, a poisoned thorn, a thorn that rankles and stays, a thorn that cannot be extracted by prayer, which retrieves all other ills. The saints who have seen most of heaven are often decreed to see most of hell. Saints who have the fullest and most transporting revelation of God, often have the saddest experience of Satan.

Paul's thorn was as much to Paul as his abundance of revelations. His thorn made him more a saint than his vision of the third heavens. Satan only lifted him higher by keeping him lower.

Satan may come to us in his own native character, the

thorn breeder and piercer. He may put in us thorns which no prayer power can extract. Thorns which will poison and pain, but the thorn will enrich grace, increase and mature humility and make infirmities strong and glorious. Satan's thorns will clothe necessities with richest attire, change distresses and persecutions into divinest pleasures, make room for God's greatest power in us and on us, make the lowest point of spiritual depression the highest point of vision, and make strength out of weakness and wealth out of poverty.

There are positions and conditions which lie open to the attacks of Satan. These points must be guarded by sleepless vigilance. The devil is a remorseless, cruel and mighty foe. To watch him with unsleeping eye, is not only a duty, but safety to life, deliverance from hell, certainty of heaven, all, and more, if more there can be, are involved in overcoming the devil. Stupidity, neglect, being off guard in the conflict, with Satan are much more than mistakes or indiscretions. They are fatal undoings, eternal and remediless losses. . . .

Much akin to the foregoing exposed position is the one which makes light of Satan. Frivolous views of him, his works, or his character, light talk or dishonoring epithets in the line of jesting—are all detrimental to any serious views of life's great work, its solemn engagements, its serious conflicts and its weighty hindrances. Presumption, self-will and foolishness are the characteristics of those who thus deal with these weighty concernments. The existence and work of the devil is a serious matter, and it is to be considered and dealt with from the most serious standpoint, and none but serious people can deal with it. And with this well accords the iterated and reiterated New Testament exhortation and note of warning, "be sober." That which gives it point and arousing power is, "Be sober, for your adversary, the devil," etc. . . .

An unforgiving spirit invites Satanic possession. His favorite realm is the spirit. To corrupt that, to incense or provoke to retaliation, revenge or unmercifulness—that is his chosen work and his most common and successful device. Paul puts it to the front so as to thwart Satan: "To whom ye forgive anything, I forgive also; for if I forgive anything, to whom I forgive it, for your sakes forgive I it in the person of Christ; lest Satan should get an advantage of us; for we are not ignorant of his devices."

When he begets an unforgiving spirit in us, then he has us, we are on his ground. Then wicked men and good men, all kinds of men, are likely to do us harm, sometimes at vital and very sensitive points. Sometimes all unconsciously they wrong us and sometimes knowingly and wilfully they wrong us. As soon as a spirit of unkindness possesses us for the wrong done, Satan has the upper hand. . . .

. . . even those who are earnestly striving after that "holiness without which no man shall see the Lord," Satan tempts them to go a little too far and their zeal degenerates into party spirit and unhallowed heat. "Strict earnestness degenerates into severity, gentleness into weakness, energetic activity into imprudent meddling and narrowness, calm moderation into careless acquiescence, bold decision maintaining its own convictions firmly becomes intolerant, self-opinionated, narrow, arbitrary, bigoted. Due regard for the peculiarities and convictions of others degenerates into paralyzing indifference and skeptical indolence. Lively trust lapses into presumption and haughtiness, a wise prudence into cowardice and hesitating anxiety," and confession and profession degenerate into and evaporate into aridity. So Satan watches and is alert always, and wary, to hold us back from the goal, or to press us by an impetuous, unkindly or vehement spirit to go beyond the goal. So all this uncovers often our strongest positions and turns them into exposed conditions.

Yoking with unbelievers in the relationship of life-ties of friendship and intimate and confiding associations with unbelievers, are exposed positions of great peril, and of which the devil takes instant and great advantage. Partnership in business, or the more sacred relation of marriage with unbelievers, is perilous to one united to Christ by close ties. . . .

An untrained body exposes readily to Satan's assaults. Even the natural, innocent appetites and passions have to be held in with bit and bridle. An apostle was aware of this: "But I keep under my body, and bring it into subjection, lest that by any means, when I have preached to others, I myself should be a castaway." An undisciplined body would hurl Paul from the apostolic heights down to the fearful abyss of apostasy. Two statements are made as to his body. "Keep under" and "bring it into subjection." The first means that part of the face under the eyes. A blow on that part of the face, a black and blue spot by the bruise of a heavy blow, restrained and suppressed by heavy blows, and its native power is broken.

The second statement means to make a slave of, to treat with severity, to subject to stern and rigid discipline. The apostle sets forth the body as an important fact in the contest for heaven, and teaches us that if it be untrained, without the strong repressing, molding hand of discipline, it becomes an easy prey to the assaults of Satan.

After the same order is the direction of Peter: "Be sober, be vigilant; because your adversary, the devil, as a roaring lion, walketh about, seeking whom he may devour. Whom resist steadfast in the faith, knowing that the same afflictions are accomplished in your brethren that are in the world." A listless, drowsy, sleepy, stupid state, gives us into Satan's power without a struggle or even a surrender, or the decency of a parley.

To the same end is the strong injunction of Christ to the drowsy and fainting disciples: "Watch and pray, that ye enter not into temptation. The spirit indeed is willing, but the flesh is weak."

Low aims in the spiritual life, satisfaction and quiescence in present conditions and attainments, is exposed condition. The devil may *visit* the highlands and mountain ranges of spiritual elevation, but he makes his *home* in the lowlands. He will attack the strongest, maturest giant form of piety, but he works his havoc and gains his spoils where the Christian slumbers in the cradle of spiritual babyhood. There is no safety but in high aims, strenuous effort and constant advance.

It is on the field of low aims and satisfied results, that the devil wins his chief victories. A spiritual growth, constant and sure spiritual development, is the surest safeguard against Satan's wiles, assaults and surprises. Constant growth is all eyes and all strength. Satan never finds it asleep, drowsy nor weak. Onward, upward, is the great battle cry. Constant advance is the steel armor in the fight with the devil.

Israel lost Canaan by not possessing Canaan. Satan has all the vantage ground when we do not maintain the aggressive.

When the Bible sounded the clarion call, "Let us go on unto perfection," it was seeking to arouse a church which had lost immensely in the vigor, manliness and fighting ability of Christian character by feeding on milk, and indulging in the lazy luxury of being children. It raises a standard and marks a point for them to gain. The point is far ahead, but it is a real point, as real as the point at which their steps had been stayed by a ruinous stay. They are called out of the cradle and away from the nursery to the strength, conflicts and perfection of a royal manhood.

The eulogy on Wesley by a great writer of being "the first of theological statesmen," pays him no high compliment; but his spiritual perception, the man of open, divine vision, is his highest eulogy, and this is evidenced by the fact that he reechoed the trumpet call of the Bible, and sounded it on every key and in every refrain, and sought to stir into a forward movement the Church, and quicken its members to seek an advanced position, which had not only dropped out of their experience, but out of their hopes and creeds. God gives religion in its beginnings, and these beginnings are glorious; but to be content with the beginnings of religion, is to forfeit not only its possibilities, but is to leave us opened, naked to Satan, a prey to his schemes. Additions to our spiritual capital are the conditions of solvency, and of the retaining of the capital, and is a victory over the devil as well. To stand still in religion is to lose it. To enter into camp at regeneration, is to forfeit regenerating grace. To stop at any other transitional advance station, is to go backward. The weakness of men is inconstancy to a great aim. The drafts of a long and exhaustive strain are intolerable. We are willing to pay the cost of nerves for a great temporal success, but the price is too dear for religious success. The tendency in religion is to be satisfied with rudiments and to die in infancy. Teething time is a perilous time for spiritual babes. The great sin of the Israelites was hugging the shores and not going up to possess the land.

The marvelous glory of their entrance into Canaan paled in the lethargy and timidity of their after advance.

A stopping, standing still, a nongrowing, nonfighting condition, is a position fully exposed to Satan. Many run well, fight well, but at some point their running and fighting cease. At once spiritual development is arrested and the devil moves at once to an easy victory. This spiritual arrest may be at the initial steps or stages of spiritual life. The raptures and triumph of the first stages may arrest advance and cause a standstill while the cradle is not out of sight, and the steps are unsteady by baby toddling. It is true that Paul calls the Corinthian saints baby saints, but this was the point where their saintship turned back to carnality and lost its odor, sanctity and strength. Their great sin and backslidings were found in their babyhood, not that they began as babes, but that they stayed babes. Baby sainthood is the popular sainthood of these days. To begin as babes is well, but to remain babes forty years is a fearful deformity.

It would be well for us if spiritual arrest belonged only to the high regions of spiritual advance. While not a few, doubtless, of those who have received a great spiritual baptism after the grace of conversion, have crystallized around this point of advance, the far greater number of people and preachers have crystallized around the initials of grace. We may have some specimens of Christian mummies who in size approach to maturity, but the number of the dwarfed and cradled ones is legion.

Spiritual arrest is not confined though to the initial steps. Its lifeblood may chill and its step halt at the point of highest advance. Many Christians are so enthusiastic over some marked advance, some higher elevation gained, that they become enchanted with the beautiful and lofty regions, and are lulled to sleep, and, like Bunyan's Pilgrim, lose their roll, and are all unconscious of their loss; and instead of pressing on with tireless steps, they but cover the future with their imaginations, and while their fancies are filled with the rich colorings of their advanced position, their feet have declined and are in the vale again. They are so happy that it is almost impossible to bring them to their senses, and make them understand that there is many a weary and toilsome step between their Red Sea deliverance and the Promised Land, and that even after the desert is crossed, and the Jordan divided, and the sanctified soil of Canaan pressed by sanctified feet, there is many a battle to be fought, and many an enemy to be destroyed before the goodly land is all possessed. A singing and shouting sanctification is good, but if it is not joined with a marching and fighting sanctification, it will sing and shout itself as thin as a ghost and as dry as a chuck. "Forgetting those things which are behind and reaching forth to those things that are before," is the divine process to hold what we have by getting more. Paul's marvelous career was simple, not complex. He sums it up in fighting, running, watching, the three elements of continuous advance. Many a great battle has been lost by the demoralizing effects of the halt caused by a partial victory in the earlier part of the conflict. It is no easy matter to keep place and march in rank when the spoils of a half-gained victory cover the ground. There is no position this side of heaven free from the dangers of spiritual arrest and secure from the devil's attacks. The conflict and vigilance of advance must mark every step till our feet are within the pearly gates.

A nongrowing piety, with an arrested spiritual development, whether the arrest is in the initial stages or at the more advanced steps, is always and everywhere an exposed position, always vulnerable to Satan's attacks.

The apostle James, in his frank, practical, earnest way, says: "Resist the devil, and he will flee from you." Resist means to set yourself against, to have no parley with, make no concession to, meet the devil only to fight him, talk with him only to withstand him. "Whom resist," says Peter, "steadfast in the faith." That is, be solid, firm, rigid in the faith. Be stalwart in orthodoxy, for heterodoxy has no devil, or only a very amiable and young one, and makes no fight against him.

The spirit of forgiveness always maintained and constantly exercised is a supreme defense against the attacks of Satan. An unforgiving spirit is not only Satan's widest door into our hearts, but it is the strongest imitation and warmest welcome. St. Paul not only urges a spirit of forgiveness as a bar to the devil's ingress, but hastens to close the door by his own readiness to forgive even in advance. "To whom ye forgive anything, I forgive also; for if I forgave anything, to whom I forgave it, for your sakes forgave I it in the person of Christ. Lest Satan should get an advantage of us; for we are not ignorant of his devices." A lofty spirit, ready and compliant with the spirit of forgiveness, free from all bitterness, revenge or retaliation, has freed itself from the conditions which invite Satan, and has effectually locked and barred his entrance. The readiest way to keep Satan out is to keep the spirit of forgiveness in. The devil is never deeper in hell nor farther removed from us than when we can pray, "Father, forgive them; they know not what they do."

The soldiers in the warfare against the devil must understand how to wear the armor of all prayer. "All prayer" in all kinds, and at all seasons, in the intensest form, with deepest sense of personal need of God, is the demand. Prayer must deepen and narrow and intensify into supplications, helped into this mighty praying, clothed with this resistless power of prayer by the Holy Spirit. This intense conflict with the devil requires sleepless vigilance, midnight vigils, a wakefulness which cannot be surprised, a perseverance which knows neither halting, fainting, nor depression, which knows by clearest spiritual intelligence what it needs, and what the illimitable provisions are to supply all those needs, and the imperative necessity of pressing the prayer till the need is supplied and the succor is secured. This praying holds itself in loving sympathy with the entire family of God, making their conflicts, perils and needs its own. It is in line of battle with the whole familyhood of God, taking in their foes, their safety and their perils. "Supplication for all saints" gives victory to every saint. The line of battle is one. Defeat or victory must come to all. It is the soldier fully equipped in God's armor, who is a veteran against the devil and invincible to all of his attacks.

It is not an easy thing to pray. Back of the praying there must lie the conditions of prayer. These conditions are possible, but they are not to be seized on in a moment by the prayerless. Present they always may be to the faithful and holy, but cannot exist in nor be met by a frivolous, negligent and laggard spirit. Prayer does not stand alone. It is not an isolated performance. Prayer stands in closest connection with all the duties of an ardent piety. It is the issuance of a character which is made up of the elements of a vigorous and commanding faith. Prayer honors God, acknowledges His being, exalts His power, adores His providence and secures His aid. A sneering half-rationalism cries out against devotion, and charges that it does nothing but pray. But to pray well, is to do all things well. If it be true that devotion does nothing but pray, then it does nothing at all.

To do nothing but pray fails to do the praying, for the antecedent, coincident and subsequent conditions of prayer are but the sum of all the energized forces of a practical working piety.

Prayer puts God in the matter with commanding force. "Ask of me things to come concerning my sons," says God, "and concerning the work of my hands, command ye me." We are charged in God's Word, "always to pray," "in everything by prayer," "continuing instant in prayer," to "pray everywhere," "praying always." The promise is as illimitable as the command is comprehensive. "All things whatsoever ye shall ask in prayer believing ye shall receive." "Whatsoever ye shall ask;" "if ye shall ask anything;" "Ye shall ask what ye will and it shall be done unto you." "Whatsoever ye ask the Father he will give it you." If there is anything not involved in "All things whatsoever," or not found in the phrase, "Ask anything," then these things may be left out of prayer. Language could not cover a wider range, nor involve more fully all minutia. These statements are but samples of the all-comprehending possibilities of prayer under the promises of God to those who meet the conditions of right praying.

These passages, though, give but a general outline of the immense regions over which prayer extends its sway. Beyond these the effect of prayer reaches and secures good from regions which cannot be traversed by language or thought. Paul exhausted language and thought in praying, but conscious of necessities not covered, and realms of good not reached, of battles not gained over enemies and not conquered, he covers these impenetrable and undiscovered regions by this general plea: "Unto him that is able to do exceeding abundantly above all that we ask or think, according to the power that worketh in us." The promise is, "Call unto me, and I will answer thee, and show thee great and mighty things, which thou knowest not."

Satan: His Personality, Power and Overthrow, Chaps. 1–16

Thanksgiving Day

Thursday, November 27, has been appointed as a day of thanksgiving by the President of the United States. Thanksgiving Day has become a settled national institution of this country. From the very foundation of our country days devoted to worship have been observed at the call of the president; but as a national observance it has come into prominence since the war.

It is a recognition of God in the beneficence of his providence over the nation's being and well-being. This is a feature that must be constantly called to mind. God rules in the natural as well as in the moral world. His providential care includes nations as well as individuals. And the recognition of this great fact is binding on national authority and national life. And to adore God in his majesty as Ruler of the universe belongs to piety as well as to adore him in the tender relation of Father to the individual.

The observance of the day ought to be in keeping with the object of the day. It ought to be religiously observed. The worship of the individual is the only method of thanksgiving. To observe the day as a national holiday will not secure its ends. To spend it in recreation, or in feasting as opposed to fasting, is not to observe it truly. It is the day for church-going and the worship of God's house.

Thanksgiving is the noblest expression of the noblest sentiment of the heart. It is gratitude flowing through the lips. It is gratitude looking up with all its generous and swelling emotions, and giving out these fragrant sacrifices to God, the author of all good, by fitting acts, and by a fitting service.

In the great mass of national life the individual is not to be lost. The whole range of temporal good, the untold benefits secured for our spiritual natures are to animate the individual into thanksgiving and praise. The wide and infinite range of the future, as well as the present and the past, is to yield up its treasures as themes of thanksgiving.

Our whole national history should be turned into prayer and praise on that day. The whole stream of national life should be turned from business, from politics, and from the world to God and heaven. The church on that Thursday should be the center of attraction, and the nation flow to God's house as by one impulse.

Christian Advocate, November 22, 1890

The World

The position of the church to the world is one of separation—a separation so sharply defined as to have in it all the elements of antagonism. The world, the flesh, and the devil are the trinity that oppose the church. The world leads the van, and is the covert for the deadly assaults of the others.

Christian Advocate, October 4, 1890

Worship

The Methodist *Discipline* is a very wise little book. It suggests many things that it does not state. It hedges against many evils without naming them. It is the product of many wise minds. It has been reviewed and approved by many more. It levees Methodist policy and practice. Methodism can be conserved only by following its directions. Loyalty to its provisions, great and small, will secure the best results.

In the Methodist *Discipline* we have a directory for worship—a law regulating the service in Methodist congregations; a law which is binding on all Methodist congregations. It is one of those rules to the observance of which Methodist preachers, as the executors of the law, are specially pledged. While to keep our rules, and neither to mend nor break them, is the bounden duty of every Methodist, upon the preacher the obligation is specific and emphatic.

That this is a little rule and about the incidentals does not license us to disregard it. He who violates the little rules will soon violate the great ones. Take care of the pennies, the pounds will take care of themselves, is a proverb of as much use in religion as it is in secular affairs. The little foxes spoil the vines. The little touches give perfection to the picture.

Our directory is a law in favor of a simple service. It is a protest as well as a fence against a showy or ritualistic service. It is negative and affirmative. Its service is to exclude as well as to include. The tendency of worship is to form and show. A sensuous worship is the death of spirituality. Right where our church erects these simple, strong embankments is the place where this worldly element comes in and perverts.

The changes that are made in our service are not in the interest of vital godliness, but in almost every case a violation of its simplicity and purity by the intrusion of showy, foreign elements—elements that abridge or discount the preaching of God's word, or are not preparatory to the devout and prayerful frame which are requisite to hear and worship to edification.

The simplicity of our worship must be preserved, and there is no way of doing it but by following our written law, which we ought to follow gladly. The firm and loyal obedience to our law will save us from all forms of ritualism as well as from the showy and elaborate service to which we are much exposed. This directory is short as well as simple—not too short, to indicate haste; not baldly short. While it does not weary nor exhaust, it does not by its complexity or magnificence bewilder, nor by its ostentation divert nor kindle strange flames. It has variety enough to relieve, and the unity is so preserved that the mind is kept to the one point, and the service not only converges to the main point, which is the preaching, but prepares the heart for the reception of the life-giving and life-maturing word.

The directory is to secure and preserve uniformity in Methodist worship. This end can only be secured by the conscientious execution of this law of worship. The frequent changes in the Methodist pastorate render this uniformity an important feature to us. We will have endless diversities or confusions, whimsical changes, if the law does not mold us into uniformity and stability at this point.

We must not be congregationalized nor the order of our worship left to the lawlessness of individual tastes, good or bad.

This directory fixes the order of worship against all the changes of the pastorate, against the variations or confusions of individual tastes or whims, against the inroads of ritualism, against a showy, worldly worship.

We give, to refresh our minds, the disciplinary service:

> The morning service shall be conducted in the following order:
> 1. Singing—the congregation standing.
> 2. Prayer—the congregation kneeling.
> 3. Reading a lesson out of the Old Testament, and another out of the New.
> 4. Singing—the congregation sitting.
> 5. Preaching.
> 6. Singing—the congregation standing.
> 7. Prayer—the congregation kneeling.
> 8. Benediction.
> The afternoon and evening service shall be the same as the morning, except that one of the lessons or both may be omitted.
> Let the Lord's Prayer be used on all occasions of public worship in concluding the first morning prayer, the congregation repeating after the minister, and the apostolic benediction (2 Cor. 13:14) in dismissing the congregation.

This directory ought to be followed minutely, conscientiously. It cannot be improved on. We have seen it violated at many points, the order deranged or mutilated—the Bible lessons are often omitted, at least one; the Lord's Prayer omitted; the congregation rarely kneel; the preacher sometimes stands as a compromise, or not to feel lonesome, being the only one on his knees. We have known at least one Methodist congregation so badly taught that they sat up in receiving the Lord's Supper. Innovations are dangerous, and should not be allowed.

What we need is not a more elaborate or showy service, but the life of the Spirit infused into the beautiful and simple forms we have; not more forms, but more life; not a richer service, but a fuller life to make that which we have glow and flame and shine.

Christian Advocate, November 15, 1890

BOOKS BY E. M. BOUNDS

The Essentials of Prayer (New York: Revell, 1925).

Heaven: A Place—A City—A Home (New York: Revell, 1921).

The Necessity of Prayer (New York: Revell, 1929).

The Possibilities of Prayer (New York: Revell, 1923).

Power Through Prayer (Nashville: Publishing House of the Methodist Episcopal Church, South, 1907). (This is a slightly revised version of *Preacher and Prayer* published first in England in London: Marshall Brothers, 1902.)

Prayer and Praying Men (New York: George Doran, 1921).

Preacher and Prayer (London: Marshall Brothers, 1902).

Purpose in Prayer (New York: Revell, 1920).

The Reality of Prayer (New York: Revell, 1924).

The Resurrection (Nashville: Publishing House of the Methodist Episcopal Church, South, 1907).

Satan: His Personality, Power and Overthrow (New York: Revell, 1922).

Weapons of Prayer (New York: Revell, 1931).

(Note: The Reverend Willis Irvin, Jr., notes in his bibliography that Homer Hodge referred at one time to a volume by Bounds entitled *A Continent of Prayer*. He also notes that Bounds prepared a book on John Wesley's teachings on the doctrine of holiness. In any case neither Irvin nor I can find any traces of these two works.)